"*Ngo 1984 ngaqala ukubona umuntu wase melika owabe ethanda ukubhala ngomoulu wabantu abamnyama. Ngiphakamisa-ke ukuthi, ukuhlangana kwami no Paul Simon, kwakuyindlela kaNkulunkulu wokuphendula umkhuleko ka Helen ayewucelele amambazo. Futhi ungowokuqala kwabasemelika ukuba ahlale phansi alalele umculo wamambazo. Ehleli phansi phakathi kwesizwe esimnyama, yena no-myeni wakhe kuyibo bodwa abelungu, belalele amambazo. Okwaze kwenza uthi sibemukele njengabantu abangebona abelungu kodwa bengabantu njengathi sonke, bemane bemhlophe ngebala. Siyawuha-lalisela umsebenzi awenzayo sithi mawuqhubeke. Akekho obhala nge-mambazo njengo-Helen. Unwele olude Helen.*"

"Helen Kivnick, whom I met in 1984, was the first American I'd seen who expressed a great interest in documenting traditional black South African music. When I later met and worked with Paul Simon I strongly believed that that was God's way of answering Helen's prayers, because it was she who had been so moved by the music that she continuously prayed for us. She also was the first American who took time and listened to Mambazo music. She and her husband Gary followed us in performances, almost all the time being the only white people in the midst of black people. That inspired us to accept them as part of us and make them honorary Mambazo, and declare them part of our black family. The work that she is doing, studying and documenting this music, is important and needs to be encouraged. Nobody else writes about us and gets it right, as she does."

—Joseph Shabalala
Leader of Ladysmith Black Mambazo

"As a child growing up in a South African ghetto, I always looked forward to the hallowed time in the evening when we children gathered around the fireside to be enthralled and regaled by my mother's stories and songs. Without this respite from the oppression, hunger, pain, and suffering that was our lot under apartheid, I couldn't have survived the inhumanity of that evil system with my sensibilities intact. The songs in *Where Is the Way* vividly and poignantly remind me of those blissful interludes. They perfectly capture the quintessence of a vibrant and indestructible African culture under apartheid."

—Mark Mathabane
Author of *Kaffir Boy*

"South Africans sing their news. They are providing the soundtrack for the history they are making. You cannot understand the freedom movement there unless you feel its rhythms, its syncopated energy, and the passion of its hymns. Helen Kivnick's book recognizes the link, the crucial link between culture and politics."

—Danny Schechter
Executive producer of *South Africa Now*,
award-winning public-television news magazine

"Those already familiar with South African music will hold their breath as they set out on Helen's exploration. Those uninitiated will be brought into the exuberance and vitality of our life through the author's narration. Her book touches our history with great sensitivity, a trait usually lacking in researchers who go into our communities."

—Nomgcobo Sangweni
Cultural liaison for *Sarafina!*

"If I have a passion, it's for the music that happens here. It seeps from the earth. I am extremely grateful for this book."
—Barney Simon
Playwright and artistic director
of the Market Theater, Johannesburg

"This book is a remarkable document, rendering the pathos, hope, and tragedy of expressive African resistance to racial domination understandable to a worldwide audience. Helen Kivnick should be commended for so sensitively meshing into the world of black musicians and singers without the pretentiousness of speaking on their behalf."
—Gerhard Schutte
Former head of the Department
of Sociology, University of
the Witwatersrand, Johannesburg, South Africa

"A brilliantly conceived and masterful resource, this publication is extremely important and carries a powerful message within the haunting refrains of liberation songs."
—Joann Watson
YWCA Office of Racial Justice

PENGUIN BOOKS

WHERE IS THE WAY

Helen Q. Kivnick's previous books include *Vital Involvement in Old Age: The Experience of Old Age in Our Time*, written together with Erik H. Erikson and Joan M. Erikson, and *The Meaning of Grandparenthood*. A clinical psychologist, she teaches at the University of Minnesota School of Social Work, maintains a private practice, and consults on aging, life-cycle development, and human relations. She also performs as a singer-songwriter. She and her husband, Gary Gardner, live in Minneapolis, Minnesota, and have co-produced two record albums of South African singing, from their own field recordings: *Mbube! Zulu Men's Singing Competition* and *Let Their Voices Be Heard: Traditional Singing in South Africa. Mbube!* received a Grammy nomination for the Best Traditional Folk Recording of 1987. About her disparate areas of expertise, Kivnick says, "I've always seen connections between the things everyone else seems to regard as unrelated. The trick is to clarify the connections and then use them in the service of social progress."

WHERE IS THE WAY

SONG AND STRUGGLE
IN SOUTH AFRICA

HELEN Q. KIVNICK

PENGUIN BOOKS

PENGUIN BOOKS
Published by the Penguin Group
Viking Penguin, a division of Penguin Books USA Inc.,
375 Hudson Street, New York, New York 10014, U.S.A.
Penguin Books Ltd, 27 Wrights Lane, London W8 5TZ, England
Penguin Books Australia Ltd, Ringwood, Victoria, Australia
Penguin Books Canada Ltd, 2801 John Street, Markham, Ontario, Canada L3R 1B4
Penguin Books (N.Z.) Ltd, 182–190 Wairau Road, Auckland 10, New Zealand

Penguin Books Ltd, Registered Offices: Harmondsworth, Middlesex, England

First published in Penguin Books 1990

1 3 5 7 9 10 8 6 4 2

Grateful acknowledgment is made for permission to use excerpts from the following works:
"Uligugu Lami," "Isigcino," "Ungikhumbule," "Nqonqotha," "Nkosi Yamakhosi," "Sivuya
Sonke," "Nomathemba," "Ngelekelele," "Amabutho," "Yimani," "Uz'ube Nami Baba,"
and "Emafini" by Joseph Shabalala. Copyright © 1973, 1978, 1982 Mavuthela Music Co.,
Johannesburg. International copyright secured. All rights reserved.
"Marching in Africa" by Gale Henry. Reprinted with permission.
"Bring Him Back Home" by Michael Timothy, Tim Daly, and Hugh Masekela.© 1985 Warner
Bros. Music Ltd./Anxious Music Ltd. Used by permission. All rights reserved.
"We are here to say . . ." speech by Dr. Alan Boesak, August 20, 1983. Used by permission.

Photographs on cover: Middle school students, KwaZulu—Gary Gardner; Ladysmith Black
Mambazo perform in migrant hostel—Helen Q. Kivnick; Abafana Bomoya, multiracial group
that performs in various migrant styles, rural KwaZulu—by permission of Jeff Thomas,
Abafana Bomoya; hillside wedding, KwaZulu—Gary Gardner.

LIBRARY OF CONGRESS CATALOGING IN PUBLICATION DATA
Kivnick, Helen Q.
Where is the way : song and struggle in South Africa / Helen Q. Kivnick.
p. cm.
Includes bibliographical references.
ISBN 0 14 01.2895 6
1. Blacks—South Africa—Music—History and criticism. 2. Popular music—South
Africa—1981–1990—History and criticism. 3. Folk music—South Africa—History and
criticism. I. Title.
ML350.5.K6 1990
780′.89968—dc20   89-49495

Printed in the United States of America
Set in Goudy Old Style and Gill Sans   Design and maps by Robert Bull Design

For

Victoria Nonyamezelo Mxenge
James Madhlope Phillips
Gary Gardner

In gratitude

ACKNOWLEDGMENTS

This book has been more than seven years in the making. As I look back, I find that I have so many people to thank, for so many different kinds of assistance, that I could fill a telephone directory with all their names and contributions. Most important are the South Africans—of all colors, ages, and walks of life—who opened their homes, hearts, and lives to me. Many of these people appear in the book, and I will not mention most of them again here. Those with the protection afforded by name recognition are clearly identified. For those without such protection, I have used biographical disguises to distance them from possible retribution for observations and opinions which are mine and for which I, alone, take full responsibility. In South Africa, people have learned to be masters at hearing what may not be spoken; I hope my profound appreciation is effectively communicated in these terms.

The early stages of this project were funded as part of my participation in the W. K. Kellogg Foundation's National Fellowship program, directed by Larraine Matusak. The United States–South Africa Leader Exchange Program provided administrative assistance. During this period Bob Fleming, Steve McDonald, Bob Rotberg, John Blacking, and David Rycroft were extremely generous with their time, knowledge, and wisdom. I also thank Mike Sinclair, Sylvia Gon, Susan and David Suzman, Arthur and Lorraine Chaskalson, Peter and Margey Larlham, Gavin and Glenda Younge, Anne Collins, David Marks, Amanda Harris, Sheena Duncan, Veit Erlmann, Jeff Thomas, Andrew Tracey, Mbongeni Ngema, and the late David Webster.

The next phase of the project was partially funded by a grant from the John and Clara Higgins Foundation, represented by Lisa Null. During this period I received technical and lo-

ACKNOWLEDGMENTS

gistical help from Mike Cogan, the San Francisco Folk Music Center, Frank Scott, Sandy and Caroline Paton, Lani Herrmann, Michael Rantho, Lydia Mahlaule, John Mutalwana, Christopher Neluvhalani, Ben Ngoako, Bernard Spong, Khabi Mngoma, Fiona Nicholson, Tshilidzi Ligege, Paulos Mfuphi, Joseph Shabalala, and Alfred Nokwe. I owe special thanks to Thamsanqa Hlatywaya who worked with me for two years, transcribing and translating the bulk of my field recordings and, in the process, contributing immeasurably to my understanding of his culture.

Throughout the long period of writing and revising the manuscript Sara Evans, Kim Thorburn, Diane Calabrese, and Prexy Nesbitt provided much-appreciated moral support. A grant from the National Academy of Recording Arts and Sciences, Inc., offered financial assistance. Rich Kirby, Ray Funk, Andrew Seidenfeld, and Bill Nowlin helped with the discography. Danny Schechter, Gerhard Schutte, Nomgcobo Sangweni, Bill Strachan, Rose Moss, and Duma Ndlovu commented on earlier versions of the manuscript. My agent, Bella Pomer, continued to believe in the book after hearing that it was unpublishable, many more times than I like to remember. My editor at Viking Penguin, David Stanford, shepherded the project through its final stages.

Finally, I want to acknowledge the very special contributions of the three people to whom this book is dedicated.

Gary Gardner provided the unflagging faith, humor, and perspective that hold everything together and make anything possible. Sometimes he became a collaborator. Always he was a fan. Without him this project would never have been completed.

Victoria Nonyamezelo Mxenge and James Madhlope Phillips: These late South African freedom fighters gave me friendship and personal encouragement when I had no right to expect either, and they accepted mine in return. One as a lawyer and one as a singer, they lived—and died—in the spirit of dedication, cooperation, and human dignity.

Ngiyabonga.

CONTENTS

CONTENTS

x

INTRODUCTION

by Mbongeni Ngema and Duma Ndlovu

In traditional societies of South Africa, long before the white man came from across the seas and disturbed every known aspect of culture, music was a way of life: a way of life in that it informed a people's culture and was, for Africans, what schools and educational institutions are to Western society today. And it did not even stop there. On the weekends, at least on days when people were at home relaxing, it was used for entertainment. In the workfields and in situations of war it provided the rhythm that inspired people to go on. Music music music. Wherever one went there was music. Funeral dirges, wedding songs, ritual chants, work songs, war songs, children's songs, songs that were used to call the rain in times of drought, fertility songs, songs that taught children their traditions. The list was endless.

South Africa has presented herself, certainly to the international community, as a very complex case study. The country has been riddled by upheavals, which escalated when the Nationalist party came to power in 1948 and rose to maddening proportions after 1976. No sooner had the Nationalists gained power than they made dividing Africans by language groups a priority. After the "divide-and-rule" system was in place, the government then instituted systems that were meant to crush any efforts promoting the use of cultural symbols as tools for struggle. Various acts of censorship were introduced to make sure that the music, one of the most utilized forms of communication for Africans, stayed nonpolitical. This succeeded in keeping recorded music and those songs meant for commercial exploitation on the safe side of the government. But you cannot keep a good song down.

Songs still poured out of homes late at night as families gathered around fires for nighttime stories. Children sang their songs in the morning on their way to school. Especially in traditional societies the music might not have openly said "let's go for our guns" but it still echoed sentiments about lands "taken away from us," about children dying of starvation because of man-created, or, more appropriately, government-created, problems.

The introduction of the Christian church in South Africa, as in the United States during the slavery period, immediately provided an avenue for Africans to express their spirituality where their traditions and customs were being discouraged. Church music took on the major responsibility of becoming a spiritual vehicle in which Africans found solace and the promise of a hereafter. Bringing into the church ancient inflections derived from chants and hollers, the Africans changed the sound of church music and made it their own. Suddenly songs became exuberant and spirited, suddenly strict Western harmonic structures were replaced by riffs that made it sound like there were five, six, or even seven loosely structured harmonic parts to each song. The South African church was never the same again. The interesting thing with the development of the black church—both in Africa and in the diaspora, particularly in the United States and South Africa—is that after Africans had accepted forced adaptation to Christianity, they settled down to the religion and made it their own. The birth, in the United States, of the African Methodist Episcopal church and, later, the Pentecostal and the Southern Baptist churches, followed the exact pattern that was taken in the founding of the various Zion Christian churches, and the Ethiopian churches in South Africa. On both continents these churches fused traditional African elements, or whatever was remembered of them, with the Western church norms, to produce a different idiom altogether.

The dynamic force of these syntheses came through mostly in the music. And nowhere was this as evident as in the music of the black church. Helen Kivnick has done an incredible job in capturing the force of this music. If anyone ever wondered how the black masses expressed their political frustrations and how they expressed their hopes for a better tomorrow in a country that seems riddled with hopelessness, all this comes through in the churches as the masses sing.

These songs sung in churches are later taken away and sung in the enclaves of people's houses as they deal with their daily struggles to find jobs, to maintain dignity in environments that seriously undermine their humanity. These church songs that speak of "Help me cross the river Jordan, my burden is too heavy for me" are not only talking of the Biblical Jordan, they are songs that also talk of the Africans' inner fight to keep their sanity in an insane world. "My hope, my hope, will it rise?"

Helen Kivnick, in her powerful chronicle of this music, found her way into the heartbeat of our culture:

"They sang not only in praise of God and Africa. They sang, too, in celebration of the pride that years of enforced servitude had not destroyed. And they sang to fan the flame of humanity, burning still, even inside the land of apartheid."

Then there are the aspects of black life that were not touched by Christianity at all. All these aspects responded to white oppression and domination in different ways. There are the male choral groups that were created in the urban areas by migrant workers from rural areas. These were mostly Zulu-speaking men from the Natal area who were given to high-spirited harmonious traditional songs that were almost always accompanied by fierce Zulu dances characterized by heavy stomping feet. But in the urban areas, because of influx laws, they could not bring women. So whenever they got together to sing in these choral groups, men had to improvise parts that were traditionally sung by women. Not only that. Because they had to hold choir practices in servants' quarters and take precautions so as not to be discovered by their employers, the heavy stomping of the *indlamu* dances had to be replaced by very quick and light movements of the feet that made the men look like they were dancing on their toes. Thus the music was given two new names: *ngomabusuku* (songs of the night) or *isicathamiya* (music accompanied by tip-toe dances). But the most important change in this music was in its moral fiber. Whereas before the preoccupations were with war and with the land (which was taken away from us), in the townships those issues could land you in jail. You would never enter a recording studio singing about that. But you could still sing about cattle and wives and girlfriends that you had left back home. Joseph Shabalala, that magnificent musicologist trained by his forefathers, leader of Ladysmith Black Mambazo, attributes this change to the changing times. "A singer writes about things that he sees around him. And today we see different things than those we used to see before. It is easier today to sing about a girl, the love of your life, while deep in your heart you are also expressing the deep feelings you have for your land. For most of our people, land is a precious thing."

Kivnick spent time with Shabalala and the members of his ten-man group, and also with other groups that sing in this particular style. Her book again manages to capture the essence of multifaceted music and the element of struggle in voices crying out to be heard. *"When you see us here / We are from far away. / We are from there / The place where times are hard."*

So it is that today, when white domination has tried to replace ancient traditions with "civilization," the black family has resorted to songs to escape from the clutches of oppression. When an avenue of escape is sought, it is to music that the black family resorts.

The government's release of Nelson Mandela from prison

in February 1990 was the single most important event that gave black South Africans reason to be optimistic. For the first time in the history of that troubled land black people were made to feel that maybe change is around the corner. Songs jumped out of everywhere, not only celebrating the occasion of Mandela's release but also speaking of a promise of a brighter future ahead. We now will see more songs that speak directly of the political situation in South Africa. But as sure as the sun rises, whenever there is an occasion to celebrate or to mourn, you can rest assured that South Africa will always sing. With tears in her eyes, she will sing. With tears of joy and eyes open wide with jubilation, she will sing. Arms spread up and thrown to the skies, praying for a better world, she will sing. Bodies in motion, celebrating this life or the next, she will sing. Songs of struggle, she will sing, songs of freedom.

March 1990

SOWETO

Meadowlands
East   Orlando
      Orlando West   Nordgesig
Mofolo   Orlando East
      Dube   Diepkloof
Jabavu
      Klipspruit

BOTSWANA

NAMIBIA

Orange River

SOUTH AFRICA

ATLANTIC OCEAN

Robben Island   • CAPE TOWN

Cape of Good Hope

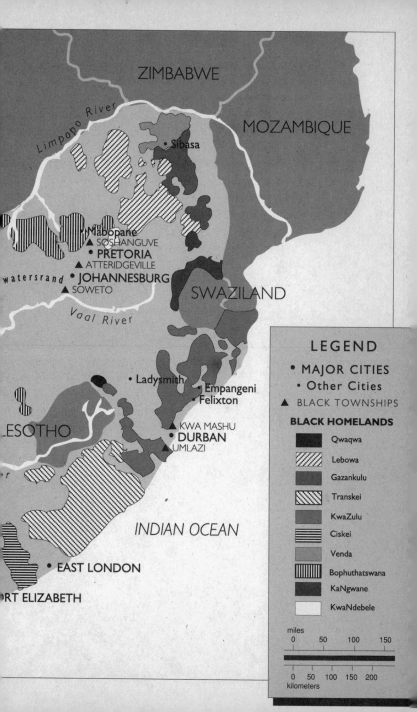

ZIMBABWE

MOZAMBIQUE

Limpopo River

• Sibasa

Mabopane
▲ SOSHANGUVE
• PRETORIA
▲ ATTERIDGEVILLE
watersrand • JOHANNESBURG
▲ SOWETO

SWAZILAND

Vaal River

• Ladysmith
• Empangeni
• Felixton

LESOTHO

▲ KWA MASHU
• DURBAN
▲ UMLAZI

INDIAN OCEAN

• EAST LONDON

RT ELIZABETH

LEGEND

- • **MAJOR CITIES**
- • **Other Cities**
- ▲ BLACK TOWNSHIPS

BLACK HOMELANDS

	Qwaqwa
	Lebowa
	Gazankulu
	Transkei
	KwaZulu
	Ciskei
	Venda
	Bophuthatswana
	KaNgwane
	KwaNdebele

miles
0   50   100   150

0   50   100   150   200
kilometers

PEOPLE
WHO
SING

SHABALALA SPEAKING

BEHIND THE SOUND

THEY ARE SINGING IN AFRICA

SHABALALA SPEAKING

A very long, earnest meeting with Joseph Shabalala was coming to an end. In just a minute or two, the leader of Ladysmith Black Mambazo would go his way and I would go mine. Outside the relative protection of this "international" Durban hotel, Joseph would move through the white city as a nameless, faceless member of his country's black majority. His clothes were better, his bearing more graceful than many. His talent and drive were unsurpassed. But to the whites who claimed South Africa as theirs alone, distinction among blacks went largely unnoticed. In the autumn of 1984 white South Africans knew little about the music of Ladysmith Black Mambazo. So the quietly imposing Joseph Shabalala would walk out of the hotel's front door to become one of his country's expendable black "boys." I would follow, anonymous but white, with my respectability un-challenged.

Like many blacks in South Africa, Shabalala is a fervent Christian. His devotion to God and to Christian humanitari-anism pervade his life and his music. He is a priest in his local church. In the white West, religious leadership may seem in-compatible with musical performance and celebrity. But in South Africa the themes I think of as "church," "kraal" (a circle of grass-and-mud huts), and "fist" run through all of black life, and music somehow weaves them together. Western Christi-anity. Rural-based African tradition. The forceful struggle for self-determination. Music is integral to all three, and South African blacks—virtually all of them—are raised to sing as a way of participating in life's richness and diversity.

Joseph had not talked with me of general black themes

or contradictions. But his account of his own singular path had told far more than one man's personal story. We stood up. I wondered how to thank him for his thoughtfulness and his wisdom. He spoke first.

"Ja. Thank you very much. We pray that we see you when we sing again. Ja."

Prayer is not part of my daily life, and I was surprised to hear myself answer in phrases that reflected the ones he had used. "Thank you. I pray that I see you sing again. Soon. And often. And after that, I pray that I will see you in America. That you come to sing in America."

I exchanged occasional letters with Joseph after my return home. Ladysmith Black Mambazo's popularity in black South Africa continued to grow. His eldest son completed a teaching course and acquired a satisfying classroom position; his second son matriculated high school and enrolled for higher education. Black Mambazo recorded the *Graceland* album with Paul Simon. They came to the United States to perform with him on "Saturday Night Live" and, later, as show-stealers in the blockbuster *Graceland* tour. Now on their own, they draw huge audiences wherever they perform.

My kitchen phone rang one night in 1986 and a familiar harsh, nasal voice identified itself at the other end. "Joseph Shabalala speaking!" He laughed heartily. "Ja! Your prayers for us, they worked. We are here!"

BEHIND
THE SOUND

Beginning with the *Graceland* album and tour, South African music has enjoyed new prominence on the international entertainment scene. Although this distinctive music has always been available to anyone who knew to look for it, suddenly Ladysmith Black Mambazo, Johnny Clegg and Savuka, Miriam Makeba and Hugh Masekela pack concert halls around the world. *Sarafina!*'s children sing out from Broadway stage and movie screen. South African recording artists find their albums selling in the tens and hundreds of thousands. They appear on the "Tonight Show"; they win Grammy Awards. Their sound is driving and exciting, conveying a determination, a hopefulness, and an ultimate indestructibility that infuse popular music with new life. In a very real sense, the music of these artists is energizing the world.

But we in the audience—who love this music today as we have loved other music in the past—must not fail to recognize that these very special sounds do not belong to these performers alone. They are truly the sounds of black South Africa. Their vitality and relentlessness are the soul of a people who, robbed of land and liberty, maintain dignity and struggle for freedom with the only resource they have: their spirit. And that spirit comes alive in song. In South Africa, music very much like what we buy from these professionals is performed as part and parcel of the everyday lives of ordinary people. Parents and children, workers and students. To these people singing is far more than an entertainment commodity, produced by a few for sale to the rest. Rather, it is a way of being together today and moving ahead, together, toward tomorrow. South African blacks grow up using song as a way to express any feeling, to share any activity.

The particular way these people sing—in overlapping parts that work, all together, to produce rhythmic and harmonic fullness—reflects a fundamental African social philosophy: an individual achieves wholeness only in interaction with others. In Zulu the saying goes *umuntu ungumuntu ngabantu* (roughly, "One can only be fully human through relationships with fellow human beings"), but similar sayings exist among every South African people.[1] It is not that individual achievement is discouraged. Instead, it is that such achievement is pursued in a way that enhances the whole community. South Africans do not perform, by and large, as soloists. On stage as off, they work together in intricate, dynamic cooperation that transcends any one person's virtuosity.

Today's South African musical celebrities are not just current stars in an entertainment industry's ever-changing galaxy. Far more important, they are international ambassadors of a people whose government denies their humanity. Their music is the voice of a people whose government presumes to speak for them abroad while fighting to silence them at home. South African performers are most fully, most musically human as they interpret the sound and soul of their people. And what lies behind their extraordinary musical sound is nothing less than their people's story.

THEY ARE SINGING IN AFRICA

I went to South Africa in 1984 because that country's black singing had been intriguing me for years. Spirited and inexplicably gripping, it had always seemed to represent something larger and more far-reaching than the words or notes of any one song. I knew something about apartheid's institutionalized system of racial oppression, and I wondered if singing hadn't, all along, been more important than we acknowledged in black people's survival within that system.

In March, on my first trip, people in the urban areas were talking about upcoming elections to the newly formed "Colored" and "Asian" Houses of Parliament. The nonracial United Democratic Front (UDF) was urging a boycott of the elections, claiming that the white government's new constitution permanently disenfranchised the country's vast black majority. Other voices called the government's new reforms a real hope for the meaningful, peaceful change needed so desperately in their country. I accompanied black people to their homes, to church, to work, to meetings. Wherever they gathered they sang; I sang along.

I returned to South Africa in early October, with my husband, Gary Gardner. Only a small minority of eligible "Coloreds" and "Asians" had voted in the parliamentary elections. Armed authorities had transformed peaceful protests into riotous occasions for violence and death. Demonstrators had been arrested, opposition leaders taken into "preventive detention." Still, people seemed to think that the opportunity for meaningful, peaceful change was not entirely gone. Students were demanding fundamental changes in government-controlled

Bantu Education. Anti-apartheid groups were staging massive work stayaways. Labor unions were organizing large-scale federations whose concerns would transcend workers in one industry, people in one region, and issues related to the shop floor, alone. Sewage still stank in the open ditches along black area streets. Black parents still left young children alone from dark to dark, struggling to hold on to the distant jobs that were the only jobs they could find. Kerosene fumes still choked black people forced to live, far too many, in small, unventilated rooms. Alongside accustomed determination and weariness, hope and excitement crackled in the air. And, as before, it was all voiced in song.

An inextricable part of traditional life, black music in South Africa clearly reflects the social foundation of that life. Thus, good singing relies on both individual excellence and group cooperation. Good performance requires a strong leader and a competent chorus, interacting in sensitive realization of the fullness that is implied whenever one voice produces a lonely melody. With voice and body, in words, rhythm, and melody, these people sing together in the spirit of brotherhood that transcends age, time, and the currents of political power. Singing marks the passing of milestones social and personal. It deepens the connection between people who have come together for reasons casual or profound. It ties any moment to every other experience of singing. With every note black South Africans proclaim themselves more than victims. Yes, they are oppressed. Yes, they are horribly violated. Yes, too, they are people of spirit, of tradition, of remarkable humanity.

In South Africa personal introductions from American friends and colleagues led me to people of diverse social, racial, and professional backgrounds. Among urban blacks who were not choir directors or professional musicians, a predictable series of exchanges quickly came to characterize the beginning of each conversation, graphically illustrating the extent to which these people take singing for granted. It is not "Singing"—something special, with a capital S; it is just part of life.

I would know something about the special commitment of the person with whom I would be sitting, and he or she would know that I was interested in black singing. Briefly we would exchange pleasantries and sip coffee. After a very few minutes, however, my host would rather impatiently say something like, "I'm really not a singer and I don't know how I can help you. Perhaps you would better spend your time talking with a real musician."

At first I was quite taken aback. Gradually I began to relax into my responses.

"You're not a singer?"

"No."

"You really don't sing?"

"Not very well."

"What about at church?"

"Well *everyone* sings at church. Of course I sing there. But I'm not in the choir."

"When you're singing in church, do you sing the main melody? Or do you sing some other part?"

"I sing my own part of course. The melody is just one part, and most people sing a different part, in harmony."

"What about at a family gathering?"

"At a family gathering of course I would sing. That is when everyone sings. The women will be in the kitchen preparing food and singing women's songs, and the men will be out singing men's songs, and the children will be outside singing children's songs. Singing is always part of such times."

"What about when you're with friends?"

"Singing is just part of being with friends. Walking together, or working in the house, or just sitting and telling stories. Sooner or later someone will start a song and then we are all singing."

"Do you sing at a wedding?"

"*Everybody* sings at a wedding. There are songs to prepare the bride, and songs to prepare the groom, and songs to welcome the bride, and songs to welcome the bride's family, and songs to welcome the groom, and songs to welcome the groom's family. Everyone sings at such a celebration. The women and the men and the children. Everyone."

"What about when you are by yourself. Walking to the bus, or driving in your car?"

"When you are walking by yourself you may be thinking about your family or your job, or you may be thinking about a problem or a sadness, and then you just notice that you are singing. Probably you are singing to yourself softly, because you are in the city, but sometimes you hear yourself quite loud and then you wonder how long you have been singing to the streets. You keep on thinking, and you keep on singing."

"Do you sing at a funeral?"

"Do you *not* sing at a funeral? How can you mourn if you do not sing together?"

I came to learn that most blacks who said they were not singers seemed to mean that they did not belong to organized choirs and, perhaps, that they were not particularly good singers. But with only one exception, they all acknowledged singing in the specific settings about which I learned to ask—settings which constitute everyday life. Those who initially denied being singers were responding as, I realized, a white American might respond if I asked about being "a speaker."

"You're really not a speaker?"

"No."

"Do you speak to your family or friends, when you are together?"

Talking is something most white Americans do whenever we are in someone else's company. While working, walking, and relaxing. At parties and at meetings. To rejoice and to console. Identifying oneself as a speaker implies a formal audience, a special ability, and a status that is somehow exalted. Few of us readily characterize ourselves this way, but we all talk.

Similarly, black South Africans take singing for granted as a way of taking part in community life. It is not that these people do not talk to one another; of course they do. But in singing they share a second way of communicating, that we in nonsinging cultures don't even imagine as possible. Inseparable from the struggle to survive and the exhilaration of living, singing is a way of expressing everything and sharing anything.

Songs speak to every aspect of black South African experience. Some celebrate. Others mourn. Some invoke distant worlds. Others protest the here and now. Many simply accompany, as Savuka's bass accompanies the band's overall performance. In social interaction singing fades in and out. Now it peppers conversation with lively, rhythmic interjections; now it yields to smoother, more linear discourse. It is to illustrate this Protean ubiquitousness that I include song fragments in my writing about South Africa. I use song fragments, as well, to convey the spark, the multifaceted richness with which life can proceed when didactic Western prose is not held as the paramount standard of communication, and when movement forward, in a straight line, is not viewed as the only form of progress.

I spent a total of three months in South Africa, searching for the soul of its haunting, ever-present singing; my search brought me to the soul of the country itself. This is a place where people of different races, different sociopolitical convictions, view the world through such different lenses that they can't even see they are not looking at one another. Somehow, music afforded clarity. In city and country, church and workplace, community hall and private living room, black people sing as an integral part of being together. Singing along allowed me, if only for isolated moments, to step inside their world. Rough, exuberant, and inspiring, that world is permeated with an intensity that concentrates joys and sorrows, hopes and terrors, almost beyond endurance. Still they endure. Understanding the singing of black South Africans is essential to understanding who these people are, what they live for, and what they are increasingly being pushed to die for.

They are singing with history—
Let us all sing along![2]

Amandla!

IN CHURCH

WORSHIP
IN SOWETO

In an auctioneer's tones the black cleric at St. Paul's Anglican Church in Soweto sang out page numbers; his congregation prayed in many languages, each with its own hymnal.

Xhosa 79!
Tswana 78!
Zulu 31!
Pedi 23!
Sotho 48!
English hymnal 72!

Everyone was included with grace and good humor. Hymns were sung—sometimes simultaneously, sometimes in sequence—in as many languages as there were hymnals. Pretoria makes much of "black on black" ethnic antagonisms. At St. Paul's I saw the way cooperation can flourish in South Africa's black urban townships when people are left to live together without government interference.

But for the Babel of foreign tongues, most of the hymns sounded a lot like those I have always loved. Chord progressions were predictable, rhythms regular, stately, and consistent around the room. Mellifluous harmonies flowed in every direction. I was enveloped in a unified choral sound that came from every voice in the church.

Let me be purified
For I have nothing in my hand.
I am naked, Lord,
As I survey Your cross.

Suddenly the quality of the singing changed as Western hymnody yielded to African idiom. Choral unison broke into multiple parts, each following its own path in complex, fine-tuned interplay with all the others. The words to these prayers were clearly religious, clearly Christian. But where the beauty of the Western hymns had expressed reverence, the rhythmic excitement of their African counterparts was creating life.

(*Pray*)
Because the road has thorns
We will pray

The congregation played with words and with the syllables that made them, repeating linguistic fragments again and again in musical celebration of their shared heritage.

Pray and pray (*Praise Him*)

They punctuated old phrases with spontaneous new ones, adding parts where, just a moment before, I would have said there was room for nothing more.

Pray and pray (*Praise Him*)
(*Because*)

It would not be precisely accurate to describe the congregation as dancing these prayers; neither would it be accurate to describe what they did with them as anything else. These Anglicans sang their Western hymns, in praise of their Lord. But they *became* their African hymns with every fiber of their beings. In voice, in body, in spirit personal and communal, so did these children of Africa celebrate their Savior.

Pray and pray (*Praise Him*)
(*Because*)
Pray and pray (*Praise Him*)
(*Because*)
Because the road, it is strewn with thorns (*Praise Him*)
We will pray and pray (*Praise Him*)
(*Because*)

My white Johannesburg hostess was still asleep when Peter Mabotho knocked at our front door. Since I was newly arrived in the country, he had agreed to come out to the city's white northern suburbs and then drive back with me into Soweto. It was Sunday morning, and Peter had decided that although he usually worships at a different church, a service at St. Paul's—led by an energetic, community-minded priest and his indomitable wife—would be a good introduction for me to the mission Christianity that is such an important theme in urban black South Africa and its music.

I fumbled with the elaborate system of locks, keys, and plugs that secured my hostess's gracious front porch. Peter and I eyed each other through the door which was, for all its locks and heavy steel bars, made largely of glass. Introduced by a mutual friend, we had spoken often by telephone; this was our first face-to-face meeting. I saw a large, dignified man of fifty dressed in dark trousers and a cream-colored embroidered African shirt. From his neck fell a slender strand of beads. Unamused, he watched a small, young-looking white woman doing clumsy battle with a ridiculous contraption. At last I got the door open and we shook hands.

IN CHURCH

Auntie, open for me
I am all alone outside
I am wet and cold
Open for me.

From the passenger's seat in my rented blue Toyota, Peter directed me through a maze of shaded suburban streets to the highway that took us south into downtown Johannesburg. One more turn, and we were heading west. The black South Western Townships of Soweto are separated from the white city by what appears to be a twenty-kilometer stretch of undeveloped no-man's-land. Each of four east-west roads provides a single entrance to the black location. In times of emergency, access is easily controlled and the whole collection of townships, unofficially said to number well over two million people, may be entirely sealed off by no more than ten roadblocks.

Peter Mabotho is a social worker and the director of his church choir. Having sung in choirs for decades, I empathized instantly with his concerns about rehearsal attendance, performance quality, and the difficulty of maintaining and expanding repertoire in the face of constantly changing personnel. We had just met, Peter and I, but when he started singing the melody of one of his choir's favorite hymns, in Sotho, I found myself pulling a harmony out of some dusty corner of my past and singing along on "ah." His stiff seriousness relaxed into a smile. "So you really do sing. And you are not shy about joining in. Now I'm sure you will understand what will be happening in this church today."

We drove along Soweto's rutted dirt roads, lined with uniform matchbox houses that stretched as far as I could see. Kitchen, living room, bedroom or two. Toilet out back, cold-water tap at the sink. If it had been winter, kerosene burners would have poured heat and smoke into rooms that were all too small, all too close.

In the heart of Jabavu, we turned into the dusty driveway of St. Paul's. Black people scattered to make way for our car, peered at my white face with some curiosity, and then resumed what we had interrupted. I had already been in South Africa for several days, but until this morning I had stayed in Johannesburg, a white city that managed, at the time, to lull inhabitants into a mistaken feeling of national white predominance. Even these few minutes of driving through Soweto reminded me that this is a country of black people. Poor people. Poorer people. People who are somewhat less poor. But *black* people, among whom white faces constitute individual curiosities or collective oppressors.

St. Paul's was in the process of building a new sanctuary, so the service was to be held elsewhere on the grounds. The main building was nearly demolished. Although it was surrounded by a fence, bits of brick and board lay everywhere. Adults walked carefully to avoid turning ankles or puncturing soles. Children scooped up these scattered fragments of the old church and used them in impromptu games of skill.

We stood outside until the final clang of the steeple bell, while Peter greeted friends he hadn't seen in many months. The late-summer sun was bright and hot. No breeze stirred the dust that hovered in the air. Language told me that this was Africa, but clothing—the women's, in particular—confirmed my initial impression that these people might have been found in any mainstream Christian church anywhere in the Western world. Timeless, proper dresses clung to breasts and hips that were already damp with perspiration. Shoes that were never meant for comfort cramped feet that were already beginning to swell. Like Peter, a few of the men wore lovely embroidered African shirts. By and large, however, the men wore suits. New suits. Old suits. Old suits that were badly frayed. Old suits that were carefully preserved. Suits whose age and fashion were unidentifiable for the tracery of wrinkles that dominated them so completely. But suits nonetheless, as a sign of respect. In Western terms. For me today was my first visit to Soweto; for these black Anglicans it was the Sabbath.

Peter led me into the temporary sanctuary, to seats a friend of his was saving. The room was so crowded that I had no idea of its size or realistic capacity. People were squashed together in pews, crowded into aisles, seated on rows of benches outside the windows, and squeezing in through the doors. Children holding infants sat on the laps of their parents. And everyone sang. Every prayer filled the hall with music.

> My hope—
> **Will it rise, rise, rise**
> **To join with the voices of heaven?**

At one point the children were all asked to leave to attend a Sunday school class outside the sanctuary. I expected the room to feel airier with so many bodies gone, but in the crush of adults the children's absence was hardly noticeable. There came a time in the service for guests to be introduced and welcomed to the community. When Peter was singled out, he rose and spoke in Sotho about the joys and sadnesses, the births and deaths, that had colored all their lives since his last visit. He had lost his wife. A friend had been blessed with a grandson. Another friend had a son in detention, in prison. Until I heard him saying my name and asking me to stand up, and until I stood and looked around, I had not realized that mine was the only white skin in the whole, crowded room.

I gazed at a vast sea of warm, welcoming black faces, and I tried to express my profound gratitude at being permitted to share this congregation's prayers. White acquaintances had warned me to expect animosity in Soweto's churches, particularly those, like St. Paul's, known for practicing community development and advocating fierce local pride. Perhaps today, with increased township tension and militarization, the animosity would be inescapable. Perhaps there was hostility that morning, as well. But I forgot to look. All I noticed was the love.

> **Love (*His love*), His love**
> **Is wondrous and surprising (*His love*)**

Shortly after the introduction of the guests, the service proceeded to the wishing of "Peace be with you," a custom Peter described as common in churches throughout Africa. At St. Paul's the congregation repeated a short phrase, and while people were singing they began to mill about the sanctuary, greeting everyone they knew, grasping each other's hands, and wishing one another "Peace be with you." Although I knew no one except Peter, I had just been introduced at large. In addition, I had been looking around during the service, catching the eye of whoever happened to be looking my way. As I drifted around the room in Peter's wake, each person with whom I had made eye contact greeted me by name and warmly grasped my hands.

"Peace be with you."
"Peace be with you."
Peace be with us all.

The children reentered the room from the rear, and they moved to the front for communion, singing in English. The whole congregation rose to sing along.

> **Every time I**
> **Feel the Spirit**
> **Moving in my heart**
> **I will pray**

Again and again the verse went around. White acquaintances had predicted that I would soon find black singing boring and repetitive, and for a moment, as I listened in silence, I was tempted to agree. But everything changed when I joined in the song. From the outside, every repetition had been a replay of what had come before; on the inside, it became an opportunity to try something new. A harmony that worked perfectly with what Peter was singing to my right. A syncopation that complemented the rhythmic way the women behind me were beating their hymnals. This simple spiritual would have to last for hours, for us to realize all its possibilities.

I asked Peter about numbers of people at the service, and he estimated eight hundred. I asked if that included the children. He laughed. "The children are a host in themselves."

And so they were. They came and came, flowing like a river, and still there were more. In all sizes. Dressed in all colors and styles. The smallest girls wore lacy stockings crocheted in pastel colors, showing the lovely dark of their legs through the openwork. All the children were clean and scrubbed, so that their faces shone to match their eyes. Some were dressed casually, in starched jeans and brightly colored T-shirts. Some wore fancier clothes—party dresses for the girls and suits for the boys. Like their parents, most had come to church in their Sunday best. All sang.

Every time I
Feel the Spirit
Moving in my heart
I will pray.

The song echoed with such force that I thought it must carry all the way to Johannesburg.

Upon the mountain
Down the valley
I will praise
My Lord!

22

I imagined blacks echoing this spiritual in Mofolo and Klip-spruit, adding their voices in Dube and Meadowlands East to help it on its way.

Upon the mountain

It gathers strength in Orlando East and Orlando West.

Down the valley

In Diepkloof. In Orlando.

I will praise

A last boost in Noordgesig and the song sails over the emptiness toward Johannesburg.

My Lord!

And I wondered who would be there, in that white City of Gold, to hear this black exultation and add to it the brotherhood that could ensure its Divine audience.

**Every time I
Feel the Spirit
Moving in my heart
I will pray———**

BLACK
IN CHRIST'S MISSION

Mission Christianity in South Africa has always been tied both to black progress and aspirations, and, paradoxically, to white conquest and control. Indigenous African life was agrarian, and in its context religious, social, economic, and political institutions were all inextricably interwoven.[1] Anthropologist David Coplan explains that by the mid-1800s, when Christian missionization had been established throughout the region, African religious converts found themselves unsuited to the complex fabric of traditional life. These people had voluntarily accepted Christ as their Lord; in so doing they had, far less knowingly, been drawn into a new world that could not help but unravel the intricately knitted life of old. Mission education introduced its African converts to Western economic and political power. Aspiring to new goals, these people migrated to the developing towns, where they modeled themselves after the whites who held power.

Christianity removed "school" Africans socially and culturally from their traditionalist countrypeople. Migration distanced them geographically, as well. But westernization never led to political or economic equality, and the population of well-educated, urbanized, mission Africans soon found themselves isolated both from the Victorian whites whose favor they were courting, and also from the black traditionalists they had learned to disdain as "primitive" and "heathen."

Oh my God,
Why have You forgotten me?

Although they failed to win white acceptance, mission-educated African professionals assumed early leadership in the expanding black urban townships. They also enjoyed a measure of economic prosperity. Particularly after the 1886 "discovery" of gold on the Witwatersrand, black teachers, clergy, and lawyers from the whole of South Africa flocked to the new urban center of Johannesburg, or *Egoli* (City of Gold), in search of westernized respectability and advancement.

Missions followed their rural converts to the city, where they shaped the development of middle-class black life. In place of traditional tribal social structure, urban churches organized general community welfare, cultural development, and social action. In place of traditional tribal schools they provided secular, cultural, and religious education. In place of segregated tribalism, churches and their schools fostered cooperation among members from many traditional heritages. Thus, social class and Christian denomination paralleled ethnic heritage and regional background as determinants of black urban identity.

Political authorities in each of South Africa's provinces governed according to a "color bar" intended to ensure the domination of the region's relatively few whites over its far more numerous black population. While Christian doctrine reinforced the commitment of urban blacks to a theology of nonracial brotherhood, the Church hierarchy itself perpetuated the color bar. Christian doctrine notwithstanding, even the most articulate, insightful, and aspiring blacks were prevented from sharing either political and economic power, or Church-related authority. And Christianity entrenched the early distance between these westernized blacks and the rural traditionalists who condemned them as traitorous tools of the Europeans.[2]

I went far away
From my father's lands
And now everyone despises me.

As early as the late 1800s, black urban leaders began to doubt the wisdom of their unqualified embrace of westernization. They began to consider bases for autonomous black political identity, autonomous black religion, and autonomous African culture. These early Africanists sought to draw on their tribal past and on their essentially Western present to synthesize these two disparate identities into something new, something that would express their unique relationship to each tradition while maintaining their independence from both. One hundred years later, this effort to develop a unified, autonomous black South African culture persists as blacks struggle to express their own integrity while avoiding white government domination and interference. Still, today, they incorporate elements from their own westernization, their own historical tribal traditions, and international black culture into an ever-changing, ever-richer body of black South African expression.

Inevitably, church singing in South Africa reflects this same overall movement—first toward unconditional westernization, and, later, in new directions derived from both Africa and the West. Complex part-singing is an important component of traditional communal life among all of South Africa's indigenous black peoples. Coplan explains that Christian converts brought a well-developed vocal proficiency to newly introduced mission singing. Although the four-part harmonic structure of European hymnody differs considerably from traditional African polyphony, black Christians offered little resistance to this new Western idiom. Never mind that Western melodies forced frequent violation of the speech tones characteristic of their indigenous languages. They sang European hymns in Zulu and Xhosa, admirably imitating Western choirs. With the stirrings of African nationalism at the end of the last century, black composers began to set religious words to syncretic singing that incorporated such African stylistic elements as call-and-response, semi-independent parts, staggered entrances, and rhythmic liveliness.[3]

Today's black mission Christians worship in musical and linguistic diversity. They sing Western hymns in tongues both European and African. They sing syncretic hymns with harmonies too Western to claim African genesis, and melodies too rough and rhythmic to be of the West. In all languages or without language altogether, they sing and stamp the prayers of Africa.

My, my, my
Jesus is my

Thus, mission-based Christianity is historically bound up in those struggles which, to this day, remain most central to black South Africans: the struggle to integrate the goals of African progress and self-determination into an overall theology of human brotherhood; the struggle to share in the progress of urban westernization while retaining or re-embracing essential elements of African tradition; and the struggle to accommodate, simultaneously, to Western values and to truncation of the aspirations fostered by those values.

My, my, my (*Oh my*)
Jesus is my (*Oh my*)
Jesus is my Savior
Day by day
My, my, my
(*Oh my*)
Jesus is my
(*Oh my!*)

OFFERING

People spilled out of the St. Paul's sanctuary, raising anew the township dust that had begun to settle during the service. Inside, a little girl had been sitting next to me. Her dress of crisp pink ruffles shone in her patent leather shoes as she climbed on and off her mother's lap. When she happened to glimpse the reflections in those gleaming shoes, her eyes widened and she squealed in gleeful fascination. Once or twice she caught me watching her. Outside, she held tight to her mother's hand as Peter formally introduced us. I started to comment on her mirror-shiny shoes, but after just these few minutes in the yard they were already gray with dust.

Peter positioned us in the middle of the path, ten or twenty feet outside the door, so that friends could find him without searching through the crowd. A group gathered around us, mostly middle-aged, as younger relatives and small children hung back and smiled at me with the shyness of people who wish one another well but have no common language for conversation. Friends pushed gently toward Peter, their warm feelings for him spilling over onto me.

"*Ngiyabonga! Ngiyabonga!*" Thank you for the service, I tried to say.

"Ja!" "Thank you very much!" "I'm very happy." They were struggling, too. Peter's resonant baritone boomed over our reedier voices.

In the center of the churchyard women were gathering. Twenty. Fifty. Nearly a hundred, they laughed and moved about purposefully. Suddenly they slid into a harsh, rural-sounding melody, one of their number loudly slapping a leather briefcase for rhythm. A shrill ululation pierced the air.

Rock of Ages

These were the same Western-looking women whose company I had been keeping for hours. But their voices were no longer sweet, their rhythm no longer anything I recognized.

Let me be purified

An undulating procession emerged from the milling mass of womanhood, slowly winding its way across the yard and back inside the sanctuary.

Until I hide in you

Reminiscent of traditional, rural ceremonies where women perform songs and dances together, grouped by age, they followed one another single file. Shoes were discarded. The whole line snaked through the courtyard. Each woman swayed gently as she moved.

Wound of Jesus

Their song was a slow wail. Two phrases repeated again and again. A soft, low tone slid up, high and loud, held fast for two or three beats, and fell off, back toward the starting pitch. Much more quickly, three tones ascended, stepwise, and returned to the first.

Blood of Jesus

Around the courtyard men stamped and clapped, echoing the leader's slow, rhythmic slapping of her briefcase. Women sang

out from all directions. Some droned; others added open harmonies whose harshness matched the tone of the song. Conversation did not entirely stop, but voices quieted to a low buzz,
accompanying the shrill female sound that was like nothing I
had heard from these same people all morning.

Let me be purified

The leader raised her briefcase high in the air. Other women
raised their hands.

I have nothing in my hand

The easy dignity of their movement, individually and together, established this procession as part of their cultural heritage. No longer were they simply Anglicans, residents of
Soweto, mothers, teachers, nurses, and the many other contemporary roles they all played. In addition, they were Xhosa
women, Sotho women—proud women of a timeless Africa.

Rock of Ages

As one they affirmed an essential cultural identity that transcends specific ethnic or linguistic lineage. As one they invoked
an ancestral spirit that admits none of apartheid's shame.

Let me be purified

The morning's sermon had been delivered by a new dea-
con. During the service Peter had identified a special collection
as the customary way of taking care of this young man and his
family. Now he explained that the congregation's women were
taking care of him in yet another way, and demonstrating care
for their people, their historical legacy, as well.

OFFERING

Until I hide in you

I had looked up at Peter during his explanation, momentarily ignoring the procession. When I looked back I saw that on her head, in the traditional manner requiring a gracefulness in the hips that must be mastered in childhood, each woman now carried some kind of household object.

Blood of Jesus

A box of laundry detergent swayed gently.

I have nothing in my hand

A roll of paper towels stood upright.

I am naked, Lord

A stack of canned soups teetered but did not fall.

I look closely

A squeeze bottle of green dishwashing liquid, translucent, caught the sun.

At the cross

A huge sack of mealie meal spread far beyond the narrow shoulders of its bearer.

IN CHURCH

In its crucifixion

Peter laughed down at me, delighted. "You see, Helen. Even in the city we do not forget our own ways of doing things. We are all very Western, here today. We are all also African."

Oh my Lord.

MY HOPE, WILL IT RISE, RISE, RISE?

Soshanguve township, in South Africa's Transvaal Province, is filled to capacity. Peter Mabotho's young friends Elisabeth and Samuel Kgapola might have waited for years before getting a house there. So rather than live with parents, they had opted for the house Chief Minister Mangope offered to blacks who would accept citizenship in the "independent homeland" of Bophuthatswana. Their house stood in the homeland location of Mabopane, divided from Soshanguve by an imaginary line. When Peter invited Gary and me (Gary had just arrived in the country) to join him for the celebration of Elisabeth's robing into the church Mothers' Union, we had no idea we were being invited to an international event.

Samuel Kgapola was in training for the priesthood at St. Barnabas Anglican Church in Soshanguve. With Elisabeth's formalized membership in the Mothers' Union, she would be spending much of her time at the church, as well. But every time they traveled from home to church or church to home, they would cross what South African maps designate as an international border. We crossed that same international border when we drove from the church service to a party at the young couple's home.

> Speak the news
> My mother's child, speak the news

In many township churches I had seen women wearing what my hosts identified as the uniform of the local Mothers' Union or Mothers' Guild—black shoes and stockings, black skirt, long-sleeved overblouse of white or red, matching hat, and, in many cases, a beaded rosary. As women are the acknowledged backbone of black South African families, so the Mothers' Guilds are recognized as central to the functioning of black churches. They accept major responsibility for the human activities that make the churches vibrant community organizations during the week. Conducting educational and social affairs. Visiting the sick. Arranging assistance for families in crisis. Organizing services for those whose special needs are not met elsewhere. These kinds of activities were once handled within tribal social structures; in the process of missionized urbanization they were assumed by the churches.

Guild Mothers pray together on weekdays, sustaining individual faith and maintaining a strong, highly visible bond between the functions the group performs for the community and the God in whose name they serve. They also conduct much of the fund-raising that keeps their churches financially solvent. Once, Peter joked that with their control over church purse strings, the women of the Guilds could probably take over the churches outright if they wanted to.

For Elisabeth, formal membership in the Mothers' Union symbolized her lifelong commitment to God, His church, and His people. It also represented her official participation in the world to which her husband had dedicated his life. Joining the Guild was an extremely important event in her life and the occasion for a major feast.

The news is not about you
The news is of Jesus

The brick of Mabopane's matchbox houses gleamed in the brilliant sun. Although the houses were set in close, featureless rows, at close range intensely colored patches of grass and garden created a sense of graciousness quite absent from older locations like Soweto. Bright canvas tents dotted Mabopane with gaiety.

Township houses are tiny; celebrations involve whole communities, and they are readily identified by the tents pitched wherever the hosts can find room. When we passed the third tent on a single street, Peter's friend Jocelyn murmured that spring was a good season for parties—the rains were finished and summer's heat had not yet set in.

> **This is it**
> **This is it**
> **This is it**

Anchored to the roof, a green canopy tented the Kgapolas' front yard, out into the street. People crowded underneath, enjoying moments of shade and then making room for others to do the same. Samuel stood just inside the tent, greeting his guests. He clapped Peter on the shoulder and roared his welcome. To Gary and me he extended his hand and laughed broadly. "Welcome to our humble matchbox. It is of course quite unique and unlike any other matchbox in the whole of South Africa!" Elisabeth stood at his side. Her placid face, framed with softly wavy hair, did not reflect her husband's mischievousness.

A banquet table stretched along the front of the house and then angled sharply away toward the street. On white linen places were set with utensils and fancifully folded pastel napkins. Platters of biscuits and chips alternated with bowls of colorful salads and pineapples stuck with cubes of meat, cheese, and fruit. While guests milled around, waiting for the feast to begin, they picked at the delicacies on display. Women from inside continually replenished supplies so that latecomers faced the same bounty that had awaited the earliest arrivals.

Ten members of the Mothers' Guild arranged themselves along the head table, and Peter and Jocelyn seated themselves and Gary and me just around the corner. A good-humored woman named Joyce, apparently the leader of the Guild, started each bowl of salad down the long table of Mothers, laughing loudly and calling out to new faces that peeked into the tent. Elisabeth sat next to her, shyly accepting the congratulations of her guests. I glanced uneasily at the tens of people still standing; the table would never accommodate them all. Jocelyn was reassuring. "Our township hospitality is not limited by a table. When we have finished our meal, our places will be set for other guests and they will be served all over again. And then again and again. By this evening many, many people will have eaten at this same table. No one will go away unsatisfied."

Without introduction Joyce started a lively chorus, clapping vigorously and encouraging the other Mothers to join in.

It is going to be like this
Like this
When we pray

They did.

It is going to be like this

Ten women in white blouses and black hats,

Like this

they sang multiple parts and clapped with a gusto that swept up everyone under the tent.

When we pray

The chorus was really just one line, in Sotho, sung again and again and lengthened by repeating and drawing out the last word in a way that turned it into a refrain all its own. In church, formal hymns had dominated the congregation's singing. Western or African in musical idiom, these hymns were conventionally structured, with many verses that worshippers followed in hymnals. Church singing also includes a repertoire of "choruses," one-line exclamations repeated over and over as parts enter at different times and sing through in lively rhythmic interplay. These choruses are easy to learn and follow without written hymnals. As such, they characterize religious singing in informal settings like this celebration.

> **When we pray**
> **When we pray**
> **When we pray**
> **When we pray**

Joyce started each repetition by calling high and then low, the third and then the low dominant, before landing on the tonic that defined both the key and the musical beginning of the line. Anonymous guests whistled. The chorus engulfed the whole celebration, including us.

As in so much South African religious singing, the vigor, physicality, and unabashed delight of this phrase seemed to contradict its devout content. Chagrined, I soon recognized this contradiction as part of my white Western expectations for prayer. For these Africans voice and body, delight and vigor are all integral to the experience of life. And prayer is part of life. Life is both with people, here, and with spirits, of other worlds and times. The Mothers' Union is an organ of mission Christianity; their prayers use Western harmonies to praise God in Western terms. But even within Western structures, these women's idioms for religious devotion also express their irrepressible Africanism.

> **It is going to be like this**
> **Like this**

Reminiscent of the "Peace be with you" ritual at St. Paul's, this chorus was, at once, a song of God and a song of humanity.

It joined Elisabeth to each of her guests, transforming a few hundred individual acquaintances into a strangely intimate community. No more were people the same strangers to us. We could not speak their language. We did not live their lives. But we were singing together, mutually sensitive and responsive as we constituted a robust choir and then delighted in our cooperative performance.

When we pray

Almost on the heels of the first song, Joyce began another.

**My dove
My dove
My dove**

Elisabeth had just raised a fork to her mouth, and she stopped, fork midair, unsure of what to do next.

**My dove of prayer
(*My dove*)**

Joyce grinned and clapped all the more vigorously.

**This is it
This is it
This is it**

Elisabeth giggled, replaced her fork, food untouched, and joined the singing.

This is the place for praying

The other Mothers followed her lead, leaving their own food on their plates.

My place
My place
My place

We found the meal delicious. As each bowl passed our way Jocelyn identified its contents and urged us to try some. She and Peter watched anxiously lest we go hungry. They needn't have worried. Like the other guests, we ate appreciatively and sang between mouthfuls.

My place of praying

The sound of the song was constantly changing as singers faded in and out of the choir at will.

This is it

A pleasant clinking of cutlery and undertone of conversation accompanied the music.

This is it

The Mothers' singing never wavered.

This is it
(*My dove*)

Supplementing the food that had been sitting out all along, women carried new platters from the kitchen. They stepped and swayed in rhythm, setting each dish at the head table and, unburdened, shaking shoulders and hips suggestively. For a few moments they joined the festivities under the tent. Then they returned inside.

These women wore the pastel uniforms of domestic servants. Indeed, they *were* domestic servants, maids for white families in Pretoria. But that was during the week. Sunday was the Sabbath, and today's kitchen labors were their gift to one of their own. They sang not only in praise of God and Africa. They sang, too, in celebration of the pride that years of enforced servitude had not destroyed. And they sang to fan the flame of humanity, burning still, even inside the land of apartheid.

> My hope
> My hope
> Will it rise?

Throughout white South Africa black domestic servants shuffle, subservient, attending to the daily maintenance of white families, gardens, and homes. A sluggish weariness characterizes most of the black women seen walking the streets of the country's white cities. Examples leap to mind. The large woman I saw trudging toward a Johannesburg corner on my first afternoon in the country, string bags bulging over both arms and a huge carton balanced on her head. The cleaning woman at the University of the Witwatersrand, who lugged pails and dust rags along academic corridors, sighing and softly moaning with each slow step. The Capetown woman, lumbering on swollen feet and ankles, who watched helplessly as her bus pulled away, knowing that she could not move quickly enough to catch it.

> My hope, my hope
> Will it rise?

To much of the white community, sluggish compliance is synonymous with black womanhood. The pervasiveness of this unflattering stereotype reflects the unfortunate effectiveness of South Africa's racial apartness. Whites are not necessarily refusing to acknowledge black energy and assertiveness because they have been trained to believe them to be impossible. More likely, what whites see of black life is still—after one hundred years of sharing the same urban areas—only a small part of black life's diversity.

For today's black adults, weary deference is what women have been socialized to show to whites. It is safe. It attracts no potentially dangerous individual attention. It camouflages rage and frustration at being forced to shoulder responsibility for the fabric of a family life worn thin by generations of legislative assault. Passively defiant, weariness and deference appear non-threatening to the whites who continue to hold all the power. These attitudes by no means characterize black women in their own worlds. But the vast majority of South African whites have no personal familiarity with or even impersonal awareness of the richness and spiritedness of black people's own worlds. They know slow dreariness, and they are taught to fear explosive violence; they do not even begin to imagine the vitality, the generosity, the all-embracing sense of community that are the essence of black South Africa.

My hope
Will it rise, rise, rise?

Of course white activists have contact with black women whose intelligence and assertiveness are unquestionable. But even these liberals often seemed to regard their black colleagues as aberrant. My discussion with a white union negotiator illustrates.

"The democracy inherent in trade unionism cultivates leadership among female trade unionists. And of course these women are smart and tough and competent. They have to be. It's their job to protect the interests of the membership. But these trade union women are different."

"Different from what?"

"From your basic black woman on the street. You said it

yourself. They are slow, and sluggish, and they always seem tired. And that's the majority. Not the few who are leaders in the trade unions."

"Do you think black women on the street are always the way we see them?"

She seemed taken aback, but she answered honestly. "Probably not. But if that's all I see, how can they expect me to know anything different? You know, they create this image themselves, by behaving the way they do. If they were more lively on white streets, then we might come to see them differently."

"If they were more lively on white streets, wouldn't they run the risk of some kind of harassment?"

"Well yes, they might. But you know, this harassment tends to be overstated. But now we're off the subject of my white image of this country's black women." She thought for a long moment before concluding. "If they behaved differently around me, then I would probably come to see them differently. As quicker and livelier. More active. But frankly, I can't quite picture it."

My hope,
My hope

In Johannesburg Thursday afternoon is generally acknowledged as Maids' Day Off, and many domestic workers use the free hours to shop in town and to pray in women's groups. No more than a block or two from the city's prominent Gold Miners' Memorial, a large, modern Methodist church houses one of these Thursday women's services, a *manyano*. I had arrived early and was waiting on the doorstep for my hostess and her church sisters. The afternoon was sunny and very hot. Looking down Rissik Street's slope, I watched the black women approaching two and three abreast—weary figures in red jackets whose brightness was somehow incongruous with the snail's pace of their progress. Slowly they trudged from the corner to the building. Puffing and sighing, they dragged themselves up the entrance stairs and through the stagnant hallway of the white church.

But as soon as they crossed the threshold of the room that was theirs for the next few hours, they were transformed. Sagging shoulders turned square. Heavy steps turned light. On the city's white streets these women had been maids, bodies too cumbersome for activity more strenuous than serving tea and saying "Yes, Madam." Inside their own room, they were an extended Mothers' Guild, a congregation that worked together and actively rejoiced in their common devotion. Here there was no need for wariness of the Madam's reactions to "her girl's" personal joy or obvious competence. Here there were no whites to be threatened by the smallest expression of black initiative. Quickly they pulled perhaps a hundred folding chairs off stationary racks and set them up in comfortable, semicircular rows. Chatting animatedly in Sotho, they arranged a table and chairs for their sisters who would lead the service. And until the service officially began, these black women sang and danced in defiance of the white stereotype they had, just moments before, embodied so completely.

My hope
Will it rise, rise, rise?
Will it join
In Heaven's praising

Now, at Elisabeth Kgapola's robing celebration, I watched the women stepping lightly between kitchen and tent. I tried to picture them trudging through the streets of Pretoria or deferentially murmuring "Yes, Madam." I imagined their Madams disdaining them as dull and sluggish, but they were too exuberant, too full of life for my imagining to be anything but ludicrous.

Now they were serving hot food. A lamb had been slaughtered for this feast, and each guest received a plate of curried mutton stew and traditional Sotho sour porridge. Peter and Jocelyn had been anticipating the sour porridge all afternoon, and other guests, too, devoured it as hungrily as if they had been breaking a long fast. But to Joyce it didn't seem to matter if the food before her was hot or cold, African or Western. Throughout the afternoon she ate almost nothing, and she left little opportunity for the other Mothers to do more than steal mouthfuls between her choruses. Whenever a member of the Guild raised fork to mouth, Joyce would sing out, laughing, clapping, and gesturing for the others to join her. Perhaps this was a display of religious fervor. Perhaps it was a joke within the Guild. Perhaps it was her personal teasing of Elisabeth, an impulsive gag that had somehow caught on and become unstoppable. Whatever its significance, the Mothers' perpetual chorus made of this feast an unforgettable experience of musical joy.

Look!
There are clouds appearing

All afternoon I had joined the singing on "la."

That died for people long ago

All afternoon I had gotten the feel of each chorus just as it was ending.

They have returned from Heaven
To bring all people together

But as the women were bringing out the trifle without which Peter and Jocelyn assured us any celebration would be incomplete, Joyce started a song that sounded strangely familiar.

> Hallelujah!
> Hallelujah to us all!
> Hallelujah!

I found myself first humming and quickly singing out loud—in English.

Show us the way to freedom

Of course! I had heard this melody at political events, sung as a freedom song. As a freedom song I had sung it around the United States myself and passed it on to performers who are popularizing it among American anti-apartheid audiences. The Mandela song.[4]

Show us to freedom now

Joyce rose from her chair to lead the Mothers in a procession around and around the tiny house.

Listen to the outcry
To awaken the dead

The kitchen women followed, in bouquets of yellow dresses, pink, blue, and green. Then came the men, hands up, feet stepping high, jackets flying out behind. And then came the other women, joining for one turn or two before returning to the shaded comfort of their chairs. They clapped and ululated.

They are invited by the Source of all fountains

It was time for us to leave. But as we thanked Samuel for his hospitality and began to move toward our car, Joyce led the procession to follow and then surround us, in their musical ecstasy.

IN CHURCH

They arise from their graves

They were still singing that song of freedom. Their words were not in English, and their intent was not of politics.

Hallelujah!

As they had all afternoon, they were singing of religious devotion.

Hallelujah to us all!

But the images of this particular hymn are those of redemption.

Hallelujah!

And the vigor and passion of their singing shattered apartheid's slavery—if only for one afternoon—with the spirit of freedom.

Show us the way to freedom
Freedom in South Africa!

BLACK CHRIST
APART

Africa, arise!
Seek your Savior.

South African black separatist Christianity reflects an assertive religious response to white domination. In mission churches a color bar infantilized blacks. Few blacks were ordained as priests, and those who succeeded found their authority subordinated to that of white superiors. Nonetheless, some urban blacks remained inside mission Christianity as they struggled to redefine African identity. Others left. Far from being monolithic, Christian separatism has always included the two very different movements of Ethiopianism and Zionism.[5]

Religious scholar Bengt Sundkler explains that in 1892 a number of black ministers seceded from the Wesleyan Methodists to found the Ethiopian Church—an interethnic denomination preaching self-government of the African church under African leadership. The Ethiopianists essentially transplanted white Christianity into black westernized communities, providing an alternative to white mission churches for the educated black urban elite. By this time many educated, professional blacks were coming to the Africanist view that their own salvation lay somewhere between the traditional African culture they had rejected and the Victorian Western Christian churches that had, in many ways, rejected them. They looked to blacks in the Western Hemisphere for inspiration, and before the turn of the century the Ethiopian Church in South Africa had united with the African Methodist Episcopal (A.M.E.) Church, based in the United States. The Ethiopianists established the Wilberforce Institute, near Johannesburg, as a South African Tuskegee. Many of their leaders studied in America. In the 1920s, during the heyday of African National Congress (ANC) activity, many leaders of this church participated in the work of the Congress.[6, 7, 8]

Not all black Christian converts joined the ranks of educated professionals; not all black urbanites became members of the middle-class elite. Particularly with the "discovery" of gold and diamonds, and the consequent boom in the mining industry, uneducated blacks flocked to newly urbanized areas in search of work. Poor and still traditional in orientation, these workers were only minimally exposed to the Victorian values and practices of their middle-class counterparts. They came to the cities for economic rather than cultural or professional reasons, and they maintained strong identification with rural life. But rural traditions were grounded in personal closeness with the land and the natural world, closeness that could flourish only in the countryside. The religious needs and aspirations of these uneducated black workers differed from those of black professionals. These needs were satisfied in Zionist rather than Ethiopianist churches.

Zionist Christianity recast in Christian rhetoric many African social and religious practices that the missionaries had proscribed as heathen. Zionists engaged in purification rites, faith healing, assorted behavior taboos, and the expulsion of evil spirits. All these were interpreted as deriving from the Old Testament.[9, 10]

Sundkler explains that in traditional African society harmonious life depended on a balance of interests between the king, the chiefs, and the people. The king owned his nation's cattle and people and was guardian of their lands; it was his responsibility to use his resources for the benefit of all. Religion revolved around the belief that spirits of the dead protect their descendants. Spirits of departed kings and chiefs were viewed as the source of communal prosperity. The king functioned as priest in important ancestral rites and ceremonies of healing; he was assisted in these functions by lesser spiritualists and herbalists.

Each Zionist church is led by its own self-identified prophet who, after receiving the divine call, serves his congregation almost as a traditional king. He is responsible for healing, for expelling evil spirits, for ritual purification, for summoning the Holy Spirit, and for maintaining the church's financial solvency. As the prophet becomes a Black Christ for his followers, references to Christ the Son tend to drop out of the congregational liturgy in favor of references to ancestral African kings.[11, 12]

> We are the first fruit
> Of the root.
> We are not in need.
> From the father of Shaka,
> Yes, comes my King.[13]

Zionist congregations are small and personal, occasionally numbering as few as ten or fifteen members who follow a charismatic leader. Many congregations are too poor to acquire permanent buildings. Indeed, Zionists have become known for worshipping out of doors, in the fields or mountains where the spirits might be expected to join them most readily. As in traditional African societies, worship has always been the most important collective activity in Zionists' lives; musical performance—singing with voice and body—is perhaps the most important feature of worship. Zionist singing draws heavily on the musical traditions of each church's membership.

As described by exiled South African anthropologist John Blacking, Zionists style their singing in the fashion of traditional spirit worship, to bring the Holy Spirit to the congregation and to accommodate the Spirit's presence—with sighs, sobs, and cries—once come. Hymns are sung slowly, and the general pitch rises with performance. Singing is ornamented and slurred, allowing expression of intensifying religious emotion. Harmony is rich and full; frequent parallel movement of parts creates a sound that reflects one massively voiced feeling. A call-and-response structure in which final notes are held to avoid rests maintains a constant stream of sound. Theoretically, a hymn may be invoked by any member of the congregation at any moment, and once a hymn is under way individual worshippers are free to slide, vary pitches, repeat short phrases in double time, or add whatever other ornamentation they are moved to produce.[14]

> **Yes, comes my King.**
> **Yes**
> **Yes Yes**
> **Yes Yes Yes**
> **Yes,**
> **Comes my King.**

In a land where racial oppression is observed more religiously than any theology, the church has represented one of few avenues through which blacks can peacefully exercise the drive for leadership. The independent Zionist churches constitute perhaps the only such avenue that has remained wholly free from white interference.[15, 16]

> **We Dingaan's people—**
> **We have heard him.**
> **The Liberator has arrived.**[17]

ZION
ON THE MOUNTAIN

In a white friend's kitchen in Johannesburg, a domestic worker followed her Madam's instruction to tell me what she knew about Zionist worship. "They sing the whole night through, up to early hours of the morning, and then from after breakfast, and then they start again.

> Hallelujah, Amen
> Hallelujah, Amen!

"After lunch they carry on again until the sun goes down. Night and day. Oh, it is wonderful! They sing and they beat the drum!

> Hallelujah, Amen
> Hallelujah, Amen!

"They do not need a church building. Any place that is open space can be a church for them. You can see them walking by the road. They will be wearing a green robe, for example, most especially with white crosses sewed on. I go there visiting because I love to hear them pray."

> Hallelujah, Amen! Hallelujah, Amen!
> Hallelujah, Amen! Hallelujah, Amen!

The woman grew more and more enthusiastic, as she relished every detail of the service she was describing. Suddenly she brought herself up short, perhaps embarrassed by her display of affinity for a group that was, by township standards, quite primitive. "Of course, myself, I'm a Roman Catholic."

Amen.

When Gary and I drove through the open country from Johannesburg to Durban, we passed small bands of Zionists. Some wore flowing robes of white, some of green, tied with cords of green or blue. Singly and in pairs, they walked along the roadside carrying large crosses and a drum. With no buildings and no other people in sight, we wondered each time we saw them how far these stalwart worshippers would have to go before reaching their religious brethren, in one direction, or their homes, in the other.

> **I know my Father who made me**
> **I know the Spirit who made me.**
> **Ehe———**
> **Hallelujah**

Depending on the day of the week and the time of day, we saw them, too, in the barren fields between Johannesburg and the surrounding townships. From our vantage point on the road, we watched them deep in the fields, formed into a ring that was now still, now whirling as worshippers encircled the spiritual center of their service.

Near sunset on the highveld as we drove toward Venda, a group snaked its way down a small hill. They swayed and sang, white robes billowing in the winds of an upcoming storm. Lightning cracked the dusky sky, and it was not difficult to imagine the spirits of the ancestors revealing themselves to this small ecstatic band.

We dance before You
Our King
By the strength of Your Kingdom.[18]

These separatist flocks bore little resemblance to township mission congregations. With their presence in the open air, their robes becoming part of the wind and the grasses, they embodied traditional African reverence for the land and the forces of nature. They invariably reminded me that every aspect of black South African life spans a stylistic spectrum that ranges from the modern Western to the traditional African and includes all combinations in between. Singing and worship are certainly not exceptions.

ZION
IN ZULU

Among the most conservative and most influential of today's Zionist congregations is the Shembe Nazareth Baptist Church, located in the Natal Province, historical home of the Zulus. This church has retained its practices of worship, unchanged, since its inception in 1911. Its prophet and founder, Isaiah Shembe, was born in 1870. In middle age he rejected mission Christianity to create a church where he could integrate mission teachings with his own supernatural visions, and with traditional Zulu social and spiritual practices. He established a church village at Ekuphakameni, north of Durban, and he instituted three annual festivals—one high on a mountain, one at the village, and one deep in Zululand. His followers came to regard him as a co-creator with Jehovah, as the Black Christ, their mediator in heaven.[19, 20]

The Shembe Nazarites have much in common with other Zionists. They observe behavior taboos, and they pray through hymns, through testimony, and through the sighing and speaking in tongues that constitute spontaneous individual expressions of the Spirit. Their hymns retain such features of traditional Zulu singing as polyphony, slow tempo, increasing volume over the course of very, very long songs, and room for individual improvisation within the overall group effort. Reflecting the importance of community in Zulu society, musical emphasis lies on group participation rather than on individual proficiency, and on group sound rather than on the quality of any one singer's voice.

> We are all standing before You
> At the gates of Ekuphakameni.
> All the generations of Heaven
> Rejoice because of you, Ekuphakameni.[21]

Managing to attend a service at Ekuphakameni required several weeks' effort. People had been talking about the Shembe Nazarites ever since my arrival in the country; all references had been laced with tantalizing mystery. A record producer noted the Nazarites' peculiar, and absolutely characteristic, hymnody, but he would be no more specific than to tell me, "You've got to hear it to understand. I really can't describe it." A professor of dramatic studies rhapsodically described the group's two-week celebration each January, atop Nhlangakazi Mountain in Zululand. The whole community is divided into four huge dancing regiments according to sex and marital status. When I asked what kind of dancing they did he shrugged. "It's like nothing you've ever seen." A television producer jealously guarded his footage documenting this celebration and the more general history of the church.

> We dance before You our King
> By the strength of Your kingdom.[22]

While showing Gary and me around Durban's KwaMashu township, our very Western friend Thandi Mphahlela had laughingly gossiped about the Shembe Zionists. "Though their community is near the city, they do not live a city life. You will see it when we go there. One of their beliefs is that they do not use medicines or chemicals of any kind. The Shembe does all of his healing with a black veil. Except that they believe in holy jelly, to use on the outside and the inside. Do you call it Vaseline? The Shembe blesses thousands of jars of this jelly every year, and these people buy many jars at their festival on the mountain." All this sounded very exotic and far removed from the black township life we were coming to know.

Thandi had taken us to her father's home where a friend of hers was waiting. She introduced Sbongile Mtetwa as a non-resident member of the Shembe church. That day was a Sunday; the Shembe Sabbath was on Saturday. Thandi was a film actress, often away on location, Sbongile a pop singer with frequent weekend gigs. It took nearly a month, and many phone calls across the country, for Thandi, Sbongile and me to arrange a Saturday on which we could all be free and in Durban, and on which the church's Rev. Dladla would approve outsiders visiting a service. By that time Gary was back in America.

The Shembe village is no farther from KwaMashu than KwaMashu is from Durban, but it is a world apart from the bustling, township house of Jonas Mphahlela. From the road out of KwaMashu, the predominant color was the overbaked gray-brown of dust and rock. Even the scrubby plants clinging to the embankments took on the color of dust. But after a very few minutes the terrain changed to green. The change was an interesting variation in degree, rather than in kind. What we saw was not the lush, forested hills and grassy knolls of the Valley of a Thousand Hills, farther west and south. Neither was it the rippling pastures and thriving fields of sugarcane that cover much of KwaZulu, farther to the north. Rather it was the same urban underbrush, just grown larger and competing more effectively for visual dominance, now that the city was farther behind and the buildings were fewer and farther between. I marveled at the inviting quality the landscape had acquired, simply by virtue of this overgrown underbrush. Shacks peeked out from the shrubbery as we drove past. Occasional concrete houses stood close to the road, often painted the pastel colors I had learned to associate with the Indian community. A billboard on our right announced the Mahatma Gandhi Clinic, reminding us that Gandhi's ashram had once thrived as a very different sort of religious community in this same vicinity.

> The springtime of the earth has come.
> You are called to Ekuphakameni.[23]

Without warning Thandi ordered me to turn off the road, into a small clearing where the stones and dust had reasserted their claim. Back from the road stood a few small buildings of naked cinderblock and brick. The upper portion of one was covered with a huge sign proclaiming, in words and pictures, "Ekuphakameni Dry Cleaners and Watch Repairs." Another sign advertised a butcher. Sbongile explained that these shops helped the community sustain itself. Driving as slowly as we could, and struggling to avoid large stones and small darting children, we threaded our way among the buildings to an open lot where Sbongile told me to park. My rented Toyota looked out of place among the battered old vans and pickup trucks in this makeshift parking lot. Far more so did the three of us look out of place among those who walked around us—we in our silky Western dresses and they in their long-sleeved white smocks and Zulu headbands of cowhide stitched in intricate designs, hung with pompons and tails of fur.

Sbongile led us to a slightly shaded porch. Thandi had noticed the difficulty I was having with the stones through my thin-soled sandals. She teased, "It's good for you we are not going farther. Beyond this point you must remove your shoes." Sbongile left us on the porch while she went off, barefoot, to confirm our welcome.

> May our feet be made strong.
> Let us dance before You forever.[24]

The service was about to begin, and villagers of all ages were streaming toward their long, barnlike sanctuary. Sbongile returned, a church elder in tow. They talked back and forth in Zulu; Thandi translated and relayed my comments back to Sbongile. The elder was clearly reluctant.

Rev. Dladla was not on the premises, and if he was the one who had organized the visit we would have to return when he was here.—But Rev. Dladla had approved my visit, and this was my last weekend in the country.

The Shembe was in Zululand, and we would have to return to join a service when he was here.—But there would be a service today, even without the Shembe, and much as I would like to meet the prophet this was my last Sabbath in the country.

We would have to leave our shoes on this porch and white girls do not like to walk barefoot.—I would be pleased to leave my shoes and try to go barefoot like the rest.

We would have to sit on the dung floor with the congregation.—I had no objection to sitting on the floor.

The elder grasped my hands and smiled. Sbongile said we were welcome. Thandi looked down at her chic white skirt and asked, giggling, if I had a cloth or a raincoat I could bring from the car. I did. We left our shoes as instructed, and my African friends darted from our porch to the sanctuary. I tried unsuccessfully to follow suit. Slowly my white, city feet picked their way across the rocky spaces between the buildings, around the goats, and along the earthen porch that ran the length of the sanctuary. The service was under way. Thandi and Sbongile beckoned from where they had settled, near the center of the congregation. As unobtrusively as possible, we spread out my raincoat. The dung floor was strewn with bits of straw, and my two Zulu friends seemed, if anything, more eager than I to avoid sitting directly on it.

The one-room sanctuary was hot, humid, and, particularly in contrast to the brilliant subtropical sunlight we had left outside, nearly dark. Walls and roof were of corrugated tin, broken only by occasional windows and doors which admitted small patches of light and air. Gradually I grew accustomed enough to the darkness to see that the room held over four hundred worshippers. We were seated amongst the young, unmarried women who occupied one whole long wall. Wrapped from head to toe in white sheets, they did not meet our eyes. To our left were the older, married women, each sitting or kneeling on a colorfully woven straw mat like those on display, unidentified, in curio shops in the white cities. These women also wore white—smocks, robes, or expansive shawls. One crawled over to offer us a prayer mat. Her smiling face was crowned with a beaded band that was the base of a traditional Zulu woman's headdress. On her robed breast dangled an icon with a framed photograph of the Shembe. She embraced us each, in turn, and quickly crawled back to her place. A second woman crawled over to offer a hymnbook. Another soon followed. Again we smiled. Again we embraced. Again, as so many times before in black South Africa, outsiders had been made welcome.

> **How do you do, my friends?**
> **May the peace of the Lord be with you.**[25]

A small boy slept upright, under the billowing arm of his father's smock. Other children sat, solemnly enfolded in their mothers' white robes.

> **The Lord called Shembe in his mother's womb**[26]

The service was led by a cadre of men. Robed to the knees, bare legs and feet protruding forward on straw mats, they took turns reading from their books or speaking from their own Christian and Zulu experience.

> **We are standing before you, our beautiful hen.**
> **Please love us and hatch us, our hen of heaven.**
> **Bring it into life, this village of Ekuphakameni,**
> **Just as a hen loves her baby chicks.**

O Jerusalem, Jerusalem!
How much I wanted to gather your children under my wing.
But they would not be gathered,
And now you are left desolate.[27]

Sometimes the congregation responded, line by line. Other times the leader read through on his own, for the whole five or ten minutes of his prayer's duration. Each recitation was followed by a long, wailing chorus. In full, complex harmony the congregation modulated slowly from chord to chord, again and again beginning the progression that, in Western music, leads to a final "Amen." Again and again the progression did not resolve as I expected, but continued onward instead. Voices slid from note to note (30 seconds). Voices wailed (90 seconds). Voices sang (150 seconds). Voices groaned (4 minutes). Louder and louder (6 minutes, or far, far more). And then without any discernible signal the chorus dissolved into a general mumbling prayer that, itself, soon dissolved into silence.

Amen.

One hymn led into another.

Aaaahhhh———

Tears streamed down faces, and the congregation sang on and on. A voice went up from somewhere in the room.

Eeeehhhh———

Joined by another and another, it became a full, dense chord.

Aaaahhhh———

From all around me worshippers slid in and out,

Oooohhhh———

sighing, groaning, and singing until the chord had, almost imperceptibly, changed into another, and, in the same way, another and another.

Aaaahhhh———

Sometimes Thandi could make out words.

Shembe, the servant of the Lord,
Will wipe the tears of his people.[28]

Sometimes voices sang different words superimposed on one another.

Today our sons and daughters are slaves
Africa, rise! And seek your Savior
Today our sons and daughters are slaves[29]

Most often she could not discern any words at all within the rich, swelling sound that seemed to fill the room with the spirit of the ancestors. Individuals moaned and cried out. But the group sound did not waver in giving voice—one massive, textured voice—to the prayers of the whole community.

All vocal movement within the sanctuary was exceedingly slow, as if these full, weighty Shembe prayers were actually stopping time. Three hours passed as three days. I wondered at these worshippers' emotional endurance; Sbongile said the service would continue until sundown. Thandi reminded us that she had to be at a rehearsal by four, and that we would have to leave quite soon. We conferred in whispers. There would be no break in the praying, no way of slipping out, no time for thanking the elders who had given us permission to be here. Sbongile offered to express our appreciation on another day.

Blushing in her short Western dress she crawled to the married women to return our mat and hymnbooks. And, at Thandi's signal, we left this congregation as we had found them, immersed in prayer to their spiritual King.

**We dance before You, our King,
By the strength of Your Kingdom.**[30]

IN
THE
COUNTRY

HOMELANDS
HISTORY

If for no other reason than that black people have always constituted a majority of South Africa's population, the "Native Policy" according to which these people are "handled" has always been a major concern of the country's white authorities. Conceived in various guises and enforced with varying degrees of zeal, such policy has consistently allowed white authorities to relate to the country's blacks through the interwoven principles of confinement, control, and capitalization. Broadly, apartheid legislation confines blacks to small, carefully demarcated areas. The lives of blacks outside these areas are minutely and meticulously controlled. The white economy manipulates a massive black labor force to perpetuate overall black confinement and control. Central to this tripartite policy are the country's ten "bantustans" or "black homelands."

Look at what is happening!
Look at what is happening to us!
Listen to the cries of the people!

Early black resistance to white colonial takeover prompted governmental preservation of "Native Reserves," rural areas that were said to correspond to historical tribal territories. Here, blacks were to retain the land ownership and political power denied them in white regions, and traditional African life was ostensibly to be practiced. But colonization and conquest continued to eat away at Reserve lands, and by the end of the last century they were reduced to bits of depleted territory within the rich expanses once roamed by African pastoralists. In 1913,

7 percent of the total land area of the country was set aside for black ownership.

Unable to survive by farming land that was, at best, overcrowded and overutilized, rural blacks sought employment outside the Reserves. Burgeoning industrialization created a need for black workers in urban factories and mines. However, unlike the mission blacks described earlier, who *came* to the cities on their own initiative, these new rural recruits *were brought* to the cities entirely to serve white interests. Mission blacks had migrated to the cities as families, and they established vital, robust communities in the black urban townships. Industrial recruits were viewed as "temporary sojourners," and they were excluded from township community life by requirements that they leave their families in the Reserves, and stay, while in town, in tightly controlled workers' compounds.[1]

Throughout this century Pretoria has legislated to restrict ongoing black influx into white South Africa, to remove numbers of blacks who are already established in white areas, and to systematize control over the rural areas to which these newly created exiles are sent. In 1959, the Promotion of Bantu Self-Government Act declared that South Africa's blacks represent " 'separate national units on the basis of language and culture.' "[2] Legislation defined certain pre-colonial groupings of chiefdoms and clans as "nations," tied these nations to existing bits of Reserve land, and called the resulting fragmented agglomerations of people and territory "bantustans" or "black homelands."

The homelands are officially said to be havens for traditional black life. However, such life involved semi-nomadic farming and grazing that today's overcrowded plots of dust and stones simply cannot support. Indeed, with the bantustans Pretoria has succeeded in emphasizing superficial aspects of traditional African culture and political structures, while destroying the foundations of these same traditions. Customs and practices once discouraged by Christian missionaries are encouraged within bantustans. These very practices are then used as ongoing confirmation both that Africans are different from one another and that they are so different from whites, "Coloreds," and Indians that a single, multifaceted society, free of enforced racial separation, is unworkable.

Various daily practices in the homelands may indeed be traditional. But these behaviors are not integrated into the tightly woven fabric of culture, religion, politics, and economics that constituted traditional African life in its period of prosperous integrity. Rather than havens for traditional revival, the homelands are artificially created labor reserves where hunger, malnutrition, and disease slowly exterminate those who are too old or too young for employment in white South Africa. In these rural wastelands, elements of tradition *do* provide spiritual richness, which must compensate for the physical poverty which would otherwise be unendurable.

According to the Surplus People Project, today's bantustans are allocated roughly 13 percent of South Africa's land; they are increasingly identified as the only legitimate political homes of the blacks who make up more than 72 percent of the country's population. Boundaries are gerrymandered in such a way as to incorporate bits of rocky, unwatered terrain into the homelands while leaving inside white South Africa the mineral resources, fertile soil, and profitable ports located in the region of a given traditional group's ancestral home. These "unified" political territories comprise noncontiguous bits of land that have nothing left to give, but with which the black dispossessed must, nonetheless, try to bargain for survival.[3]

> We protest for our land
> That was taken from us by the wolves.

In pursuit of Pretoria's goal of " 'no more black South Africans,' "[4] legislation for "separate development" has encouraged each bantustan to move toward political independence from the Republic of South Africa. Although roughly 45 percent of the African population lives within South Africa's borders, every black South African is assigned bantustan citizenship. Many such people automatically lose South African citizenship with bantustan independence, even if they live in urban townships and have never set foot in "their" homelands. In this way, universal bantustan independence would free South Africa of its black majority and of black claims on its resources.[5]

It is certainly true that South African citizenship has never guaranteed blacks reliable rights to political participation, a fair share of economic wealth, or residence in urban areas. However, the loss of this citizenship seriously diminishes such residential rights as do exist, and it wholly eliminates previously legitimate *claims* to any rights whatsoever. Loss of South African citizenship also transfers from the wealthy Pretoria government to ill-provided bantustan administrations the ultimate responsibility for paying pensions, unemployment insurance, and workmen's compensation—in spite of the fact that the *work* supporting these claims has probably all been performed inside South Africa. Thus, instead of twenty-eight million Africans[6] clamoring for political rights, the homelands create an image of a series of dispersed and numerically less threatening ethnic groups, a " 'plurality of minorities.' "[7] Far more easily than could one unified, incontrovertible majority, this collection of diverse minorities has been excluded from national wealth and power.

Zulu, Xhosa, Sotho—Unite!

Pretoria has relentlessly pursued a policy of massive consolidation, redrawing bantustan borders along less implausible lines, eliminating "black spots" (black-owned land lying in areas designated as "white") and analogous "white spots," and relocating black people, both physically and administratively, into their putative homelands. Physical relocation involves the straightforward moving of whole communities from one place to another. Buildings are destroyed, land expropriated. Compensation, if any, is determined by Pretoria. Administrative relocation takes place when a given community is declared to be part of a bantustan rather than of South Africa, or part of one bantustan rather than another. For example, in the early 1980s Durban's black townships of Umlazi and KwaMashu were excised from South Africa and annexed to KwaZulu. Township residents instantly became citizens of KwaZulu, subject to the authority of controversial Chief Minister Gatsha Buthelezi and in danger of losing their South African citizenship altogether should his government accept political independence.

Impoverished bantustan administrations vie with one another for the land and financial assistance that Pretoria reserves the right to distribute among them. This competition fosters interethnic rivalries, distracting blacks from fundamental grievances against white domination. Pretoria fans black-on-black competition into violence, and then uses such violence to discredit the threatening political messages of African unity and of a democratic society in a common South Africa.

The homelands have never been economically viable. In 1960, 55.4 percent of the homelands' GNP was generated outside homeland boundaries; by 1976 this percentage had risen to 71.6.[8] Estimated 1987/88 sources of homeland revenue suggest that only two of the ten homelands generated more than 50 percent of their total revenues from internal sources.[9] So why have four of these specious countries opted for the political independence that releases Pretoria from official responsibility for their economic survival?

The answer to this question would seem to lie with local governments that are, like everything else about the bantustans, designed by Pretoria to preserve superficialities of African tradition while violating the essence of Africanism. Homeland governments were modeled after South Africa's Westminster system, and members of traditional royal families were chosen to run these Western-style administrations. However, royal families are large, and any one member's hereditary claim to authority has far less influence on maintaining a government position than does willingness to cooperate with Pretoria.

Chief Tshivhase
Resisted the new laws and our punishment.
He was deported to die in Pretoria.

In exchange for their treachery, appointed officials enjoy large salaries and luxurious amenities that contrast ostentatiously with surrounding communities struggling to survive on primitive subsistence agriculture.

Homeland officials are also empowered to allocate land, welfare, business and professional licenses, health and educational services, and development money in their districts. We must remember that indigenous African economies thrived on the basis of communal access to vast expanses of land. Even early colonial restrictions on Africans' lands seriously challenged traditional economies. The fragmented, already overutilized Reserves of the 1950s have been forced to accommodate larger and larger populations as more and more blacks are denied permission to live elsewhere. Since relatively constant amounts of land must sustain ever-increasing numbers of people, power over allocating land is congruent to power over survival or starvation. Similarly, the power over pensions, licenses, and services is tantamount to control over life itself. The officials who wield such power are in a strong position to command support and tribute from their subordinates; their personal stake in continued white supremacy is unquestionable. Thus, with few exceptions, Pretoria has succeeded in transforming rural black leaders from colonial-era spearheads of resistance against white domination to contemporary representatives of the white government's interests.[10]

> Two princes were in contest to be chief.
> The people cried
> "This is not the rightful chief.
> He uses our voices for his own celebration."

RABBIT
AND WOLF

"We have got something in our Venda tradition which is a story and a song. You tell a story and when you reach a certain point you start singing, and then you get to another certain point and you talk again, and then you sing again, going into a chorus. When I was a kid my grandmother would tell a story, and then she would start singing, and we would join with her in the chorus. This is a thing which happens in every family, most especially in summer. We push the night to go on and on, because even though we are tired we do not want to stop sitting all together around the grandmother and singing as a family gathered all around.

"My grandmother used to tell one such story, and I always loved it. It is a Venda story. There were a wolf and a rabbit, and they decided to cook each other in a pot to see who would make the sweeter soup. The rabbit had little round fruits like tomatoes. So she climbed into her pot and started cooking, and she squeezed the tomatoes in. And then they both climbed out and they drank the soups, and the rabbit's soup was sweeter than the soup of the wolf. But the rabbit was still a rabbit and the wolf was still a wolf, and then and there the rabbit decided, 'No, I will kill the wolf in the pot. Just leave him there and be safe from him forever.' So they both climbed back in, and the rabbit just jumped out and put the lid on the wolf's pot. And the wolf started saying,

I am burning
I am burning!

Can't you open the pot for me?
Can't you let me out?

"So the rabbit answered,

Keep boiling.
Then your soup will be sweeter.

"We would always sing along with that, and even today I love singing along with that story. Ja. My kids love it too. You watch a child listening to that. He chuckles and enjoys it. And the whole thing is beautiful."

Our Venda storyteller was a thirty-year-old schoolteacher named Luvhengo. She concluded wistfully. "But more and more today, the child will be watching television and ignoring the old grandmother and her Venda stories."

Keep boiling.
Then your soup will be sweeter.

The previous morning this tall, smartly dressed young woman had introduced herself as Rosalie—westernized, educated, and remote. She had spent the day driving with Gary and me around the "independent" homeland of Venda, in South Africa's far northeast. Together we had searched out the best musicians in the villages that dot the red hills of the region with thatched huts and scrawny crops. After a few hours she admitted her early suspicion that our professed interest in Venda singing was really a bid for an invitation to the *domba*, the young women's initiation ceremony that is sexually caricatured by white outsiders who titillate one another at black expense. By evening Rosalie had become Luvhengo, and suspicion had yielded to pride in her identity as a Venda woman and a black South African.

I wondered how she reconciled her regret for the passing

of Venda traditions with her pursuit of the modern accoutrements she also seemed to relish. She fingered the red electroplate earring that flirted from her right ear. Her voice hardened. "You know, for you who have lost the traditional life, you want to go back. For us who haven't reached the modern life, we still want to go forward."

If she was baiting, Gary bit. "I don't think anyone has the right to say that one should want to live in poverty or under dangerous conditions in terms of public health standards. And one of the outrages of this country is the way one affluent minority keeps the majority under just such terrible conditions, and then tries to justify doing that. But after the essential needs are met, then there are other aspects of life which may be modern, but they're not necessarily better."

I don't know what Luvhengo had expected to hear, but Gary's words seemed to take her by surprise. She started to break in on him, stopped herself, and thought for a long moment after he had finished. "I started to be unfair to you, my friend. In this country white people talk about how beautiful it is for us to live a traditional life out in the rural areas, and they never mention that in these same areas we are starving and our children are dying from malnutrition. A few of us are lucky." Again her fingers found her earring. "But most are just sick and starving. You know, even our own leaders talk like that, praising our traditions to serve their own reasons. For a moment I thought you would be saying something like that. Around such people, black or white, I cannot speak proudly of our songs or stories or our old ways of life.

I am burning!
Can't you let me out?

"I'm now living in a modern house. Electricity. Everything plugs into the wall. And I'm telling you I'm missing— Just to smell the smoke of a kitchen! My kids don't know how I grew up. I used to carry water on my head. I used to cook with a pot on the floor. I would cook pap right on the floor, and dish it out with a plate. Just imagine if you were going to roast eggs, or cook meat, you would do it in an earthen pot on the fire.

"You know, that way of cooking is more tasty than what we are doing now. But if you tell anyone I said that, I will say you are telling a lie!"

VENDA
SONG

The mountainous region that is Vendaland lies in South Africa's far northeastern corner, nestled just inside the military staging area where the Zimbabwe and Mozambique borders meet. Venda was the third of South Africa's bantustans to accept political independence; the Republic of Venda was born in September 1979.[11]

Independence!
We have got it!
Telephone code 210!
Aheee! He aa!

For 1983/84 at least 72 percent of the new "country's" national revenues comprised "aid" from South Africa,[12] and the Venda government is reported to have spent nearly 2 percent of these revenues on luxury cars for its officials. It was reported that only 8 percent of the population over the age of five was literate and that the President himself had been educated only to Standard Five (roughly equivalent to American seventh grade). Dr. Alex Boraine, of South Africa's Progressive Federal Party, described Venda as a land of " 'hunger, corruption and sudden death' where the President lived in 'obscene affluence,' . . . where the opposition was in gaol, and where the majority of the people starved on R20 a month."[13] Particularly to the rural, landless people of this remote, impoverished place, singing represents a link with past glory lost and a vision of future glory still to be won. Singing expresses the pride, the ingenuity, the cooperative mastery that all support endurance in the face of seemingly inevitable demise. And even this resource—more personal than land, more precious than cattle—the authorities struggle to co-opt in their own interests.

Independence!
Aheee! Haaa!

In the mid-to-late 1700s, the mountainous area of Vendaland was populated by a number of politically autonomous, mutually interdependent, "aboriginal" clans. Their culture was rich and varied, focusing on religion, magic, and rainmaking. Roughly one hundred fifty to two hundred years ago these people were invaded by clans from across the Limpopo who imposed their own chieftainship and military systems, but who, unlike conventional conquerors, adopted many of the cultural and religious practices of their new subjects. Perhaps due to mountainous terrain, perhaps to a loose political system offering no paramount chief to speak for the whole nation, the Venda were the last of South Africa's Bantu-speaking peoples to submit, in 1899, to South African authority.[14, 15]

John Blacking's work offers the West's most comprehensive understanding of Venda culture and the role of singing within it. He explains that among the Venda music is a social activity. Performed communally to mark the cycle of seasons and the development of human lives in harmony with the earth's cycles, music expresses the overriding value of Venda solidarity. Music permeates every social activity, from birth to death. People sing in the groups that constitute Venda society—children, male initiates, female initiates, men working, women working, family groups, religious groups—simultaneously demonstrating societal organization and training individuals in the responsibilities of every level of societal membership. And when people sing, they sing all together. With *tshikona*, the national dance in which everyone participates, the Venda epitomize their underlying notion that an individual exists at his or her fullest when functioning in common purpose, along with the whole community. Human kindness and cooperation are integrally connected with the balance of forces that govern the world.

In Venda tradition every newborn heralds the return of an ancestral spirit, and every "fulfilled" person who dies is said to give birth to a new ancestral spirit. Personal "fulfillment" is a function of fruitful individual life in community. Thus, the very cycle of existence relies on self-realization in cooperation with other wholly realized selves; without this delicate balance, the supply of spirits available for rebirth would soon be exhausted. The spirit world is inextricable from the world of people. Immersing oneself in communal song provides momentary access to the spirits of the ancestors. In addition, it allows each individual to move toward the fulfillment that will permit his or her ultimate transformation from human to spirit.

Venda music is founded not on melody, but on rhythmic expression of the whole body. Indeed, when the Venda speak of their "music," they refer to singing, dancing, and rhythmic recitation. It is not that they fail to recognize differences among musical forms. It is, instead, that they emphasize social function far more than musical style. Since song, dance, and recitation serve a common social purpose, they are all described as music. Speech tones are important in the Venda language, as in many tongues in the Bantu family. When songs are composed, melodies build on the speech tones and rhythm of the early words, and subsequent lines follow these initial patterns. But more important than any particular melody or set of lyrics is the process of participating in communal song.[16, 17, 18]

Good performance is characterized by vigor and excitement, regardless of style. Blacking cites a dancer being praised for " 'dig[ging] a hole in the ground' " or " 'lick[ing] the clouds,' " and a singer for " 'nearly burst[ing] his diaphragm' " or for singing him- or herself hoarse.[19] Energetic involvement may characterize audience members as well as performers. Every individual masters the elements of Venda music as part of growing up in the society. Thus, every spectator is competent to bring fullness to a given performer's work by adding a chorus of rhythmic clapping, dancing, stamping, and harmonic shouting. Among the Venda even personal performance may become communal. As one, audience and performer assert their shared identity by engaging in the medium of music.

Pretoria declares that the bantustans are havens for African traditionalism, that within bantustan borders ethnic groups may exercise political and cultural freedom without pressure to accommodate to the ways of other groups, black or white. In Venda this policy of "separate development" leads contemporary authorities to violate the solidarity, cooperation, and mutual responsibility that are fundamental to Venda culture, indeed, that are the essence of Venda spirit itself. And along the way, these authorities may prostitute, for their own ends, the music that has always given that essential Venda spirit its voice.

> **Independence!**
> **We have got it!**
> **Aheee! He aa!**

THE SONG
IS MY SOUL

Rosalie Ralushai met Gary and me in the lobby of our hotel in Venda's capital city, Sibasa. Through a complicated network of friends and acquaintances it had been arranged that this confident young schoolteacher would accompany us for the next few days, through the remote Venda and Shangaan homelands. She presented herself, tall and slim, in a straight black skirt and tailored white blouse. Her smile was businesslike; her tone guaranteed competence without promising friendship. "I am Rosalie, and you must be Helen and Gary. Just now we must go and collect my friend Gibson, who has organized for us to hear Venda singing today. Gibson is a philosopher and a playwright. He is well known among our people and has written many books. He works at the university, but since it is now closed by the disturbances he can spend today with us."

She watched our faces closely, making certain we were suitably impressed with her friend's credentials. The state university of the Republic of Venda claims high academic standards and assumes the role of preserver of traditional Venda culture. "Ja. Gibson works at the university. As a janitor."

> My heart is like the river
> Which roars right through the night.

We drove to the campus under Rosalie's direction and parked outside a boxy building. We waited. And we waited. Eventually a small, bearded black man ran up to our car, brightly striped necktie streaming over the shoulder of his worn, dark suit jacket. He greeted Rosalie and me, in back, through the window, and he climbed into the passenger's seat beside Gary, in front. Rosalie's professional reserve contrasted with Gibson's unwary expressiveness. His bearing was exuberant, his smile angelic and guileless, but his eyes reflected an ancient sadness. He carried a manila mailing envelope stuffed with papers. He apologized for keeping us waiting; he had been reading a manuscript for a friend in Johannesburg and had lost track of time. In a voice low and intense, he described his friend's masterful use of the Venda language, and the nobility of this man's ideas.

Rosalie whispered to me that Gibson was far too modest. He himself was known for his command of Venda and of the imagery and cultural history that this language conveys with its every phrase. Her tone was anxious and protective. He was her friend, but she often felt more like his student—or his mother—than his equal. With a jolt I remembered that he was not a professor, or a teacher like Rosalie. He was a janitor. To the University of Venda this man was not a source of wisdom. To the official bastion of Venda culture he was nothing more than a pair of working hands.

Rosalie forced a laugh and interrupted Gibson's literary monologue to introduce us all around and get the day under way. "Gibson, Helen, and Gary. You are all G and H but for me."

Thinking of what I had just learned of this man's commitment to the Venda language, I tried to pronounce the name I had seen written on his manuscript mailer. "Does that envelope say Tshifiwe? Is that your Venda name?"

"Tshifiwe. Yes." He looked at Rosalie and laughed a small laugh. "One has no secrets around those who see."

"What would you like us to call you, then? Would you prefer one name to the other?"

Gibson took Gary's question seriously, and he deliberated before answering. "White people do not call me Tshifiwe. But if you would like to use that name, I think I would like that very much." He looked from white face to black, adding, "And perhaps for today Rosalie will remember that even among white people she, too, has a Venda name."

She blushed and hesitated, her veneer of Western confidence cracking momentarily. Between these two their names, English and Venda, clearly stood for something more. Rosalie broke her own silence. "All right, my friend. Since you are Tshifiwe then I will be Luvhengo. And now we can be off." Gary and I looked at one another and at our two Venda hosts. For a moment the sadness seemed to fade from Tshifiwe's eyes. Rosalie's stiff reserve seemed to relax. Something meaningful had just been settled.

Indeed, my heart is like the river.

As soon as we drove out of Sibasa we left the tarmac behind. Unlike the bleached yellow-gray of the Natal, the earth in Venda is red and it dominates the landscape. Mountains claim the horizon, sharing the foreground with wide valleys and rolling, sparsely wooded hills. All are dotted with clusters of the thatched rondavels that are traditional Venda dwellings. Between the huts and the rows of planted crops in the distance, between the individual tufts of grass at the fore, and along the length of each dirt road that winds through these dramatic northern hills the pervasive red reminds that this soil is tired and overworked. It cannot support lush crops or natural vegetation to color the landscape green. It cannot produce the wealth to buy cities that would cover large areas with angular blocks of gray and black. So it provides an inhospitable home for the villages and the vegetation that have been given nowhere else to try to grow. The huts take on the color of the dust that always seems to blow. The roads leave tires and feet the color of the mud that truly rules this region. And for all that, the land is beautiful.

We stopped at a curve in the mountain road. Scanty grasses and occasional trees grew up the hill. Below, thatched roofs seemed to cower under cover of whatever greenery the hills afforded. Tshifiwe had guided us here in search of a Venda musician who, he said, still plays and sings in the old style. Before African languages were written, cultural history and wisdom were transmitted entirely orally, in songs and praise poems emanating from the chief's kraal. Those who composed and performed these songs were, in a sense, custodians of the tribal soul.

He explained, "This is a type of singing which is poetry. You hear the mothers praising our mountains or praising our chiefs, or singing about the morals and the values of our people. The men used to praise places or events or cattle, mostly. And they would praise themselves for a certain deed that they have performed bravely. If I had lived in another age, perhaps I would have fallen in this category, you know, because it really appeals in my eyes." He paused. "Today the authorities prefer that our music should be more Western, or that our singers should praise *them* or sing the values that *they* wish to encourage."

Once there was a place with a beautiful old name.
There we were staying happily.
Today that old place has a new name
And the spirit of the new name bewitches even the park.

Tshifiwe spoke of the lyrics of old-style Venda songs. "These songs really tell you something. Even if it's kids playing, you find it has a meaning in it. And when those kids are playing and singing their own songs, they are practicing, so to say, for the music of our people. Even when they are just playing, their songs are teaching them to be Vendas. With us it's not just a song for the purpose of enjoying yourself. It always has a meaning, our Venda songs. These old-style songs are really the soul of our people."

IN THE COUNTRY

To sing well
One needs assistance from other singers
To sing is to work together.

Tshifiwe's musician worked the night shift for the Venda Public Works Department. While Gary and I waited with Luvhengo, Tshifiwe ran far down the hill, through the grasses, toward the village, looking for this man. We three walked around the road's bend, scanning for Tshifiwe's sprightly form among the distant huts. We saw no trace of him, but our shoes picked up a thick layer of red dust. A large truck drove up the hill, dousing the road surface to settle the dust; each step now caked our shoes with new red mud. Women walked barefoot down the road, wearing Western rags and carrying huge parcels on their heads. Luvhengo was little more familiar with this remote area than we, and her fashionable black pumps fared worse in the mud than our clumsier shoes. She was leaning on me, wiping one shoe at a time on the uphill grasses when Tshifiwe burst through the lower underbrush. He had located the musician's hut and spoken with his wife, but the man himself was already off on his daily rounds. Apparently he slept for a few hours each morning after work, and then he set off with his instrument in search of prospective audiences or drinking companions in local beer halls.

Tshifiwe was disturbed by the all-day drinking to which he felt European values and a culturally bankrupt administration had driven this traditional artist. "Once I asked him why does he drink this much. He said to me, 'A man at my age, what else can I do? If it was in the olden days I would be found in the chief's kraal, entertaining the chief. But today the only place for my song is the beer hall.' I looked at him and I was thinking, 'There is something which is gone now in the life of our people, and because of that his own life is dry and hollow.'"

> In the olden days
> We were well settled.
> In the olden days.
> But they are not here any longer.

All morning we drove through the hills, stopping periodically for Tshifiwe to run off and inquire about his musician. The last time he returned to us, he led a lanky man without teeth, carrying a variant of the one-stringed, bowed instrument that is common throughout South Africa. He called it a *tshinzholo*. At one end, a sturdy three-foot length of bamboo was attached to a large, squarish metal can that served as a resonator. A thick dowel served as a tuning peg, fitting crosswise in a hole through the free end of the bamboo. A single wire ran, taut, from dowel to can. A small bow dangled from the dowel and somehow did not fall off. In Venda this is a personal, rather than communal, instrument. Unlike the large drums and reed pipes played at community celebrations, the *tshinzholo* is used by a single musician, to accompany the songs that express personal involvement in what it means to be Venda.

The man wore his Public Works jacket and looked to have been awake for days on end. He was introduced as Petros Mabilu. He grasped Gary's and my hands in turn, stringing together barely intelligible English words in sequences from which I could derive no meaning whatsoever. I realized that I didn't know even a single word in Venda.

Tshifiwe spoke with the musician in spirited Venda, gesturing widely. He reported that Petros liked to sing with a particular woman, and that if we would take him to find her, they would gladly perform for us. Luvhengo disassembled our morning newspaper and spread it on the car floor in a futile attempt at protection from the mud that now ran halfway up the car doors, and that coated all of our feet, shoes, and ankles. For some time we five drove in silence along the dirt road. Each time we saw a woman walking, Petros shook his head and sighed. Then, up ahead we saw a fragile-looking female figure, and he howled out to Tshifiwe. Although this was not the woman he had wanted, she would be an acceptable substitute. We drove up slowly behind her as she walked along the side of the road, oblivious to our presence. On her head she carried a twenty-five-pound sack of grain. Her feet were bare. Her thin sweater was full of holes. Tied around her waist, her skirt was a dark, fringed blanket. She continued to walk.

Petros scrambled out of the car to talk with her. Tshifiwe followed behind. After some conversation the woman turned around and walked with Petros, back in the direction from which she had come. Tshifiwe reported that we would return to the remains of a fallen tree, back by the last curve in the road. Since our car could only accommodate five, Petros was walking back with his friend. We would bring the *tshinzholo*.

As we drove, Tshifiwe talked with us about a proper performer fee. More accurately, he argued with himself, out loud. "In our tradition we do not sing for money. We sing for a reward from the community. We sing to clear our souls. To share our philosophy. I know he needs money, with a wife and a family. But I don't like it that he demands money, as if the depth of our culture can be bought for rands. And it's not right for him to be greedy, just because you are from overseas."

We knew we could never soothe Tshifiwe's pain at the effects of twentieth-century commercialism and bantustan politics on Venda tradition. But we tried to ease his mind about Petros's demand to be paid. "Folk artists all over the world starve because people think that only commercial music is worth paying for, and that's not fair. If he were playing at the hotel in Sibasa, tourists would pay to listen, just like they pay to buy traditional Venda pottery in the tourist shop. The fact that he wants us to pay for his art doesn't have to make you feel bad, and we're glad to do whatever you and he decide is appropriate."

We had reached the fallen tree. Tshifiwe took the *tshin-*

zholo to the two musicians and spoke with them briefly. When he faced us once more, his angelic smile had returned. "This is going to be a very good day, I think."

Petros Mabilu was a consummate performer. With a deceptively casual gesture he swung the *tshinzholo*'s resonator over his right shoulder. Where the wire was attached he grasped one end of the dowel between the middle and ring fingers of his left hand. His left thumb and index finger were free to move along the musical string, regulating its pitch. His right hand grasped the small bow and sawed rapidly, producing tones which were initially harsh to our Western ears but which, after a few minutes, took on their own beauty.

> **My wife has returned**
> **To her family in Mutale.**
> **She has left me**
> **And I have followed her.**

The woman knelt on the ground, up against the fallen tree that was the backdrop for the performance. A lizard skittered across her body and onto the dead wood. Her eyes were cast down and to one side. Her hands clasped one another, off that same side of her lap. Still. Silent. Sculpted. Her lines were those of the Venda hills.

> **I have followed her.**

Petros acknowledged our applause and Tshifiwe's enthusiastic cheering with a performer's familiar appreciation. He signaled to the woman and began to play again. She rose as he began to sing.

IN THE COUNTRY

> We must look at the headman
> For the last time.
> He is leaving for Tshandama.

Petros's hands raced around his instrument. In strident coun-
terpoint the woman sang out her own melody.

> Our bird is flying to Tshandama
> Where he will drink the liquor
> That we are forbidden to brew.

Back and forth they played and sang. The woman stood small
and neat, hands clasped before her waist. Her face was sweet,
her expression shy, reminiscent of a schoolgirl timid to perform
in front of strangers, but too obedient to refuse. Only her mouth
moved. Her voice was surprisingly strong and clear.

> For his own reasons
> The new chief
> Forbids our brewing.

Petros played behind closed eyelids but his face was lively as if,
in his own small darkness, he was watching the traditional
headman break free of newly imposed constraints. He added a
final chant to the woman's song.

> Our bird is flying.
> Our bird is flying.

This time Tshifiwe did not cheer alone. During the last
song passersby had stopped to listen, and by now our audience
numbered nearly twenty. Among the women, several wore
bracelets Luvhengo identified as a Venda tradition. Tens of
delicate metal bangles decorated calves and forearms, ankle to
knee, wrist to elbow. For a moment these people left behind

their weariness and hunger, savoring the artistry of their Venda heritage. They were undoubtedly enjoying the performance. But more than that, they immersed themselves in the songs that transformed them, one by one, from starving peasants into proud Vendas. They cheered their musicians in their own language, celebrating the culture they had to rely on, so completely, to sustain them against both poverty and treachery. Bangles clinked and rattled as the women stamped their feet and waved their hands.

> **Ahee**
> **He aa**
> **Ahee!**

Petros warmed to his expanding audience. Playing ever more wildly he looked each of us squarely in the eye. We cheered, in Venda and English, and he soared to greater and greater heights. The woman sang along, strangely distant from the performer's dynamic and exaggerated Venda enthusiasm which were giving Petros such energy. She made eye contact with no one but him. Her expression never changed. A diminutive, self-contained figure, she seemed to produce that powerful voice from nowhere. And suddenly an ear-splitting ululation issued forth and did not stop. She had twisted her tongue ninety degrees, from horizontal to vertical, and she wagged it quickly back and forth until audience cheers drowned out the music.

> **To sing is to work together.**
> **It is better to be ugly**
> **And to entertain others**
> **Than to be beautiful**
> **And be selfish.**

By now our numbers had swelled to forty or fifty. For the most part these people were barefoot and clothed in the threadbare garments and blankets that suggest difficulty in keeping themselves clothed at all. One man had been riding a bicycle. He wore shoes and clean clothes, and at first he stood somewhat apart from the rest. But like Gary and me, he soon seemed to lose track of the enormous gulfs that divided our audience. The bicycle rider had a job and a full belly; so did we and our two Venda hosts. I guessed that most of the others had neither. We had come from different worlds, and after the final song we would continue along our different paths. Perhaps it was a wish to prolong the nearly palpable group intimacy that led the musicians to sing on and on as they did. Their songs called forth dignity from backs that were tired. They revived identity in minds that were preoccupied. They rekindled love and mutual responsibility in hearts that were too often manipulated into jealousy.

To sing is to help one another.
One is the leader
And others join in
To fill out the song.

From the women's rags and the filthy faces of the babies blanketed to their backs, I guessed that this music was providing unexpected respite from the struggle that was every today and tomorrow. More important, it offered a spiritual nourishment that would continue to sustain, long after the physical tones had faded. The babies, too, were receiving cultural sustenance. They were absorbing the music and their mothers' rhythmic responses. Tiny as they were, they were beginning to learn the musical skills that would enable them to link music to daily life in the manner of the Vendas they had been born. We could communicate nothing but our smiles, these women and I. We shared nothing but our involvement in the moment. But while these two old-style performers were singing, we were all together in the soul of Venda.

THE SONG IS MY SOUL

**My heart is like the river
Which roars right through the whole night.**

Tshifiwe watched the musicians with tears in his eyes. Finally they had sung the last song, and the audience had cheered the last cheer. Payment had been made, and hands had been shaken. Audience members walked off in ones and twos, singing where they had been silent before. Petros grinned his toothless grin and carried his *tshinzholo* off into the grasses. The woman replaced the sack of grain on her head and proceeded down the road, toward—and then past—the spot where we had interrupted her progress a few hours before. Only the four of us remained by the fallen tree when Tshifiwe murmured, "In your country of America, everyone is free to make a contribution."

SHANGAAN CALLS

The bantustan of Gazankulu comprises three or four noncontiguous pieces of land in the northeastern Transvaal. This place is identified as home to South Africa's Shangaan- (also called Tsonga- or Thonga-) speaking people, although even after extensive government relocations no more than 43 percent of these people actually live there.[20] Its history, as described by the Surplus People Project, illustrates the ethnic manipulation through which Pretoria has pursued the policy of separate development.

> **Giants will kill me, Mama.**
> **They are sharpening their blade.**

In small clans, related to one another only by loose linguistic links among their dialects, the Shangaan migrated into South Africa throughout the nineteenth century. Most of them came from Gaza province in Portuguese East Africa (now Mozambique)—hence the contemporary homeland name Gazankulu ("large Gaza"). Eventually they settled in the eastern and northeastern Transvaal. Though they became subjects of powerful local Venda and Sotho chiefs, they retained primary cultural similarity to Shangaan clans remaining in Gaza, on the Portuguese side of the border.

Pretoria drew preliminary bantustan boundaries in 1959, and at that time the Shangaan were not regarded as important enough to warrant their own homeland. Flagrantly violating its own policy of bantustan ethnic homogeneity, Pretoria sited in the northeastern Transvaal a single bantustan that would incorporate both the Shangaan and the Venda. It also located the homeland of Lebowa in this same area, to accommodate the Northern Sotho and the Northern Ndebele. For generations the Shangaan had been living among the Venda and the Northern Sotho without conflict. However, the rising ethnic chauvinism that accompanied bantustan establishment soon engendered conflict. Impoverished bantustan administrations are said to discriminate against ethnic aliens in assigning the small business licenses and development grants, civil service jobs, living space, and agricultural land that are in perpetually short supply. The Shangaan in Venda-Shangaan began to complain of discrimination at the hands of Venda chiefs; those whose homes had been incorporated into Lebowa complained of discrimination at the hands of the Northern Sotho. In response to these complaints, the Venda-Shangaan homeland was divided, in 1963, into the two bantustans of Venda and Gazankulu. [21]

Since then borders have been drawn and redrawn as tracts of land from South Africa and from Venda, Gazankulu, and Lebowa are traded back and forth. [22] People living on these tracts are removed in the service of ethnic purity, or repatriated, regardless of ethnic identity, at Pretoria's capricious discretion. Shangaan communities removed from South African "black spots" must be accommodated in Gazankulu, even when the homeland has no more land to allocate. Thus, the Surplus People Project describes areas throughout Gazankulu where one drives past settlement after settlement, each village separated from the last by only a kilometer or two. Although these are farming communities that require agricultural land for survival, the homeland does not have fields for all of its people. In addition to blacks who are rendered landless when they are removed from white South Africa, Gazankulu has, since 1983, taken in tens of thousands of Shangaan fleeing Gaza province in Mozambique. [23] In the last century the Shangaan fled invading Zulus; today they run from violence perpetrated by the NMR,

South Africa–backed guerrillas seeking to overthrow Mozambique's elected government.[24] Gazankulu was granted "self-governing status" in 1973; currently its Chief Minister still refuses to accept "independence" from South Africa.

Go well to Mozambique.
Tell your relatives to grab two knobkerries.
We shall arrive at sunrise.

Descriptions of Shangaan music and culture are provided by ethnomusicologist Thomas Johnston, based on fieldwork from 1968 to 1970. As with the Venda, music is an essential part of Shangaan social life. All men, women, and children participate in music making as part of involvement in other cultural activities. From childhood, the Shangaan learn the principles of their music as part of the overall process of socialization, and they develop musical skills as a by-product of learning the other skills necessary to social and biological maturation. Traditional village life is largely communal, with social, religious, and work activities taking place in groups. Because most such activities include song and dance, there is nearly always some form of musical performance taking place in any given village. Communal singing reaffirms social and cultural allegiance. Singing together reminds people that they are living together, working together, and finding fulfillment in the ways they perform in concert.

Among the Shangaan, traditional beer is a negotiable commodity that forms the basis for much of the economy. Brewed in large quantities from local grain (maize, sorghum, or millet) and from the marula fruit, such beer is low in alcohol and high in nutritional content, and it constitutes the culinary mainstay of communal celebrations. Beer-drinking songs permeate social life, with vocal parts related to seating arrangements of different groups of singers. In the agricultural milieu of traditional Shangaan society, time is marked according to the seasonal cycle. Holidays celebrate agricultural milestones and the work that contributes to each season's success. Associated songs reinforce the extent to which individual life is inseparable from community, and community life is inseparable from the natural world within which it unfolds.

The vast majority of Shangaan songs are structured in a call-and-response style. The call ("small voice") is generally sung by someone who occupies a respected musical role in the village, knows the culture's repertoire of traditional songs, and possesses a powerful voice. Since most Shangaan singing is performed outdoors, often accompanied by loud drums, vocal volume is essential in a song caller. The response ("big voice") is provided by a chorus, generally sung in unison. The musical form of the first line of a Shangaan song is strongly influenced by the speech tones of the lyrics, and by the length and rhythmic stress of the syllables. After this first line is set, however, subsequent lines may be influenced by musical as well as linguistic forces. In particular, Shangaan songs are uniformly characterized by an overall descent in pitch, from the first note to the last. Songs are constructed around a pentatonic scale, and melodic descents occur in a series of musical plateaus. This structure is assisted by the introduction of specific "nonsense words" that are free from obligatory speech tones.

You will be a wanderer!
Huwelele iyooha!

Shangaan music, like the traditional lore of any strong culture, fulfills the overall functions of asserting cultural unity and assisting in societal integration. For a politically weak, geographically dispersed, still-immigrating people, such unity is particularly important to cultural survival. Shangaan folklore is known for its heroic, anthropomorphic animal and bird characters, and songs frequently concern these same characters. In addition, the culture is rich in story-songs like the one about the wolf and the rabbit, that Luvhengo told us from her Venda grandmother's repertoire.

The Shangaan are known among their neighbors for their extensive body of folklore, and they ensure that their children learn it properly. They are also famed for lengthy recitations of genealogy and tribal history. Music is intimately related to all of this oral literature. Children learn game- and story-songs from older children during the day. They learn other kinds of songs in adult company at night, and they master the art of chorus singing as part of this oral cultural schooling. It is the women who are generally regarded as guardians of Shangaan cultural heritage. Like this people's century-old aspirations for genuine political independence and for adequate, watered farmland, Shangaan folklore, genealogy, history, and the process of proclaiming them in song are all part of each generation's bequest to the children who are—as in every culture—their people's future.[25]

> **Mama, hard times lie ahead**
> **Huwelele iyooha!**
> **Huwelele ahoo!**

THE CHIEF
AND THE LADIES

Luvhengo came by our hotel early, to confirm that she would be accompanying us to the Shangaan resettlement village of Makuleke, where Chief Makuleke himself had agreed to have the women of his village sing for us. "I have some things to organize in the next hour or so, and after that, darlings, I am all yours." She giggled. "But before I return you must go and find a present to give to the chief."

The last time I had given a present to a ruling African chief must have been in a previous incarnation. I had not an inkling of what an appropriate gift might be. From my elementary school memories rose embarrassing images of British colonists placing ropes of glass beads around the necks of unspecified natives, and presenting them with pouches of tobacco. Gary's expression was confused, and we looked to Luvhengo for advice. She giggled again. "Sorry, darlings. If I gave you suggestions I would spoil your fun."

Over the next hour we looked for a gift, but most of the shops around the hotel were closed. A drugstore offered men's cologne. A small market displayed candy and packaged biscuits. Finally we found an African curio shop like those that cater to white customers throughout South Africa. Familiar tribal faces smiled out from the ubiquitous English- and Afrikaans-captioned CNA postcards. Bowls and serving spoons carved from exotic woods filled one shelf. Huge lacquered ostrich eggs filled another. Woven woolen pillow covers and wall hangings dangled from the ceiling. Large straw baskets were piled in one corner, along with cone-shaped Sotho hats, and colorful woven prayer mats. For all the jumble and the essential sameness of these tourist shops from one region to another, we found some of the crafted objects quite beautiful. But would the chief find them beautiful? Or laughable? Or, even worse, insulting? Would they signify our respect and gratitude, or would they, instead, remind him of the white government's self-serving manipulation of African traditionalism?

> **The wizard kills even chiefs.**
> **Oh our chief!**
> **They would kill for no reason.**

At the back of the shop, on a top shelf, a large, heavy china pitcher sat in a matching basin. Painted with tiny pink flowers, it resembled a Victorian washing set. It wasn't to our taste and we couldn't know if the chief would like it, but at least it wouldn't violate his sensibilities about his own culture. We had been looking for over an hour, it was time to meet Luvhengo, and this was the best we could do. We took it.

As the shopkeeper climbed up to retrieve our selection, we deliberated about gifts for the women who would be singing for us. Again we grappled with questions of individual taste and cultural appropriateness. Again we struggled to use available materials to express personal appreciation without unwittingly violating social convention. In some ways these dilemmas were no different from those attending all cross-cultural interactions among strangers. But here we were not simply foreign strangers. Here we were white in a place where all black-white relations are suffused with history and emotion that transcend any one encounter. My eye fell on a pyramid of pleasantly decorated tins of Taverner's sucking candies. Thinking of the women's throats, I added these to our larger, more formal purchase and we ran off to meet Luvhengo.

The three of us drove northeast from Sibasa, heading out of Venda and toward the village of Makuleke, in neighboring

Gazankulu. Luvhengo continued the playful teasing with which she had started the morning. "Well, darlings, did you have fun shopping for this chief?"

She left no time for a reply, pointing immediately to two men in tattered jackets and trousers, walking, single file, along the edge of the road. "They are going to walk, maybe three or four more hours. You wouldn't manage it, but they have no choice. When you find Vendas and you say to them, 'How far are you going?' they will say 'Around the corner,' because they hate thinking of how far they have to go. Those two people will be coming to a village we will pass later on. They hate to think it's far, for then they will be lazy to start walking. You know, if you ask a stranger how long you will have to walk, he will say, 'It's around the corner.' You feel energetic. You keep walking. And then you see around the corner, and it isn't there and you think, 'He meant another corner.' And at the next corner you think it must be the next corner further on. Then you keep walking, and you are energetic, even though you realize it has been a *long* way."

For quite some time, we drove on rough dirt roads that wound generally uphill. The red earth of Venda shaded into northern Gazankulu's bleached, rocky terrain. We saw neither villages nor cultivated fields. Structures were small and of scrap, set back from the road. Finally, after a long, barren stretch, our road ended at a clean, square stucco house. Brightly colored flowers grew in a carefully staked-out garden. Luvhengo pointed out the new green plants that would, in several months' time, become this season's summer vegetables. A tall, dignified middle-aged man came toward us from the front door. Luvhengo walked over to talk with him while we watched and waited for further instructions.

Some distance beyond the house, on a smooth, clear flat of dirt, stood an arrangement of rondavels—round mud huts with low walls and high, pointed, smoothly thatched roofs. Women moved among the huts, performing the tasks of cooking and cleaning that are women's work the world over. In shifting pairs, half-naked children darted up to our car. They stared with huge dark eyes, giggled to one another, and darted off again, their ragged clothes disappearing into the muted colors of the village's geometry. Luvhengo's tall man looked ill-suited to this place. His clean chino trousers and crisp navy windbreaker might have arrived that morning from the current *Lands' End* catalog. His shoes were of good leather, styled, like the rest of his outfit, in the classic lines of understated Western affluence. A heavy watch flashed on his wrist.

After a brief conversation he followed Luvhengo to our car, gravely shook our hands, and turned to reenter his house. He was not unfriendly, but black men of his apparent age and economic station usually greeted us with a gregariousness he simply did not show. We asked who he was and whether we had done anything to offend him. Struggling to contain her laughter, Luvhengo steered us away from his house.

"That was the chief, and he must be very modern to come over and shake your hand. And my hand even more. In Venda I wouldn't even come near him. I would have to send somebody to go and talk to him. I would have to sit down and talk to somebody. And somebody talks to somebody. And somebody talks to the chief. But I took a chance here, because I knew he knows I'm a Venda, and I don't know anyway how one approaches a Shangaan chief."

The women were not yet ready to sing, but the chief had urged us to walk around the village in the meantime. We welcomed the opportunity. In South Africa's urban townships we had seen a great deal of material poverty, and we had been consistently impressed with the richness of spirit that pervades even the most dismal of physical circumstances. But this remote northeast region was quite different. Here the environment is mostly rural and primitive, and, at least superficially, daily life here is as different from that in Soweto as life in Soweto is different from that in the affluent white suburbs. On the path before us two small boys drove a Bible-era mule-drawn plow back in from a field. The boys wore nothing but the shreds of old, oversized shirts. One carried a long stick with which he prodded the mule as the plow dragged heavily behind.

In a pasture on the far side of a fence, needle-shaped anthills reached six feet into the air. Luvhengo told us, "The ants of that ant hill—tall and skinny, skinny—they are very deep and you cannot find them easily. So the people don't eat those ants. Normally they go for these round, heaped hills, where the ants are easier to find."

The scarcity of bread
And of money.
Oh how I wish for more!

Many children gathered around the carcass of a pickup truck that lay outside the perimeter of the rondavels. The truck had once been bold and yellow; now its twisted, misshapen cab suggested final catastrophe. Stripped of everything except the remnants of its paint, it served as an all-purpose play structure for the community's smallest members. One little girl perched on the right front of the hood, swinging her bare heels in and out of the headlight sockets and staring at us with an unabashed grin. Another hopped delicately along the front bumper. A boy stood where the driver had once sat, making the sounds of an engine and miming the job of steering. A group of larger boys swarmed over the whole truck, singing. Having failed to interrupt the little girl from her game on the front bumper, a big boy pulled her up to the roof. He joined her there, and together they jumped and hopped. Their feet banged in rhythm. The truck rattled and echoed, and the other children squealed and sang.

IN THE COUNTRY

The young doves
Fly in the tree.
In and out,
Thanking the summer.

They were putting on a fine show for the strangers in their midst, and they were delighted with themselves.

Luvhengo had said that this was a resettlement village, and I compared it with what I had seen of other such communities. Nowhere were the infamous tin toilets, the rows of closely spaced shacks with corrugated roofs that I had come to associate with resettlement. Nowhere the flimsy one-room structures that admit the wind, trap the heat, and amplify the sound of rain until it clatters in perpetual percussion. But for the chief's house, Makuleke's structures were all rondavels, built from what looked to be traditional materials in what looked to be a traditional manner. The thick mud walls were smooth and whitewashed inside and out, decorated with the wide, horizontal stripes of color that are characteristic of the Shangaan. The walls stood roughly five feet high, and the thatching added perhaps another five feet. From a distance, these huts had looked fragile and doll-like. Up close they were substantial and almost spacious. Inside, a scaffolding of thick branches was lashed together to support the heavy thatch. Despite the heat of the day, the air inside was cool and fresh. These structures had been developed in this part of the world, and they were clearly suited to its climate.

This community had been resettled here a good many years before, and the people had had time and materials to build their own village to approximate a traditional, subsistence-farming way of life. More important, they had also been allocated fields. Adjoining many of the rondavels were vegetable gardens, surrounded by smooth mud walls to protect against the universal scavenging of goats and scratching of chickens. The green shoots in each small garden indicated that the soil was still fertile. On all of these counts, this relocated community was in a far better position than many others. This village was certainly primitive. And its people appeared to be quite poor and to work very hard. But their environment seemed to permit the subsistence that looms as an unattainable luxury in other resettlement areas.

In contrast to the children's drab tatters, the clothing of the women was startlingly colorful, consisting largely of flowing printed cloths tied about their bodies. Luvhengo chatted with a woman on the path. She wore a large yellow cloth printed with a shining sun motif in black and red knotted like a sarong over one shoulder. Under the sarong was an orange shirt and over it a bright green blanket that bound her child to her back. Her head scarf was of pink and orange. Inside the nearest garden knelt a woman with a chartreuse and fuchsia cloth knotted about her waist. Her shirt was purple and her head scarf was red and yellow. I commented on the brightness of their clothing and Luvhengo chuckled with urban sophistication. "The Shangaanis are known for how bright their colors are, and for how they don't match. If I would wear a red dress in Johannesburg and maybe I would be wearing a blue belt with it, or yellow with yellow earrings, then my friends would point at me and say, 'Iiiiiii! Rosalie is wearing her Shangaans!' "

Perhaps it was this explicit attention to the women of the village that made me suddenly aware that from the moment we left the chief's company, we had seen not a single man. Of course. As in rural villages throughout South Africa, the men of Makuleke work as migrants in the white cities as long as they are strong enough to be employable.

We are waiting for those men
Who have been working in town.
We are waiting.

Perhaps there were old men, and sick, in the village today. But as dependents they did not participate in the maintenance activity that bustled around us, and we never saw them. Although Makuleke may be a village *for* all of its members, it is certainly a village *of* its women. This community does seem to be able to grow enough food to fend off starvation. But the people must have capital to pay taxes and to buy the clothing and supplies they cannot produce themselves; this capital comes from the wages of husbands and fathers who live at a distance and visit their families a few times a year at most. Makuleke's men all work in Johannesburg. By train the trip takes thirteen hours.

What kind of family life do these women have, who see their husbands three or four times a year? And the children who know their fathers as occasional visitors bringing sweets from the city—what are they learning about parenthood and marriage?

> **Goodbye, my mother's child.**
> **Mitarini came home with a child**
> **From Johannesburg.**

One woman spoke with Luvhengo at special length. Although the men were gone from the village, marriage and its woes nonetheless dominated her story. Of Sotho descent, she was born in Johannesburg and met her Shangaan husband there, where he works as a migrant. Tradition demands that she live with his family, so after the marriage she moved to their village, here in Gazankulu. In six years of marriage she has spent a total of six months with her husband. She spends the days caring for their two children, and for his aging mother. This woman considers herself lucky, for her husband's family have welcomed her and made her life among them as pleasant as possible. And when her husband comes home he is kind and loving. She sighs that others in the village are not as fortunate as she. Their husbands may be cruel, their families unwelcoming. Without one's husband or with him, she laments, marriage can be bitter.

> A beautiful lover!
> I enter strange countries, Mother.
> You will be a wanderer.

We returned to the chief's house, where a dozen women had gathered with their children. Four chairs had been arranged outside the front door, and the chief gestured for us to sit in three of them. He took the fourth and, without introduction, the singing began. One woman sang out with strident vigor. Before she had finished her phrase the others answered, harmonizing in an open fifth and holding their last note until she was well into her next phrase.

> You must be satisfied
> Huwelele
> You must behave well
> Huwelele
> So your children will be happy.

Like calls and responses we had been hearing throughout the country, this song was traded back and forth seamlessly, between leader and chorus. As the chief holds traditional responsibility for the well-being of the entire community, so the song leader is responsible for the strength and integrity of the group's song. It is the spirit and vigor of the caller's singing that allow the rest of the group to constitute a coordinated, effective chorus—a chorus that is somehow more than a sum of its individual voices. The women of Makuleke live together in a community structured largely along traditional lines. On various levels, their call-and-response singing reflects the relationships that order their daily lives. Suddenly the chorus held a high note and slid down into nothing. The song was over.

We applauded, taking our cue from the chief. To my surprise the women seemed more embarrassed than appreciative. They looked at one another and down at the ground, scuffing heels and toes in the dirt. One whispered something to the caller, and the three or four who heard burst into giggles. The women's tittering contrasted with the powerful sounds they had just produced. It seemed more appropriate to the little girls, sitting off to one side and peeking at us through their fingers, than to these women who could sing so lustily and run the village with such competence. They squeezed one another's hands and began singing again. Shyness evaporated. Their voices were strong. Their spirit drove the song home.

> **When we were still in love**
> **In Johannesburg**
> **It was fine.**
> **Awulele.**

One song led into another, and another, with breaks just long enough for the caller to catch her breath and sound the first line of something new.

> **Be still, my heart.**
> **Be free from anger,**
> **From the gossip of others,**
> **Pain!**

Traditional Shangaan songs give voice to matters of village life. However, the practice of singing about daily life encompasses more than rural tradition. When daily life concerns buses to and from Johannesburg, the scarcity of cash, and treacherous chiefs, then these issues, too, enter the repertoire of songs.

Colorfully dressed Shangaan woman poses outside migrant hostel, Atteridgeville.

Gary Gardner

Ladysmith Black Mambazo perform in migrant hostel.

Helen Q. Kivnick

Audience at Ladysmith Black Mambazo concert in migrant hostel.
Helen Q. Kivnick

Middle school students imitate Ladysmith Black Mambazo, KwaZulu.
Gary Gardner

The Lucky Stars perform at singing competition, Dalton Road Hostel, Durban.

Helen Q. Kivnick

Sign outside Dalton Road Hostel, Durban. Nonresidents are forbidden, in three languages, from entering without written permission from the superintendent.

Gary Gardner

The Shining Stars (above) and the NKA Special (below)
at singing competition, Dalton Road Hostel, Durban.

Helen Q. Kivnick

Communal drumming outside migrant hostel, Atteridgeville.
Gary Gardner

Migrant workers rest from communal music-making and pose
for the camera outside migrant hostel, Atteridgeville.
Gary Gardner

Animalistic dancing during communal music outside migrant hostel, Atteridgeville.

Gary Gardner

Shop carrying *sangoma* supplies in migrant market, Johannesburg.
Helen Q. Kivnick

A shebeen (extralegal beer hall) in migrant market, Johannesburg.
Helen Q. Kivnick

> On Wednesdays we go to the bus stop.
> The bus comes only Wednesday.
> Truly, yes!

After their first awkward pause, the women seemed almost to have forgotten our presence. No longer were they singing for strangers. No more were they performing for the chief. Now they were singing for themselves and for one another. With each song their voices grew stronger, the bond among them more nearly palpable.

> The light from afar
> She is like the bright light.
> You are worrying.
> Stay calm.
> The child is crying.

Under skirts, sarongs, and dresses, several of the women wore a thickly pleated, multilayered underskirt, a *tsibilani*, that added considerable girth and imparted an improbable, exaggerated pear shape. At one point the caller removed her outer dress to reveal a brightly striped blouse and her heavy, knee-length *tsibilani*. In caricatured Shangaan style, she tied the first dress around her waist as a cummerbund, and without interrupting her singing she began to dance. The *tsibilani* swayed and fell heavily, accentuating the quick, tightly controlled hip movements of her dancing. The other women clapped and stamped as they continued to sing. Two little girls ran off and returned wearing their own miniature *tsibilani*s over their other clothes. They joined the dancer in the center of what had become a semicircle, and the delight on their small faces competed with the smile the somber chief could not banish from the corners of his mouth.

IN THE COUNTRY

> How is our Chief?
> Without him we are in trouble.
> Without him we are killed.

Luvhengo was moved by one song, in particular, and she returned to it when the women took a long needed break.

> Our chief must be angry
> To see us moved
> Out of our country,
> Into another place.
> Makuleke must bring a gun.

I listened to her repeat that song, over and over, and I wondered whether these women had been praising their chief's loyalty or crying for a heroism he had never shown.

> Makuleke!
> Let him come and fight for us.

The singing resumed. As in small, closed communities throughout the world, gossip, jealousy, and infidelity are sources of personal pain and general speculation in this village. Here, as elsewhere, these issues pervade the songs that offer women some personal relief as they make public that which is otherwise suffered in private.

> Gossiping woman
> You are a liar.
> Quarrelsome and spiteful.
> Hayi!

In the absence of their men, these women have learned to heal their own wounds. Alone together for eleven months of the year, they have learned to look to one another for the support that no outsider can provide in intermittent visits—even an outsider called "husband," "father," or "brother." Jealousies notwithstanding, the sisterhood of the women of Makuleke shines as an inspiring example of strength and solidarity from within, resolute in the face of fragmentation deliberately imposed from without.

> **Things are in disorder**
> **And I must shout at the top of my voice**
> **To tell you**
> **That things are out of balance.**

The women had been singing and dancing for over an hour. Their chorus was beginning to sound ragged. The caller had been coughing for quite some time, but she had refused to give in, choosing, instead, to sing over the increasing roughness in her throat. Luvhengo whispered that it was time for me to go and bring the chief's gift from the car. I returned with my arms full, and the singing stopped. Luvhengo prompted me to make our presentation to the chief. He stood, ever-solemn, accepting our English and Luvhengo's line-by-line translation into Shangaan. With equal solemnity he accepted our gift and then reversed the communication process, speaking to us, line by line, in Shangaan with Luvhengo translating to English.

We asked Luvhengo to tell him that we had brought a gift for the women as well. Surprise and something akin to annoyance crossed his face, but he nodded and, in the end, did not seem displeased at our showing gratitude to the performers as well as to their chief. The sound of the women's throats convinced me that the sucking candies had been a good choice for them. I remained uncertain of his pitcher.

A few of the women clustered around the chief, examining the pitcher and basin. Others crowded around those who held the candies, jostling and laughing as they moved off toward their own rondavels. It was time for us, too, to depart. Through

Luvhengo we said our goodbyes and repeated our appreciation; through her the chief reciprocated. And then it was over. The women were gone. The chief was inside his house. We were in our car, driving away from Makuleke and back toward Sibasa. Luvhengo reported, "Your gifts were a hit, darlings. I heard the chief and his first wife arguing about who would get to keep the pitcher."

IV

MIGRANTS

ON YOUR TOES

BLACK MAMBAZO

BLACK TURF, WHITE TURF

WHITE MAMBAZO

LAST NIGHT, EARLY IN THE MORNING

WALK STEALTHILY, BOYS

ON
YOUR TOES

A significant segment of South Africa's labor force consists of migrant workers. But unlike migrants in America, South African migrants do not follow *work* that moves. Rather, they work at jobs that are quite stationary, but they must leave home in order to do so. These are the industrial recruits mentioned earlier, required to make their homes in overcrowded, underdeveloped rural bantustans that can neither support subsistence farming nor provide paid employment. Existing jobs are located near distant white urban centers, to which black men may bring families only after meeting elaborate residency requirements. So in order to support wives, children, and parents, rural men are often forced to leave them for year-long work contracts. Pretoria's solution for the problem of migrant labor is, as noted earlier, to grant political independence to the ten bantustans. Then these migrant workers will be temporary aliens like the Italians in Germany, the Chileans in Argentina, and the citizens of impoverished Mozambique and Zimbabwe who labor without security in the wealthy neighboring Republic of South Africa.

> We come from far away
> Where times are hard.
> We are here because we need money.

While they are in the cities, most migrants live in rigidly controlled, single-sex workers' compounds or hostels that isolate them from integral participation in black community life and prevent their real urbanization. To my white American sensibilities, hostels resemble hybrid army barracks/prisons/detention camps. Doors and gates are tightly guarded, and they may be locked at night, prohibiting all entry or exit. Non-"inmates" are required to carry written permission even to visit; this requirement is taken quite seriously and its violation may be cause for arrest and imprisonment. Conditions inside the hostels range from simply overcrowded and austere, to grossly underserved and appallingly filthy. Lack of privacy, rudimentary heat and light, pervasive dirt, and substandard washroom and toilet facilities—perhaps all of these are expectable in settings where people are confined and disciplined in connection with criminal punishment or military training. But for South Africa's migrants these living conditions are concomitants of behavior no more aberrant or aggressive than working to support one's family.

> Help me
> My father's child
> Help me.

Migrant workers have developed a style of singing known, over the course of this century, as *mbube* (lion), *ingomabusuku* (night song), *cothozamfana* (walk steadily, boys), or *isicathamiya* (to walk stealthily or on one's toes). This singing is performed by male "choirs" averaging ten or twelve members and comprising a lead singer, one voice on each of two other high parts, and a large number of basses. The resulting low, rumbling, lionlike sound, and the characteristic catlike, stalking movements are related to several of the style's names.

Every Saturday night choirs compete against one another for prizes; during the week they practice whenever they can find time and space. Although they try to rehearse in secret, to protect performance innovations, privacy in migrant hostels is all but impossible. Zulu music teacher Marcus Nzimande, now near retirement, tells of visiting a compound in his youth. When he entered the toilet block he found one group perfecting stepping routines under the showers, and another practicing songs while its eleven members crowded into a single toilet stall.

Marcus was involved in the postwar organization of city-wide Saturday night competitions, and he gladly reminisced for us about their history. In the early days, he recalled, performing choirs were brought into the migrant hostels for entertainment. Inmates organized themselves into groups patterned after these choirs, and they practiced throughout the year to sing for their families when they returned home at Christmas, at the end of each year's work contract. Since migrants are recruited in their rural homes, it is not unusual that many men from any given village will work for the same urban employer and live in the same hostel. According to an informal "home-boy" structure, inmates from the same rural district may organize a burial society, drinking club, savings organization, choir, dance team, and more.[1] This home-boy structure encourages the formation of choirs that practice and compete together all year long in the city, and return home together at year's end.

As the hostel-based singing groups, or men's choirs, increased in number and proficiency, they began to sing against one another during the course of the year, within their urban compounds. Gradually formal competitions were organized so that groups would be able to rely on a weekly venue for performing. With Sunday as the day most migrants are free from work, the competitions have settled into a Saturday night schedule, located in hostel recreation halls. Choirs begin to sing in the middle of the evening. The formal competitions run well into Sunday morning, if necessary, until all entrants have performed.

For the singers these weekend competitions provide a constructive focus for spare time throughout the week, and a source of recreation on Saturday night. They also offer an arena for demonstrating creativity and mastery, a structure for consolidating identity and alleviating loneliness, and an opportunity to compete for meaningful recognition. Otherwise these are all but absent from the artificially constricted, stifled lives apartheid has designed for these men. To the authorities the competitions are valuable for reasons more closely related to increased worker productivity, inmate control, and the prevention of violence. Singing and competing offer emotional outlets to relieve the raging frustration and resentment inevitably engendered by migrant life. The competitions themselves keep large numbers of inmates out of trouble on Saturday night. And inmates who sleep at the competitions' end will be occupied for a good deal of Sunday, as well.

Choirs pay entrance fees to compete for prizes of cash or, until quite recently, for a live beast. Marcus laughingly told of the havoc wrought by one frightened prize ox, perhaps ten or fifteen years ago. At some point during the evening, the animal broke loose while a group was performing on stage.

I mean the two of us,
Baby,
We keep and stay together.

It stampeded the hall,

The two of us,

bellowing loudly, scattering chairs,

Baby,

and, at very least, startling the audience.

We keep and stay together.

People ran this way and that, some trying to get out of the ox's way, others trying to capture it. The commotion increased the ox's fear and confusion, and it began to mark the hall as its own territory, using those personal, biological markers available to all animals. Finally the ox was caught, calmed, and secured outside. People pitched in to clean up the hall and reclaim it as the province of men. The floor was quickly washed. Chairs were rearranged in rows. Only then did people notice that up on stage, the choir that had been singing when the ox began its stampede was still doing so, apparently without ever having broken stride.

> The two of us,
> Baby,
> We keep and stay together.

In Durban competitions are held, simultaneously, in several different venues around the city, and a choir may make the rounds, competing in as many as it chooses. Choirs gather to warm up and entertain their friends at eight or nine o'clock on Saturday evening. Audience members pay admission, and during the warm-up hours they pay again to request selections from their favorite groups. Audiences are almost entirely black, with the critical exception of the adjudicator, invariably white, who arrives between 1:00 and 3:00 A.M. to begin the official competition.

As an attempt at legislating impartiality, it was decided long ago that adjudicators would have to be white. They must not ever have sung with any of the competing choirs. They must not be friendlier with some choirs than with others. They must not be related to members of any competing group. In any urban area, the only people who were likely to meet all of these criteria were whites. For no matter what the socioeconomic status of any randomly selected white, it was nearly certain that he or she would never have had the kind of contact with blacks that might have resulted in the development of friendship, in mutual participation in each other's recreational activities, or in social contact with one another's families. All of this was reasoned out several decades ago; it remains largely true today.

Winning singing competitions is a very serious business, and Marcus explained that it is not unusual for a choir to bring its own *sangoma* (spirit medium) along. This practice is said to be another reason for the insistence on white adjudicators. For whites are believed to be less susceptible than blacks to the *sangoma*'s spells and incantations.

The decision for whites to evaluate a black performance medium has two obvious drawbacks. The first, that since very few whites have even a passing familiarity with any African language, the odds are extremely high that a given judge will not understand more than a word or two of what is being sung. Indeed, this factor has led choirs to incorporate English and Afrikaans into their performances in an attempt to impress adjudicators. The second drawback is that since the vast majority of whites lack even the most superficial knowledge of black cultural traditions, they are not likely to be competent to assign greater or lesser merit to specific performances within those traditions. Nonetheless in a country in which bribery and deception thrive—at all levels, across and within all racial groups, concerning matters large and small, issues political, economic, and social—the decision still stands that the most important quality for competition adjudicators is that they be impartial.

Who are the whites who adjudicate these black men's singing competitions? According to local folklore they are people for whom spending the night in a warm hall, drinking coffee, smoking cigarettes, and perhaps receiving a hot meal are more desirable than whatever else they would have been doing with that time. Hobos sleeping on park benches, drunks hunched in doorways, and convicts released from prison late on a Saturday afternoon all find themselves "tapped" for this task. Marcus told of receiving a special dispensation from the city police, so that he and a white musicologist could travel together, followed by a carload of black choir leaders, in search of prospective adjudicators. He laughed while recalling the way a sleeping hobo might jump up and scream for the police when he saw he was being watched by a black man, though sleeping in the park was, itself, illegal. Without laughter Marcus added that before the dispensation, responding police officers had most often jailed himself or the choir leaders, assuming that if a white man was screaming a black man had committed a crime.

> **Your home is not here.**
> **Your home is where the roofs are peaked,**
> **As far away as the stars.**

Writing in 1968, Zulu anthropologist Elkin Sithole emphasized the strong links between what he called *ingomabusuku* music and the traditional Zulu singing that is part of the very lifeblood of the men who developed the genre. He noted the open fourths and fifths of *ingomabusuku* harmonies and the shrill falsetto of the high voices. He stressed the importance of the leader in this particular form of polyphony. He described the competent, playfully improvised melodies exchanged between leader and choir at the beginning of each performance. These musical dialogues allowed a leader to size up his competitors, change a prearranged set of songs, and give his choir last-minute stylistic instructions, all while entertaining the audience and dazzling the judges.[2] Today *isicathamiya* has incorporated elements from the diversity of music played on the radio over the last twenty years. Tin Pan Alley, rock and roll, gospel, Latin, country, Negro spirituals, Wesleyan hymnody, and more are all discernible in the *isicathamiya* repertoire. Improvised musical dialogue has, in part, yielded to more formal, carefully rehearsed introductory exchanges. Still, the genre's Zulu roots predominate, and its sound and structure are inseparable from this African tradition.[3]

Isicathamiya choirs often take names that recall their rural homes. Groups competing in Durban today call themselves the

Harding Morning Stars, the Mtwalume Young Ages, and
Utrecht, for example, to celebrate their family homes in distant
regions of the Natal. Choir names also reflect the Zulu tradition
of extravagant self-praise, and they focus on such qualities as
physical strength and valor (the Jabula Home Defenders), urban
savoir-faire (the Easy Walkers), fearsome reputation (the Danger Boys), musical prowess (the Greytown Evening Birds), and
general excellence (the Shining Stars).

Each choir enters the hall from the rear and dances its
way down an aisle and up onto the stage, singing all the while.
The judge is seated just below the stage, facing forward. The
judge may not turn around to look at the entering choir, on
suspicion of having his or her opinion illegally influenced by
members of the audience. A choir is given roughly ten minutes
to perform onstage, and it fills that time with a combination of
singing, rhythmic movement, and caricatured pleading for the
judge's favor. After performing, the choir sings its way down
from the stage and out of the hall.

A group's music is most often composed and arranged by
its leader. Song lyrics may refer to specific people or places from
this man's home village, to life in the city, or to the competition
itself. Lyrics may concern the most trivial of personal activities,
or the achievements of cultural or political heroes. They may
refer to current local events, to general circumstances, to scraps
of conversation, to longings for distant family and customs, to
memories of deceased elders or lost ethnic glory. They may also
refer to religion—Christian or traditional Zulu—or philosophy,
to politics, or to values and social relations. Songs are characterized by a playfulness with words. Lyrics often contain
high-spirited strings of nonsense syllables; words, phrases, and
paragraphs are repeated at will. In addition, in echoing any
given word, singers may accent first one syllable and then another, until the word almost seems to lose its designated meaning and become, instead, a vehicle for perpetuating the process
of singing.

Appear, appear
Appear——pear——pear
Appear, my tears of the Ages!

Like song, dance accompanies the communal celebrations that mark life's milestones in traditional African life. Like songs, dances are characterized by social function and segregated by gender, and perhaps by marital status and age, as well. We have seen how the creative energies and frustrations of rootless men confined for months at a time in single-sex, urban compounds spawned *isicathamiya* singing. This same creative process gave rise to the development of various male team dancing forms, as Durban migrants in the 1920s and 1930s used the indigenous cultural idiom of dance to respond to the social, political, and economic forces that led to their virtual incarceration in urban compounds.

Best known as South Africa's first white to professionalize Zulu song and dance, anthropologist, and, more recently, international music star, Johnny Clegg traces one form of contemporary Zulu folk dancing, *isishameni*, to traditional stick fighting in the rural Natal. In this region, conflict between different administrative districts was largely managed through the *umgangela*, a prearranged, ritualized stick fighting competition. Male companies would sing and shout their war cries, and under the direction of their war captains, they would move in rhythm. Together and apart. Together and apart. Well-known fighters from each company would break out from the group and demonstrate individual skill with weapons. Each district participated as a proclamation of its men's ability to defend themselves and defeat adversaries. Warriors could challenge one another and engage in actual battle. The rules of *umgangela* were strict, and casualties were minimized. Until white farms appropriated black administrative districts and began evicting large numbers of families, this ritualized fighting allowed groups to air conflicts, challenge rivals, and settle scores with honor.

In so doing, it served to contain serious inter-district opposition and avert spontaneous outbursts of hostility that would surely have been far more destructive.[4]

Forced to leave the land for mine and factory, migrants performed traditional dances as a familiar means of socializing and a reassuring expression of manhood and identity. They organized dance teams as part of ongoing home-boy structures. Migrants found themselves crowded into hostel dormitories with men from other clans. This tense, close contact intensified the competition that had always underlain much traditional male dancing. White employers soon involved themselves with hostel dancing, sponsoring teams and organizing competitions. In so doing they capitalized on the dancers' recreation and influenced subsequent stylistic development of migrant dance forms.[5] It is important to note that in traditional performance competition, all participants strove to achieve a community standard of excellence. Competition in which individuals or teams strive to outdo one another is an artifact of Western intervention.[6]

Corporate sponsorship paid for dance teams' elaborate costumes and bought dancers release time for rehearsal. In return, teams were named for their corporate sponsors and they developed performance routines to suit corporate tastes and, insofar as possible, to provide informal advertising. Clegg emphasizes that these dance competitions were judged by whites, giving more weight to criteria that white industry and government thought appropriate for black dance than those that black dancers themselves might have valued. In particular, choreography, regimentation, and spectacle have assumed far more importance in evolving migrant dance forms than they ever held in rural-based tradition.

As described by drama scholar Peter Larlham, today's dance competitions are organized by white employers in co-operation with the tourism industry. They are staged on Sunday afternoons in urban stadia, before audiences of white tourists, with large cash prizes at stake. Teams dress in costly, modern adaptations of traditional Zulu garb. The basic costume includes a cowhide apron fastened at the waist, brushed woolen leg decorations tied just below the knee, and some form of headdress fashioned from hide and feathers. Each man will often carry a long dancing stick and small cowhide shield. In their opening sequences, company-sponsored teams perform elaborate gestures and formations to advertise the products and names of their sponsors.

While competition dancers attract white attention, non-competition teams organize without corporate sponsorship. It is primarily these informal teams that maintain the original, sociocultural functions that African dance served for the early migrants. These teams dance without elaborate costume, wherever they can find flat space. Often they gather in dusty compound courtyards, or on gravelly driveways, or in the spaces between buildings and the fences that perpetually remind hostel inmates of their confinement. They perform for one another and for whatever "accidental" black people may wander by and be attracted by their activity. Less carefully polished than its establishment-sponsored counterpart, this noncompetition dancing involves considerable improvisation. Dances are modified as individuals adapt ideas from other teams and from rural relatives. Personnel are perpetually changing, as teams gain and lose members to the notorious instability of black employment. Paradoxically, personnel changes also contribute to the ongoing development of dance forms.[7]

White Zulu scholar Jeff Thomas identifies the dynamic *ingoma* or *indlamu* as another style developed among rural Zulus working in the cities. Himself an *ingoma* dancer with the performing group Abafana Bomoya, Thomas describes the style as deriving from the Natal's Zulu countryside and as being popular today among rural youth who pride themselves on their traditionalism.[8] *Ingoma* is performed by young men in lines of eight or ten. The dance features high, stamping steps performed in unison by the whole team. Exaggerated leg lifts and caricatured, surprisingly graceful stamps are highlighted as individual dancers take turns demonstrating their virtuosity. Following Zulu tradition, the team leader remains in front of the line throughout, although he may move to one side as other members take turns coming forward.

High, stamping steps and line formations characterize most of the urban folk dance styles popular among today's migrants. A routine typically consists of an opening sequence—essentially a warmup—followed by the main dance. Traditionally provided by singers and clappers other than the dancers themselves, the rhythm for the main dance is established by short sentences or highly rhythmic songs, repeated for the duration of the sequence. Larlham identifies these rhythmic foundations as "bullets," viewed by each team as its ammunition against rivals. As the routine progresses, dancers perform increasingly complicated sequences, each grounded in the words, syllabic emphases, and rhythmic intricacies of its own bullet. The end of most dances is marked by the performers suddenly throwing themselves to the ground in stylized collapse.

Perhaps it is the shields and dancing sticks, perhaps the stamps and kicks that lead white urbanites to mistake these recreational forms for Zulu war dancing. Perhaps, instead, it is the difference between African and Western notions of competition. Indeed, black urban folk dance has adopted some of the vocabulary, as well as the accoutrements, of battle. Teams use musical bullets against their rivals; team members are called *amasosha* (soldiers).[9] But urban folk dance remains an expression of African culture. As such, even when it enacts competition and conflict, it functions far more powerfully to unite than to divide dancers. Belying superficial military symbolism, team dancing holds praise and admiration as the object of the battle. And such kudos are not directed toward particular dancers or teams alone. Along with individual, momentary recognition, team dancing expresses universal pride and participation in cultural tradition, and it demonstrates the tradition's ongoing, vibrant evolution. Most important, it allows dancers to assert their active identification with Africa, regardless of the circumstantial indignities imposed by the West's invention of apartheid.

> Hail, young man!
> Here is the King.
> We say Hail! Hail!
> O Lion of the Nation.

BLACK MAMBAZO

The phone in our Durban hotel room rang twice and a harsh, nasal voice identified itself at the other end. "Joseph Shabalala speaking!" This Zulu singer had been a kind of musical hero to us from the moment we heard our first Ladysmith Black Mambazo album. That was after my first trip to South Africa, in March 1984. During that trip I had spent an evening talking with Johnny Clegg. In a few hours Johnny had given me a private lecture-demonstration of traditional Zulu music, and he had named several performers whose music I would have to hear in order to get a feel for contemporary black popular singing. Ladysmith Black Mambazo, the Mahotella Queens, Amaswazi Emvelo, Obed Ngobeni, and Johnny's own group at the time, Juluka. At Johnny's suggestion I spent a whole morning in Kohinoor, a record shop run by Indians, carrying the most comprehensive collection of black singing to be found in Johannesburg. All morning I listened. Finally I bought six Black Mambazo albums to carry home along with selections by every other artist who had been recommended over the previous month. All of the singers I had chosen were good, the young black clerk told me, but Ladysmith Black Mambazo were unequaled. Their albums were all gold.

When I stepped off the plane in San Francisco, my carry-on bag bulged with twenty or thirty record albums I identified as "research materials" for the customs agents. Taking my bag, Gary groaned at this typical expression of my inability to make choices. "Couldn't you have bought just *one* album by each performer, rather than everything the store had to sell?"

His question changed after we had listened to Black Mambazo. "You mean you only bought six of their records, and not all thirteen?"

Ladysmith Black Mambazo became our instant favorite. Belying album jackets that pictured ten or twelve Zulu warriors in traditional regalia, the group's unaccompanied vocal sound was mellow, rich, and exquisitely polished. Their harmonies were tight. Their timing was precise. And through all the professionalism, through the Zulu we could neither pronounce nor translate, rang a warmth and an appealing sense of playfulness.

I had written to Joseph Shabalala immediately, recounting Gary's second question to me and asking if he might meet with us on our October return to his country. To my surprise, this glittering star of South Africa's black music scene wrote back immediately and expressed a willingness to help my work in any way he could. The result of that exchange was the breakfast meeting arranged for this particular morning.

Through the opening door of the elevator we saw three black men sitting on a wicker bench in the bustling lobby of Durban's "international" Holiday Inn. Two were boys, really, with faces young and smooth. They looked guileless in their school uniforms, and they squirmed under the stares of vacationing beachgoers. The third, their father, bore himself with confidence. He wore a track suit proclaiming "Ladysmith Black Mambazo," and he watched the vacationers with amusement. Although the hotel's international status meant that guests of all colors were accommodated, in fact the faces that stared at Joseph Shabalala without recognition would all have been designated "white" or "Asian" under South Africa's laws of racial classification.

We introduced ourselves, and Joseph introduced his two sons, Vivian and Innocent, who had come along to compensate for their father's then-scanty English. We shook hands all around and Joseph smiled the biggest smile I had ever seen. I wondered whom we should have invited, to compensate for our all but nonexistent Zulu.

Inside the hotel dining room, Joseph Shabalala created what would have been, if I had thought to think about it beforehand, a totally predictable sensation. For although the hotel's guests and administrative staff were Asian and white, the dining room staff were entirely black. Waiters in gold-trimmed jackets abandoned both their clients and their professionalism, to giggle with one another and point at our table. Every waiter in the room brought us coffee. At least once. Every busboy cleared our plates and replaced them with new ones. Before we had eaten. Joseph autographed the napkins held respectfully before him, and his sons looked on with admiration. Vivian, the elder, murmured, "It's wonderful, how they love him."

While Joseph continued to perform the duties of his celebrity, we talked with Vivian about his own life. He was a student at a teacher training college in the township of KwaMashu, and he told us how much he looked forward to teaching children. In a land in which the government mandates inferior education for black children, in which many black high school teachers themselves have only an eighth-grade education—in such a land there is a crying need for well-trained, sincere black teachers. Vivian is the first of eight Shabalala children, and from early boyhood he has assumed responsibility for his younger siblings. His face was proud when he spoke of them, and I found myself thinking that regardless of the factionalism that pervades black education, particularly in his KwaZulu homeland, this young man is someone his students will be better off for having known.

> **I live with hopes.**
> **I am convinced they are true,**
> **And I will not be disappointed.**[10, 11]

South Africa is a country of many languages and little direct communication. People speak in Zulu, Xhosa, Sotho, Tswana, Shangaan, Venda, Afrikaans, English, and more. But when they communicate most clearly, they often do so outside words. We told Joseph that we were planning to attend a fundraising concert the following weekend, at which Black Mambazo would join other musicians in singing to raise money for black student scholarships. He chuckled. "Ah, you know Milk Afrika Concert?"

"We know it, and we already have tickets. But what we really want to know is where we can see Black Mambazo do a whole concert by yourselves. Not just one set in a long afternoon of music."

Joseph's chuckle died. "Friday night we sing in Felixton. White people do not come there." Closed.

Joseph had written out what he wanted to remember to tell us about his group's history. At first he tried to answer our specific questions. But once we gave him the opening he had been waiting for, he unfolded a paper from his breast pocket.

Thought by thought, he read aloud in the Zulu that always sounds, to my white American ears, more like singing than like ordinary talking. Thought by thought, Vivian and Innocent debated in Zulu and explained, in English, what their father was trying to say.

Joseph Shabalala grew up in Ladysmith, a white place in Natal province, perhaps two or three hours' drive northwest of Durban. Like most black communities in South Africa, the Ladysmith township of Joseph's childhood was suffused with singing that functioned as a powerful social glue. The whole community sang for a wedding in any of its families. Religious services and celebrations relied on singing for the joy and fervor that sustained worshippers from service to service. Children's school choirs packed the community hall with parents and relatives for performances and choral competitions.

As a boy, Joseph would sing while he herded cattle, alone, in the rural countryside of the late 1940s. These fleeting, solitary songs were a source of comfort and a product of inspiration. Melodies would come to him from the blue skies that reached down to meet the lush, waving grasses of Zululand, and he would hum them aloud to dispel the inevitable loneliness of a herdboy.

Joseph's father was a migrant worker, away from the family for eleven months out of the year. He sang with an *mbube* choir of home boys, and when these men returned to their families in Ladysmith each Christmas, the Shabalala household, indeed the whole black township, was filled with the sound of *mbube*.

> **Knock, knock**
> **So we can enter**
> **And pass our regards**
> **To everybody.**

Even in his teens, Joseph Shabalala recognized that something was not quite right with the way the *mbube* choirs were singing. But he could never either identify the problem or figure out a way to solve it. For one year he sang with a group called the Durban Choir, about whom he told us, "They were not in good manner. Their voice was irregular. My ear *told* me that they were irregular, but I had no way to organize their voice. My failure to the Durban Choir led me to leave *mbube*."

In 1959 Joseph left Ladysmith for the city of Durban, where he found work at a cotton factory. For several years he spent his days spinning yarn and weaving cloth. His nights he spent singing. His father's older brother led the popular *mbube* choir the Highlanders, and when Joseph was asked to join the group, his lifelong enthusiasm for this unaccompanied group singing overwhelmed his recent retreat from it. However, as he had with the Durban Choir a few years before, he soon recognized that there was something not quite right about the way the Highlanders were singing. Once again he found himself unable to direct their improvement.

Joseph had several brothers and cousins working, like himself, in Durban's factories. Frustrated with his inability to refine the Highlanders to his satisfaction, he recruited these brothers and cousins in 1961 for membership in his own, newly formed *cothozamfana* choir Ladysmith Black Mambazo. This original name, now nearly thirty years old, embodies Joseph Shabalala's multiple sensitivities—to audience reaction, to Zulu tradition, and to the larger secular community. Together, these sensitivities have enabled this Zulu singer to achieve astonishing international success as a popular entertainer while remaining true to the traditional idiom that has always been his musical soul. He explains, "You must excite the audience. In your name you must tell them something interesting to them, something they already know, but also something new. So the name Black Mambazo. When we are performing, black is the most beautiful. More beautiful than other colors. And *mambazo* means an axe. An axe is powerful. It can destroy everything. So Black Mambazo is a group that must be beautiful and powerful. It must be in the first position in the competition. It must beat everyone else with its black beauty." Black Mambazo. Named for the white town of Ladysmith and the power of black singing.

Here are the boys of the axe.
Beware!
Here are the boys of the axe.[12]

For three years Joseph Shabalala and Black Mambazo struggled first to identify and then to achieve elusive vocal perfection. But something was persistently wrong with their—and every other choir's—tone. In 1964 Joseph began having recurring dreams about how to sing and, gradually, about how to teach others to sing. The dreams all showed young people in clouds of heavenly brightness, singing wonderful songs with an ethereal, hymnlike quality. Joseph always stood apart, cast as the lonely spectator left below to look up at this higher vision. Listening carefully, he heard the angelic hymns calling him to retire from current pursuits. After one such dream he awoke with the feeling that now, for the first time, he knew how to proceed. For the next two years he trained Black Mambazo.

Let me see You, my King.
I must ascend to You.[13]

The imagery of Joseph's early visionary dreams appears on the jackets of at least five Black Mambazo albums. Singers emerge, joyful, from the turbulence of clouds or ocean waves, to bask in a heavenly light. On looking back, Joseph now believes that God sent angels to bring him their music. When his group sings, they are bringing the music of angels to people who must live on the earth.

We asked him to put into words exactly what he had learned from his dreams, but his reply was more a sequence of impressions than an explanation. Perhaps he was trying to oblige our request, and somewhere, from Zulu to English, from Joseph to Vivian and Innocent to us, the essence of his meaning evaporated. Perhaps, instead, he was not even trying to put into words that which he himself had learned only through visual image and internal muscle sensation. Perhaps he shared with us only what he wanted us to know. Repeatedly he started, in Zulu, to talk about how Ladysmith Black Mambazo sings, gesturing with his hands and illustrating with exaggerated movements of lips, tongue, and jaw. Vivian and Innocent tried to translate, but, we realized when Joseph seemed to disagree with their English words, they are not members of Black Mambazo. They have not undergone their father's rigorous training; they have not sung under his direction every day for nearly thirty years. Perhaps they do, and perhaps they do not quite, understand the process he seemed to be trying to describe.

Something that has always set Ladysmith Black Mambazo apart from other *cothozamfana* choirs, even before Mambazo's international stardom, is the amount of time they spend in highly disciplined rehearsal. Joseph is a perfectionist, and from the moment he knew what he wanted to hear he trained his singers to produce it. Other choirs sound, as Joseph describes it, "irregular." Not only are isolated voices occasionally slightly out of time with the others, but also the tone of the group as a whole is highly variable. In any choir's ten-minute performance, there are likely to be moments of golden purity, followed by moments of some harshness or roughness, and moments of sound that are pretty but not glorious. Much of this irregularity might be eliminated by long hours of rigorous rehearsal, but most choirs cannot or do not make that kind of time.

In the notes to his albums *Iscathamiya* and *Mbube Roots*, musicologist Veit Erlmann explains that at the time of Joseph's early dreams, a singing style called "bombing" dominated *cothozamfana* performances. This style calls for each man to sing at the very top of his voice, and for the whole choir to sing in unison. Almost by definition this sound is raw and uncontrolled, a product of mortal exertion rather than angelic serenity. Joseph moved Black Mambazo away from bombing. He replaced raw unison with velvet harmony, and he trained the group to control and modulate tone production, even at the extremes of each man's vocal range.

In addition to discipline, Joseph teaches his singers a particular usage of mouth, throat, and tongue. The Zulu language, itself, places sounds in parts of the mouth and throat that English simply does not use. Zulu is a tonal language; syllabic pitch affects meaning. The language also uses clicks that are nonexistent in English, accomplished with tongue, teeth, cheeks, and palate. The clicks combine with round vowels to produce resonant sounds that appear in English, if at all, in sung rather than spoken form.

Joseph watched Gary's face as he laughed at something Vivian had said. "If you sing with me, I teach you how to use your mouth. First to speak in Zulu. After that to sing like Black Mambazo."

Gary fell silent, aware that what his next words were would

be less important than how he uttered them. Joseph pointed to his own mouth, stretched his lips, and produced a soft, throaty roar like the resonant rumbling of lions across the highveld in the darkest hour of night.

> The tiger is beautiful with colors.
> With camouflage the tiger catches its prey.
> The tiger eats with its colors.[14]

For two years Joseph worked with Black Mambazo, training them to sing like the angels of his dreams. At last their new sound was ready, and the group began to win the weekly *cothozamfana* competitions. Their reputation spread throughout the Natal. Vivian speaks with a mixture of pride and wistfulness as he recalls Black Mambazo's success during these years of his childhood. "My father was in Durban, working in the factory, and he would come home to Ladysmith only at Christmas. But I was so proud of Black Mambazo! They would return at Christmas, and they would be singing all the time, and I would know that was my father. It was wonderful. And people would come from all over to ask for songs, and no matter how tired he was, my father would sing. The people have always loved him!"

It was some years later that Joseph had another dream whose image again profoundly changed Ladysmith Black Mambazo's performance. The group had been working on a new song about the training of the young men of Black Mambazo, and they were accompanying the song with the rhythmic movements and stealthy walking on toes characteristic of *cothozamfana*. In his dream Joseph saw an energetic, tightly choreographed style of movement that he instantly recognized as belonging with the group's new, more polished singing. The group members were all living in the same hostel, and although it was well after midnight when Joseph awoke from his dream, he immediately roused the others to teach them the new movements—dancing, really, apparently adapted from the Zulu *ingoma*—that would soon come to characterize them on stage.

As he had done with their singing, Joseph now rehearsed Black Mambazo unmercifully to perfect their new overall performing style. This rehearsal had much in common with athletic training. The singers were required not only to master Joseph's adaptations of familiar *ingoma* dance movements, and not only to coordinate these movements with their newly learned style of *cothozamfana* singing. In addition, they had to develop the physical endurance to execute prolonged, stylish performances of *ingoma*'s energetic stamps and kicks at the same time as they were singing in the highly disciplined, tightly controlled fashion Joseph had developed for them.

Again they came out of rehearsal victorious, and they rapidly became undefeatable in the weekly competitions. Quite apart from the unequaled quality of their singing—which is, after all, what competition judges are instructed to evaluate— the group's overall performance stood out as unique among the tens of choirs singing in the Natal in the late 1960s and early 1970s. Their sound was so smooth and their diction so precise that the whole choir sounded as one infinitely rich voice. And the dancing with which they had replaced *mbube*'s traditionally smaller-scale movements was both familiar to their black audiences and wholly innovative in conjunction with their singing.

Finally their singular success and acclaim outstripped what the hostel competitions could bear. People would be so impressed with Black Mambazo's performance that they were rudely inattentive to other choirs. Audiences would come to hear Black Mambazo, and walk out as soon as they were finished, leaving subsequent performers to sing to an empty hall. Eventually the other choirs refused to compete against Black Mambazo, and in 1972 the group was barred from the competitions that were their roots. As the only alternative to giving up performing altogether, they decided to go professional. In 1973 they issued their first record album, *Amabutho* (Warriors). The album was a success and they quit their factory jobs to sing full time.

> **Here are the boys of the axe.**
> **They are! They are!**
> **They are! They are!**
> **Take care!**
> **Here are the boys of the axe.**[15]

For nearly ten years Joseph had been developing his talents for music and leadership. Now manager as well as musical director of a newly professional ensemble, he quickly developed the additional skill of responding artistically to demands in the market. He told us, "You are guided by the people in singing and in writing. What they want and what they love. The people love the religious songs. They always demand the religious songs, and so we sing for them."

Indeed, from the outset Black Mambazo were well received throughout South Africa's black community. But even from early enthusiasts Joseph received requests that the choir add religious songs to their repertoire. He acceded with the group's fifth album, *Ukukhanya Kwelanga* (The Rising of the Sun; or "The brilliance of the sun as it shines with all its glory throughout the universe with all the blessing bestowed upon mankind by the Creator").[16]

This first religious album was produced in 1975, three years after the choir's professional debut. It marked a shift not only in the focus of Black Mambazo's lyrics, but also in the focus of Joseph Shabalala's personal life. All along he had felt that he owed his extraordinary musical popularity to God; now he began to feel the need to pay public musical homage for this blessing. He also began to pay more consistent private homage, devoting more and more energy to the Church. He assumed directorship of his church choir. He began to teach Sunday school. In 1981, he proudly told us, he became a priest in his church, the Church of God of the Prophets.

Interestingly, to the Western listener the religious theme that has dominated Black Mambazo's singing for nearly fifteen years now is not immediately identifiable in either the structural or the dance components of their performance. As the group moved beyond organized competitions, so they transcended conventional Zulu song and dance forms, and conventional Western forms, as well, to create hybrids that have consistently captured the imagination of South Africa's variegated black community. The discipline, the smooth, silky tone, and the Western harmonies of much of their singing all set what is now the vocal standard for *isicathamiya* choirs. Their on-stage performance integrates many of the physically energetic elements of *ingoma* into the conventionally far lower key stage presence of *isicathamiya*. And perhaps most interesting, their unique composite style integrates Christian religion with Zulu cultural forms and with entertainment business savvy. Although English translations and frequent Western-sounding harmonies do identify Black Mambazo's songs as praises and pleas to the Christian God, the rhythms, song structures, and physical accompaniments are all those of Zulu or Zulu-derived performance traditions.

> **King of Kings**
> **We kneel before you.**
> **How long will the sun rise and set**
> **Until you appear,**
> **Oh Mighty One?**[17]

As the leader of a commercially successful ensemble, Joseph gauges his material to continue to please existing audiences and attract new fans. As spiritual leader of a religious congregation he writes of inspiration, singing songs that he hopes will speak to all people as the spirit of God speaks to him. But how can the words of Christian hymnody be in any way congruous with the dancing of traditional Zulu ancestor worship and the entertaining of secular audiences? How can faith in the Christian God be compatible with the traditional Zulu spirit worship that is consistently condemned by Christian authorities? Like the independent Christian churches discussed earlier, Black Mambazo draws from both Western and African traditions to create new forms of expression that are unique to contemporary black South Africa.

In addition, we must remember that for black South Africans the act of singing is an integral part of any aspect of daily life. A song is an appropriate vehicle for expressing any feeling—personal or general, passing or enduring, spiritual or secular. We must also remember that in this culture, singing and dancing are inseparable parts of the same process. In the racial-cultural mix that will prove to be either South Africa's greatest asset or the source of her ultimate self-destruction, it becomes eminently plausible that black entertainers offer fervent Christian devotion in the medium of Zulu-based performance. In these terms of cultural contradiction and combination, Joseph Shabalala may be seen as one example of the vital integration that is twentieth-century South Africa's hope for the future. He is African and Western, sacred and secular, spiritual and commercial. He is an artist, both Christian and Zulu, who employs the plethora of cultural idioms that have become his own, effectively expressing his personal visions in a way that resonates within audiences across the country and, increasingly, throughout the world as a whole.

Joseph describes his early songs as "having memories" of everything Zulu. Some speak of ancient Zulu history. Some praise King Shaka, who, in the second decade of the nineteenth century, amalgamated the disparate Nguni tribes of the Natal into a unified Zulu nation, transforming casual bands of spear-throwing herders into the deadly, disciplined regiments of the Zulu army. One song recalls the calling up of the warriors,

challenging Zulus in the audience to identify with the regiments
(Castle-of-the-Lion; Horn-of-the-Elephant; Lift-the-Crocodile)
into which each male, to this day, is born. But there is more
to the Zulu of Joseph's songs than military tribal history; they
teach the Zulu philosophy and values of everyday living. He
admonishes children to respect their parents. He sings of nature
and the physical environment. He celebrates contemporary personal heroes, like Paul Simon, who have influenced his life and
work. And, like all *isicathamiya* songwriters, he sings of the
migrant life in which he established his musical voice.

> Mother is cooking squash.
> The boys are slaughtering a sheep
> Near the kraal.
> Oh my son,
> We have been missing you.[18]

On Black Mambazo's recent Warner Bros. albums, Joseph
translates traditional Zulu values into modern Western idioms.
He chronicles the group's success. And, in keeping with his
commitment to the Church, he performs songs, in Zulu and
English, that will "cause people to worship God and the angels
become happy."

"But where do the songs come from?" we wondered aloud.
"Do you sit down and figure out what you need to say to the
people? Do you write *isicathamiya*-style music for hymns that
already exist?"

Vivian watched closely for his father's reaction. Joseph
nodded, sighed, and closed his eyes. Vivian clarified. "He is
thinking of how to explain to you. It means he takes your
question seriously."

After a time Joseph opened his eyes, and he and his two
sons constructed the following, thoughtful description of his
creative inspiration. "Where do songs come from? Ja. Songs
come in a different time. They arrive like an enemy to attack

you unaware. They come when you are asleep and when you are awake. When you are in a crowd and when you are alone. When you are at leisure and when you are too busy and have no time."

Innocent, reticent for most of the meal, laughed softly and interjected his own observation. "He is *always* too busy, with no time."

The three Shabalalas continued to translate Joseph's words. "Some songs come to tell you to pass a message to the people. It means, to remind them of something they have forgotten. Some songs come in a dream as a hymn without words. And it is your duty to find the words that will sustain the hymn. You must be alone, and you catch the voice of God. And you must write it down or sing it and record it right away, and then go and teach it to the group. The voice comes only once, and if you let it pass it may not come again.

"You start with a strong feeling, very strong, very powerful. Perhaps loneliness that is so strong it brings the tears. And then you compose the song to console. Most of the people believe that when you sing you communicate with God. And then no need for so much worry. No need for tears or shouting."

In a land of polarization, Ladysmith Black Mambazo are faulted by some on the political left for their avoidance of politics. Others accuse them of outright collusion with Pretoria. Their records have long been broadcast on Radio Zulu, a branch of the government-controlled South African Broadcasting Corporation (SABC), while artists who sing out for brotherhood and equality are banned. Their rhapsodizing on the glories of rural life and their outspoken faith in religious salvation are both in keeping with Pretoria's view of appropriate black behavior. By not using their status to voice explicit political protest, some critics argue, Black Mambazo are perpetuating Pretoria's image of blacks who are primitive, simple, docile, and infinitely faithful. Others insist that they are collaborating with the government by default, economically benefitting from existing apartheid structures without doing anything to change them.

Like most issues in South Africa, this one is far too complicated to be understood in terms of the stark black and white in which it is most often framed. Black Mambazo sing of the daily lives of migrant workers and their rural families. They sing of migrants' homesickness in the white cities, of their need for money to send back to their villages, of their fear of the *tsotsis*, the urban criminals for whom newly arrived blacks are easy prey. They sing of families starving in impoverished homelands. They sing of rural women aching for the men who have left to work in the cities and who may, or may not, ever return. All these painful circumstances, like the migrant labor system itself, are products of apartheid legislation. Do Black Mambazo's musical laments express simplistic black wishes to earn money and return to the countryside? Or, in a land where organized resistance is always scrutinized and its practitioners harshly silenced, might their music be seen, more appropriately, as eloquent, personal expressions of objection? Black South Africans traditionally sing of the experiences that constitute everyday life. When the circumstances of everyday life are, themselves, to be protested, who can draw a meaningful line between this traditional practice, on the one hand, and contemporary resistance, on the other?

> **You and I, my darling**
> **We will be devoured**
> **By the mine dumps of Johannesburg.**[19]

Not all black artists identified with public protest voice condemnation for Black Mambazo. Playwright/actor Mbongeni Ngema shrugs. Known worldwide for his performance in *Woza Albert!* and nominated for a Tony Award for his Broadway hit *Sarafina!*, Ngema has long admired Black Mambazo. "They are simply not political people, and we would be wrong to insist that they try to be what they are not. Besides, there is nobody in the world as good as they are at what they do. They should just do it. And we should just leave them alone."

In South Africa, westernized, educated, urban blacks are not far removed from the African traditions their American counterparts might well dismiss as primitive superstition. Consider Ngema himself, by his own admission a "political person." Over the past five or six years he has spent so much time overseas that he must now feel nearly as comfortable in New York, on Broadway, as in the ramshackle halls and dusty streets of the black townships at home. Nonetheless, he does not wholly reject the realms of spirituality and prayer that are Joseph Shabalala's métier. When Ngema moved into a new house in a Durban township, he invited Joseph to come and bless the structure before he moved in.

> **When the storms vie for my life**
> **And evil power wins out**
> **You must remember me.**[20]

Perhaps more important than politics, Ladysmith Black Mambazo have always provided moral and spiritual sustenance to members of South Africa's black community. Their songs give voice to the feelings and beliefs of black audiences around their own country. In their glory on stage and their success in the marketplace, they represent a rare source of contemporary pride to their black countrypeople. And now, with widespread recognition achieved through *Graceland* and extended, independently, via album tours for *Shaka Zulu* and *Journey of Dreams*, they are helping to gain for black South African culture an international awareness and stature that were unimaginable just a few years ago.

When I left South Africa after Thanksgiving in 1984, whites were all but ignorant of this black ensemble. In the white community I spent my time with people who were devoting their lives to justice in their country. Lawyers. Clergy. Administrators of organizations dedicated to social change. And even among this relatively small population of activist white liberals, I met few people who had heard of—and even fewer who had actually *heard*—the music of Ladysmith Black Mambazo. Joseph Shabalala may have dominated Radio Zulu even then, but his voice never rode the white airwaves. South African apartheid is an intricate system of legislated apartness, keeping races so separate that even those whites of good will, who spend their lives working for social justice, find themselves wholly unaware of the most basic elements of the popular culture that underlies everyday black life. Politically active or not, Black Mambazo is destroying a bit of that apartness.

Although Joseph does not speak of politics, he did discuss his own role and that of the group in the black community that endures apartheid. "Each person has his own task. In the black community people are helping one another. And they are singing together all the time. There is a relation among people, and they help one another to solve problems, and we sing to help them. Our church is working to support the people. We visit a sick brother in the hospital and sing for him. We praise God together and praise one another to be strong. And our singing is also a help." As Joseph Shabalala sings in his own voice, so he helps with his own hand.

Again Innocent interrupted his father to make a point for himself. "It means when he walks in the town people stare, and they love him, and they ask him for a blessing. He is always giving something to the people."

Joseph beamed at his son's praise. Unlike those entertainers who profess a wish for offstage anonymity, he enjoys being recognized and he greatly values the sense of being loved by people who pass him on the street. He feels that with his music and his priesthood he is making a valuable contribution to his people, and he works tirelessly to increase the magnitude of that contribution. He concluded his interrupted thought. "We pray to God when we awake. We pray before doing any kind of work. We pray to thank God after success."

Joseph was silent for a long moment, and his smile stiffened slightly, failing completely to mask some unbidden inner deliberation. We had been together for several hours, and it was time for all of us to move on. The moment of indecision passed. Joseph shook our hands warmly, and when he bade us farewell Gary and I were no longer numbered among the whites who "do not come" to Felixton's black hall. "Ja. Thank you very much," he said. "We pray that we see you on Friday night when we sing in Felixton."

BLACK TURF, WHITE TURF

North from Durban, Route 2 narrows to two paved lanes without shoulders. For a distance the road hugs the coast, and the northbound driver is flanked by the Indian Ocean on the right and the deep green hills and grasses of KwaZulu on the left. Then the road noses inland, and the landscape shades from field to forest and back. The roadbed rises and falls, and flatbed trucks challenge the ancestors as they take blind curves too fast and too wide. Stalks of sugarcane litter the road. Driving this route always leaves my back in knots.

A few kilometers before the turnoff for the University of Zululand, large, hand-screened red-and-blue signs began to announce from tree trunks and telephone poles,

BLACK MAMBAZO.
OCTOBER 26. 8 PM.
FELIXTON.

Even as he finally invited us to this concert, earlier in the week, Joseph had remained uneasy about our attendance. "White people do not go there . . . But I am inviting you . . . You must come. It will be OK. Ja." All week long our excitement about the upcoming performance had battled the apprehension raised by Joseph's anxious invitation. Was he trying to warn us? Was he simply thinking out loud, weighing the potential problems that attend every encounter between black and white in this country of apartness? Was he really asking us not to come at all? Would our presence somehow put him in danger? Would we be endangering ourselves? Did our apprehension itself indicate that we were succumbing to the fear of things black that seemed to pervade the white community, all but preventing those very interactions in which true mutuality and good will might flourish?

Traditional Zulu rondavels nestled down below the roadbed, sheltered by steep embankments. At a distance, beyond the fields of sugarcane, kraals stood as they might have been sited for centuries. Scrawny cattle grazed everywhere. A black woman walked along the edge of the road, one arm steadying the long sheaf of cane she carried on her head. A small boy walked with two goats, just off the road. Men trudged toward us, two and three abreast. Feet bare, clothes ragged, they leapt into the tall roadside grasses as the pickup ahead of us veered toward them and then, at the last minute, away.

In the town of Empangeni concrete and blacktop replaced the greenery that had colored the landscape a few kilometers back. We pulled into a Shell station, in search of a pay phone. Although much of this region constitutes the homeland of KwaZulu, most cities and towns are white and, as such, remain part of South Africa. Too well-developed and too valuable to be removed as "white spots," these towns exist like holes in Swiss cheese, carved out from bantustan territory. Black attendants in dirty coveralls washed our windows, looking frequently in the direction of their white employer who sat just behind the glass door of his office.

An officious white woman peered at me through the cashier's window. This establishment had no pay phone, but when she saw her black workers servicing our car she agreed to place a local call for me. She dialed the number I gave her, of the home of a white professor at the University of Zululand. However, when the phone was answered by someone I assume was a domestic worker, the cashier conducted the conversation herself rather than handing the receiver to me.

"Is the Madam at home?

"The MADAM.

"Then put your Master on.

"The Master.

"The BAAS.

"Do you know when the Master will return?

"Do you know what the Master's NAME is?"

She glanced up at me with conspiratorial exasperation.

"The Master's NAME!

"You must tell the Master you're a very naughty girl. And stupid.

"Very well then."

She hung up and sighed deeply. When she faced me again, it was with the mixture of annoyance, pity, and triumph I had come to recognize in whites who saw me witness their frustrating interactions with blacks. "Now you know what we are up against."

That was my cue to commiserate. Wordlessly I declined. What was I now supposed to know about who was up against what?

On another afternoon in a different city, an Afrikaner shopkeeper had expanded on a similar declaration. While waiting to pay for a bag of oranges I had seen him bark instructions at a black clerk who apparently neither understood her employer's wishes nor felt free to ask for clarification. The clerk finally retreated to the stock room, and the shopkeeper turned to me. "When you see us trying to deal with them, then you can understand what we are facing over here. They can't speak. They won't answer. They are incapable of learning. They are like small children. And you Americans seem to think we should hand over our country to them." He chuckled. "What we really need is for people like you to go home and tell your newspapers what you've just seen. Just that little conversation. It isn't that we hate our black people. It's that we *understand* them, and we know what they are and are not capable of doing. You must *explain* that they are not like your American blacks." In conversation with me the shopkeeper's tone was pleasant and comfortably familiar, a tone appropriate for exchanges between equals. Seen through his lens, the world included whites, assumed to be intelligent and sympathetic until proven otherwise, and blacks, who were otherwise, by definition. What this man couldn't see was that through other lenses—mine, his clerk's—the world looked quite different.

It was in a restaurant in Johannesburg's elegant Carlton Center that my friend Lindiwe had articulated the other side of this prototypic white-black, master-servant encounter. She was explaining the frustration of domestic workers like her aunt and like the woman who had apparently been on the other end of the phone conversation in Empangeni. "She is supposed to be working for the Madam, and caring for the Madam's children, and cooking for the Madam's food, and tidying the Madam's house. And she has received many instructions about protecting the Madam's privacy. When the telephone rings, perhaps the connection is poor and she cannot hear the person at the other end. Perhaps this person is speaking quickly and the children are crying and my auntie cannot make out what is being said. Perhaps this person is asking for information my auntie does not know anything about. Or perhaps he is asking questions she has been told not to answer. If he is not satisfied, this person will grow angry and he will insult my auntie and scold her. How can she explain that she is trying to do her job, when he is already calling her stupid and lazy? But should it really be part of her job, to be insulted in this way?"

**Help me
My father's child.
Protect me**[21, 22]

The white woman behind her cashier's window gave me one more opportunity to acknowledge her predicament. And to express my gratitude. After all, she had just placed a phone call for me, and she had endured a measure of frustration on my behalf. "Now you can really understand our situation," she said.

Once more I declined to confuse appreciation with affirmation. "How much do I owe you for the phone call?" I replied.

We had been planning to have dinner with the man we had just tried to phone, and he had promised to get us safely to the Black Mambazo concert. Unable to reach him, we realized that we had not thought to notice where the performance would take place. We returned to Route 2 for another look at the publicity signs.

BLACK MAMBAZO.
OCTOBER 26. 8 PM.
FELIXTON.

No street. No number. No building name. Joseph's comment that white people would not attend this concert took on new meaning, for it now seemed that the only people who were really welcome were those who already knew where to find it. The publicity gave them necessary information about time and date. And it neatly excluded everyone else.

Do you know Castle-of-the-Lion?
Do you know Horn-of-the-Elephant?[23]

We decided to use the last hours of daylight to drive through Felixton and locate the concert hall. Like Empangeni, the town of Felixton has been administratively excised from KwaZulu to remain part of South Africa. British colonial-looking bungalows stood behind carefully manicured lawns and gardens. A few structures were larger than the rest, and these were identified by discreet wooden signs as community buildings. An art center. A church. A school. The whole town appeared to sit on a single, one-way lane that made a long, graceful U away from Route 2 and back to it again. Several slow, careful drives along this lane showed nothing that looked remotely like a concert hall. In fact, we saw no structure that could even pretend to house an audience of the size we had been led to believe Black Mambazo would attract on their home turf.

For Gary, finding things by himself exercises self-reliance. At home he will drive into an unfamiliar city of any size, and, with or without a map, he will invariably proceed directly to at least the immediate vicinity of whatever it is we happen to be looking for. But this was Africa, and eventually even Gary agreed to stop and ask for directions. A boxy hypermarket stood just off Route 2; we went inside. Members of a white family prowled the aisles, watching black customers with accusing eyes and looking for shoplifters. The family's patriarch sat on a plat-form in a kind of glass cage. Through a system of mirrors he watched his offspring maintain surveillance over his customers.

We asked random black shoppers if they could tell us where Ladysmith Black Mambazo were performing tonight. No one gave information. With varying measures of impatience and regret, everyone we approached shrugged and turned back to the shelves. Did they not understand our English? Were they afraid to be seen talking to white strangers? Were they trying to protect their concert from unknown—and by definition sus-picious—white outsiders? Again and again I berated myself for not having learned to say more than "Hello," "Goodbye," and "Thank you" in Zulu. Where was my sense of reality when I convinced myself that I could come into a country without speaking any of the languages of power, and expect to be able to get around?

Do you know Mountain-of-Heaven?
Were you there at KwaZulu?[24]

In the big cities, white shop personnel usually treated us with at least a veneer of helpfulness. Many reflexively cast us as allies in their perceived struggle for survival. They answered our questions and treated our polite gratitude as an invitation to explain themselves and glorify their country. These small-town shopkeepers were different. When asked where we might find a town hall or if they knew where Ladysmith Black Mambazo were playing tonight they answered laconically. "No."

The one white family who appeared to be shopping in the store offered no greater assistance. Their British accents assured us that they could understand our questions. But they were either unable or unwilling to provide more than halfhearted directions to what they described as a small hall housing a white art exhibition, located just behind the market. We had seen and dismissed that building on our first pass through the town.

Felixton is a tiny place, and it is completely surrounded by the black communities of KwaZulu. That these whites can maintain such unblemished ignorance of the black people in whose midst they conduct the minutest details of their daily lives illustrates the deep entrenchment of Pretoria's apartheid. In matters great and small, political and cultural, personal and impersonal, blacks and whites are kept so much apart that even those who find themselves living close enough to one another to be neighbors are familiar with little more than the color of one another's respective skins.

Finally we thought to approach the black man who was pumping gas for black and white drivers in the lot outside the hyperstore. "Excuse me, sir," I hollered like a deaf person. "Do you know where Ladysmith Black Mambazo are singing tonight?" I was hoping to be overheard by any English speakers, black or white, in the waiting cars.

Gary cringed with embarrassment. We all stood in uncomfortable silence while the attendant studied the gauge on his gas pump. As it turned out, both he and several customers knew exactly where the concert would be. Patching English phrases together with Zulu, they eventually told us to look for the large hall inside the workers' compound of the sugarcane factory, ". . . down, down, down at the very bottom of the road just here." They grew solemn. "Not good for you to go there at night. Not good."

Again we drove along the lane we thought we had covered so carefully nearly an hour earlier. And at the far end, by the crook in the U, we found what looked like a driveway leading through a gate, down a small incline, and into what must be the sugarcane factory. We followed the driveway as it wound, unpaved, around and between buildings, across a railroad track, and out onto a large, dusty flat. We avoided the eyes of the men sitting in official-looking cars that seemed to be patrolling the area. Telling each other that no one would stop us if we appeared to know where we were going, we continued blindly across the flat. A motorcyclist shot across the tracks behind us, pulled out in front, and beckoned us to follow. We all stopped at a heavy wire fence enclosing a large circle of buildings. The gate was chained shut. This must be the workers' compound.

The young cyclist removed his helmet and shook out his shoulder-length blond hair. He pointed to the other side of the fence. "The concert will be in there," he told us. "I come here sometimes for the music. Sometimes they play inside that building over there. Sometimes out here on the grass. They open the gates about an hour before the music is scheduled. It's very crowded. If you want to see, you must come well before they open the gates."

He shook his head when we asked if he'd be returning later. "Some of the guards like to give me a hard time. I don't think I'll make it tonight."

An official car drove lazily in our direction. Pulling his helmet back on, our self-appointed guide reassured us. "You're driving a rental car and you look respectable. I spotted you right off, in the gas queue. Just tell them you got lost." And he was off.

I was uneasy at the prospect of our waiting for an hour or two as the only whites in what might become an enormous crowd of Zulu-speaking blacks. The thought gave me new appreciation for the feelings of isolation that must have been—and perhaps still are—part of daily life for every black American who has succeeded in gaining entry to a hitherto all-white setting. Beneath isolation, however, lurked our recognition of a mob's potential for irrational violence. This was the first time we would be entering a black setting unaccompanied by a black host whose very presence vouched for our trustworthiness. With our three or four phrases in Zulu, we would have no way of understanding what anyone might be saying about us, or of allaying people's suspicions before anything got out of control.

> **Do you know Castle-of-the-Lion?**
> **Were you there**
> **When they called up the regiments?**[25]

Over dinner, back in Empangeni, we debated the integrity versus foolhardiness of returning to the compound. We considered the wisdom versus cowardice of attending a thirty-sixth anniversary party for a friend in the nearby village of Kwa-Dlangezwa, instead. We decided on the concert. When else would we be able to count on three uninterrupted hours of Ladysmith Black Mambazo live? When else would we see them in the workers' compounds, back in the Zulu migrant community that had given first life to their group and their whole style of singing? Besides, Joseph had invited us, and he was probably expecting us.

WHITE MAMBAZO

It was dark by the time we returned to Felixton. The sky was black as liquid tar, and the roads were unlit. We retraced our way to the factory driveway and tried to avoid the road's sharp stones as we wound between buildings and across the railroad tracks. A car seemed to be following us, and I turned in my seat to get a direct look. Headlights flashed to bright, momentarily blinding me and, we suddenly realized, spotlighting my white face. Government authority, community leader, or anonymous *isicathamiya* aficionado, whoever was driving that car now knew for sure that at least one white person was inside the factory grounds and driving toward the compound. When we reached the gate we hurried to the recreation hall, hoping to remain inconspicuous until the music began.

Four rands apiece bought admission to a large, high-ceilinged room where a few fluorescent lights tinged everything a sickly green. At one end chairs were stacked from floor to ceiling. At the other, a bare stage reached from side to side. The walls were of concrete and cinderblock, painted a light color on top, and a rich, dark brown at the bottom. The floor was tiled dark and light, and homemade curtains hung at regular intervals along the walls. We stood uneasily by the stacked chairs, watching people watch us, and wondering from whom we should take our cues about appropriate audience behavior in this setting. Occasional men sauntered in our direction and then away.

"*Sawubona*, Baba."

"Hey, *Madoda*."

A belligerent edge belied the friendly greetings.

Large women in white summer dresses flashed motherly smiles in my direction. Smaller women in faded dresses and shabby sweaters clung to their men and stared at me, dark and stony. People in the gathering audience seemed to be of two social sorts. Predominant were the migrants who lived in this compound and moved about the hall with a proprietary air.

> Do you know
> Wake-Up-and-Grab-It?[26, 27]

Also represented were those more fortunate husbands and wives who managed to live in this region as families. These people clustered by the walls, looking almost as uncertain of protocol as we were.

> Do you know
> Lift-the-Crocodile?
> Were you there, young man?[28]

For the migrants this concert was a break in the drab brutality of daily life. For the others it was an evening out. And what should all of these black people be making of us—two innocuous-looking whites standing in a place where whites do not come for innocuous reasons?

> Do you know Drive-the-Bull-from-the-Kraal?
> Were you there, young man?
> Were you there
> When they called up the regiments?[29]

A young man with beer on his breath circled us several times and positioned himself a few feet away. Loudly he summoned others, and they all glared and pointed at us with suspicion, increasing their numbers, one by one, with the migrants who entered the hall alone, looking for companions. The ambient noise escalated and with it our uneasiness. Someone shouted from the front of the hall. A voice answered from the back. Tens of arms seemed to point suddenly in our direction. Chairs skidded and people fell silent as someone in a warmup suit bounded toward us. Joseph! He embraced Gary and then me. "Hey, man! You are here! Ja!"

To us at that moment, Joseph Shabalala was a savior in the wilderness. To everyone else in the hall he was an entertainment superstar. When he led Gary and me down front to seats beside his wife, the wilderness evaporated and we needed no more protection.

Nellie Shabalala watched proudly as her husband and her eldest son arranged loudspeakers and microphones on the stage. The wife of one of South Africa's black superstars, she herself conveys no air of stardom. While Joseph enjoys the attention of countless admirers, Nellie prefers to look on from the shadows. Where Joseph flashes the bright, easy smile of a celebrity, Nellie faces the world with the sweetness and devotion of a madonna. She showed us photographs of her youngest sons. We asked if they sing with their father.

"Ja. They know every song. They sing along with Radio Zulu. And they dance. They are White Mambazo."

Her quiet warmth put us at an ease we had not before felt in South Africa, and Gary risked a joke in response. "No." He pointed to his white face and his head of frizzy, dark curls. "*I'm* White Mambazo."

Nellie looked puzzled; she had not expected disagreement. Then she burst into giggles and replied, with the lovely *r*'s that roll through African pronunciation of English, "You are r-rright! They are *Gr-r-reen* Mambazo!"

Behind us the hall had filled to capacity. Perhaps five or six hundred people crowded into closely spaced rows of chairs. Nearly a hundred more stood in the aisles and doorways. Without introduction, eight men in red sport shirts and black trousers loped onto the stage, singing. Their voices reverberated in the stark hall and the microphones whistled, but an explosion of cheering and applause made acoustics irrelevant.

> **Stand!**
> **Have courage!**
> **Be warriors**
> **And fight for your king.**[30]

Once on stage Black Mambazo arranged themselves in pairs behind four microphones. Each man crossed his arms over his chest. Heads cocked to one side. Joseph stood third from the left, singing lead with the clear, slightly nasal voice we recognized from their records. He sounded the first call.

> **You must not leave me**[31]

The group echoed, and in distinctive, smooth, tight harmony, they slid up to the highest note in the phrase and down again.

> **(*You must not leave me*
> *My Jesus*)**[32]

Joseph repeated his call, invoking the playfulness with words that is so typical of *isicathamiya*.

> **You must not leave mmm**

And the group answered his playfulness,

> **(*eeee, my Jesus*).**[33]

Maintaining their silky sound, Black Mambazo sang on in a verbal unison that contrasted sharply with the independent-voice style that characterizes so much of South African singing.

The performers swayed slightly, bending at the knee in small, choreographed, side-to-side movements.

> **My friends will leave me**
> **And my relatives will leave me**
> **And my parents are going to leave me.**[34]

Even at this relatively staid level of hymn singing, the group's tone lacked the angelic purity of their studio recordings. In leaving the studio for the migrant stage, they had traded ethereal perfection for the necessarily imperfect sound of the human voice in a human body. What they gained in the exchange was energy. The song grew more lively as it flowed into the group's usual call-and-response.

> **My King! (*I thank you*)**
> **(*I thank you*)**
> **(*I thank you*)**
>
> **My Savior! (*I thank you*)**
> **(*I thank you*)**
> **(*I thank you*)**[35]

As their singing acquired animation, so did the group's physical movements involve more and more of the body. Gentle swaying and bending of knees gave way to small, precise dance steps. Eight right feet in soft white shoes pointed, lifted, and pointed again. Eight left feet stood firm. Eight men shifted from left foot to right, arms raised and clasped above their heads, knees bent.

My Liberator! (*I thank you*)
            (*I thank you*)
            (*I thank you*)

My Jesus! (*I thank you*)
        (*I thank you*)
        (*I thank you*)[36]

By now other voices were playing with Joseph's lead calling, and the call itself reached higher and higher. Physical gestures grew ever more expressive. Small shifts from foot to foot became larger, more definitive dance steps, and hips began to grind forward and back, with precise seductiveness.

God the mighty! (*I thank you*)
             (*I thank you*)
            (*I thank you*)[37]

If the group had earlier shifted from low to medium gear, now they eased into high. Joseph wailed at the top of his range and the group answered, setting up a rhythmic call-and-response figure that would repeat for several minutes. The audience apparently recognized the establishment of this figure, the bullet, as the song's climax, for they clapped and cheered when its shape became apparent.

You must be with me, Father.   (*You must be with me*)
You must be with me, Father.   (*You must be with me*)
You must be with me, Father.   (*You must be with me*)
You must be with me, Father.   (*You must be with me*)[38]

Joseph stepped out of his position in the group's formation and stalked to the end of the line.

You must be with me, Father.   *(You must be with me)*
You must be with me, Father.   *(You must be with me)*[39]

Steps became stomps, and he led the group in a caricatured march, around and around the stage.

You must be with me, Father.   *(You must be with me)*
You must be with me, Father.   *(You must be with me)*[40]

One march around, and Joseph began to vary his own vocal part. By then the dancing had taken on a life of its own.

You must not leave me, my king   *(You must be with me)*
   Except in Your paradise.   *(You must be with me)*[41]

Stomps became leaps, and when the group had re-formed their original line they were fully engaged in the *ingoma*-like movements that look so warlike to whites. In unison the group stamped first one foot and then the other.

   You must not leave me   *(You must be with me)*[42]

But their control was such that, as with a ballerina's leap, even the most vigorous stamping failed to thud against the hollow stage.

   You must not leave me   *(You must be with me)*[43]

Higher and higher they lifted each leg.

   You must not leave me   *(You must be with me)*[44]

Arms forward, knees bent.

> You must not leave me   (*You must be with me*)[45]

Knees raised waist-high.

> You must not leave me   (*You must be with me*)[46]

Knees raised chest-high.

> You must not leave me   (*You must be with me*)[47]

Arms down, leg straight up, foot over head.

> You must not leave me, my king   (*You must be with me*)
>   Except in Your paradise.   (*You must be with me*)[48]

Arms out, foot down, one last unison repetition—and the dance was over.

> You must be with me
> You must be with me, Father[49]

The group resumed their original stance behind four microphones.

> You must not leave me
> My Jesus.[50]

They reclaimed the silky tone that they now seemed to have abandoned a world ago, and they concluded their hymn.

> My friends will leave me
> And this body in which I stay
> This body will leave me.

> But it is my pride to know
> You will not leave me
> My Jesus.
> Amen
> Allelujah
> Ameni.[51]

After several songs Nellie whispered that Joseph was about to announce an intermission. He came onstage alone, zipped into a warmup suit and puffing slightly to catch his breath. For several minutes he addressed the audience in rapid, melodic-sounding Zulu, eliciting bursts of laughter and applause. Suddenly the whole hall seemed to be looking at Gary and me, and Nellie was pushing us to our feet. We caught a few words in English, "Friends from overseas, Gary and Helen," apparently added to attract our attention before widespread applause gave way to a general intermission.

Joseph's claiming us as friends earlier in the evening had transformed us from intruders to guests. His introducing us from the stage now made us minor celebrities. As people milled about the hall, they approached us to voice personal welcome.

"Welcome, hehey!"

"Overseas. From America? Ja!"

"Good music? Ja!"

"*Sawubona*, Baba."

Gone was the belligerence that had challenged us at the outset. A round man in a white suit grinned at Gary. "Hallo, Baas. I follow you all the way from the main road. You lead me here. I thank you."

We were dumbfounded. "But why did you think we knew where we were going? And what made you think we were coming here?"

He laughed. "If a white man drive in this area tonight, I think he must come here. And if you lead me wrong, I think we find the way together."

> Listen all people!
> In this world
> There is still time.[52]

Over the course of their three-hour performance Black Mambazo changed costume, and some personnel, several times. Always they would begin a set, fresh and dry, posed behind microphones. They stood straight and dignified, two men to a mike, arms entwined in twos and threes in caricatured imitation of Renaissance portraiture. Always this initially serious, exaggeratedly staged setup would give way to the playfulness, the vitality, and the bold physical prowess that distinguished the body of their performance.

When they came onstage for the final set, they were dressed in traditional Zulu costume. All evening they had worn clothes of the West. Sport shirts cut from permanent-press fabrics. T-shirts with the group's name stenciled on front and back. Black cotton trousers. Red nylon socks and white crepe-soled shoes. But now, as the hour approached eleven and audience members were preparing to return to the cramped, dirty quarters in which current circumstances forced most of them to live, Black Mambazo took the stage wearing the clothing of Africa. Loins were girded with cowhides and fluffy animal tails. Calves and upper arms were tied with brushed wool. Ankle rattles of goatskin and cocoons clattered above bare feet, and ornaments of hide and beads encircled heads and necks. For the first time since we had crossed the ambiguous border into KwaZulu, we were inescapably aware of the deep connection between the flora and fauna of the landscape, and the people who have, for centuries, also been a part of this land.

For the last time Black Mambazo posed, still, and sang sweetly into four microphones. For the last time they raised arms and pointed toes in unison, playfully recalling the gospel groups whose music has contributed so much to their repertoire. And for the last time they drew audience applause as they set up the figure that would be the bullet for the body of their main dance.

Listen
All people in the world
Listen (*Listen*)
(*Listen*)
(*Listen*)[53]

They used their arms to emphasize light, intricate footsteps. Up, like the horns of an ox; down, like a hoof testing the ground. No colleagues sang or clapped from offstage. Just nine men, they provided their own rhythm, melody, and dance. Crouching, leaping, turning, and circling the microphones, they delighted the audience with their adaptation of the movements of *ingoma* to the entertainment stage. For us the dancing was still unfamiliar enough to be exciting for its novelty alone. From the tension and small twitches in the bodies seated close around us, we guessed that for most of the predominantly male audience, *ingoma*, like the Zulu language itself, was part of the culture that was their essence.

Listen! (*Listen*)
(*Listen*)
(*Listen*)

Listen! (*Listen*)
(*Listen*)
(*Listen*)

The nine bodies of Black Mambazo glistened with sweat. Large and powerful, they leapt and stamped, and throughout it all they continued to sing.

Listen, all people in the world
Listen (*Listen*)
(*Listen*)
(*Listen*)[54]

In our earlier conversation Joseph had mentioned that he was considering retirement. He and several of the group's original members were probably nearing fifty, and performing was a tiring business for middle-aged men. At the time I had assumed he was referring to the strains of hot lights, late hours, and prolonged road trips. We had discussed his interest in business or public relations, and, with anticipatory regret for the passing of a musical sound I loved, I had pictured him, five years hence, in jacket and tie as an executive in the black recording industry. Now I understood what he had meant by a tiring business; I found myself wondering what else, from the hours and hours I was spending in conversation with black South Africans, I was unknowingly misinterpreting through white American ignorance.

Listen! (*Listen*)
(*Listen*)
(*Listen*)

At this moment Black Mambazo were not a team of middle-aged performers. On the stage before me they were infinitely strong and exultant, and I do not think I exaggerate in suggesting that they were an invigorating symbol of pride and hope for every person in the hall.

Listen, all people in this world!
Listen!
There is still time.[55]

LAST NIGHT, EARLY
IN THE MORNING

It was nearly three o'clock Sunday morning, very late Saturday night, and Gary and I were sitting in the lobby of the Holiday Inn, waiting to be taken to adjudicate the men's singing competition at the Dalton Road Hostel. Early in the week I had phoned a professor at the University of Natal, following up on a tip we had been given at the inaugural meeting of Durban's new, multiracial arts association. As soon as my words "singing competition" had come through his receiver, Wesley Hanforth had interrupted with a barrage.

"You've never seen or heard anything like it. I guarantee you. I'll arrange for you to adjudicate at Dalton Road. If they're sure of a judge this far ahead, the competition will be a good one and a lot of choirs will enter. The organizer is a friend of mine. A Zulu named Paulos Mfuphi. A very gentle man. Very responsible. You'll be perfectly safe. He'll pick you up at your hotel. And you can have him drop you off at my house for a chat afterward. I'll go down there straightaway to make sure he hasn't found someone else in the meantime. But I'm sure he'll be delighted. Ring me back tomorrow to confirm. But I'm sure it will be all right. He's a very gentle man. Very gentle. Takes the responsibility of organizing very seriously. You really will be perfectly safe. Nothing to worry about. Ta."

Last night, early in the morning
I love you.
I don't know why.
Hallelujah. Amen.

Unlike most migrant hostels, the one on Dalton Road is not located in a black township. Rather, it stands within the boundaries of the white city, just off the railroad tracks in the old warehouse and industrial district, three or four blocks inland from the Bay of Natal. Seen from Dalton Road the compound buildings rise over a white fence—a wall, really—made of heavy, overlapping metal slats and standing six or seven feet high. Two rows of buildings face each other across a long driveway. On the right one-story bungalows crouch low to the ground, mostly white stucco with roofs of red clay shingles. In summer air conditioners drip from tightly closed windows. The barracks stand on the left, three-story red brick structures trimmed in white, with small, high windows of textured, barely translucent glass. Only a few windows seem to open for ventilation, despite Durban's suffocating summers. The compound stretches back a full block or two from the road. More distant buildings look dingier than those nearer the entrance; the innermost barracks appear to be without windows altogether. Atop the fence, by the gate that regulates access to the driveway, a large, slightly discolored sign proclaims in English, Afrikaans, and Zulu:

> NO PERSON OTHER THAN AN AUTHORISED RESIDENT
> MAY ENTER OR REMAIN IN THIS LOCATION WITHOUT
> THE WRITTEN PERMISSION OF THE SUPERINTENDENT.

Wesley had phoned to confirm our appointment as the week's adjudicators. Paulos had been told we were staying at the Holiday Inn. We had eaten dinner early and gone to bed by 9:00 in an attempt to get at least a few hours' sleep before entering the world of *isicathamiya*. We had washed, dressed, and drunk coffee by 2:45, and now we were waiting. At precisely 3:00 A.M. a long black car pulled up to the hotel entrance. A small black man with a barrel chest and an extremely sweet face hurried through the door. Wearing pressed trousers, long-sleeved shirt and neatly tacked necktie, he conveyed a sense of formal responsibility.

"Paulos?"

"Helen and Gary? Ja!"

His smile was bright, his handshake firm. He led us to where his driver was waiting, dressed in a black suit with a jaunty red handkerchief folded in his breast pocket. The car was brightly polished outside. Inside it was lined with soft white sheepskin. A large pair of dice and a small, bikini-clad white doll hung from the rearview mirror. The driver shook our hands as he helped us into the backseat; his right thumb was missing.

As we rode, Paulos and the driver tried to speak to us in English. We tried to respond with at least one Zulu word per sentence.

"*Sawubona!*"

"You see for dance, for dress, for sing."

"We love *isicathamiya* singing."

"You judge for sing."

"We have heard *isicathamiya* warmup at the Lamontville Hostel last week."

"Not for dance. Not for dress."

"For this opportunity we say *siyabonga*."

"*Jebo.*"

By this time we were driving into the compound. We thought we had just been told that although choirs would be wearing special costumes, and although they would be performing flashy dance routines, we were to adjudicate winners on the basis of their singing alone.

Much of the driveway was brightly lit. The car pulled partway into the shadows alongside a pile of lumber, by a building with no windows. The recreation hall was the next building over, and just outside its door eight or nine men swayed together in matching dark blazers and white gloves, singing. When they paused for breath we could hear the singing from inside. Paulos patted Gary on the shoulder and indicated that we should wait in the car until they were ready for us inside. He would come back for us. He rolled down the back windows enough to give us a bit of air, locked all the doors, and disappeared with the driver into the hall.

At this hour only a few loners walked the driveway, up and down, carrying *knobkerries* (traditional, slender, ball-tipped clubs), cans of beer, or silenced ghetto blasters. Strains of singing continued to filter through the closed door of the hall. No one seemed to notice us. We spoke to each other in near-whispers, trying to contain our impatience to be out of the car and inside the hall with the singing.

> **The audience is calling us.**
> **You can call us,**
> **And we will be there.**

Angry voices passed by, outside the car. Two large, uniformed guards were dragging a thrashing man toward the compound office, the bungalow just inside the fence, two buildings away from the recreation hall. A heavy chain trailed out of the man's pocket, and he roared his indignation. From nowhere, white-shirted figures appeared in the shadows between buildings. They huddled in tight, silent clusters, now disappearing, now emerging again to watch the developing excitement.

An alarm sounded. Guards ran this way and that. A pair of them dragged a man toward the office, shirt half off. A second pair dragged a woman in a flowered dress; I saw her lose one shoe to a pothole. The clusters of men in the shadows grew larger and less silent, and they moved toward where the offenders were being taken.

A small white man in baggy coveralls strode purposefully toward the office. His face was vicious, and he seemed to relish slapping a nightstick into his open palm. His red-gold hair was tousled and wet, his beard the same. But he stopped before he reached the office, to bang on the half-closed window that offered Gary and me an illusion of separation from the trouble brewing in the driveway. He banged and he barked. "Identification!"

I was so much involved in wondering what would happen outside that it didn't register, at first, that this furious official was raging at us.

"Get out of that car and let me see your identification! Don't you know it's illegal for Europeans to be in here without permission?" He grabbed at my sleeve through the half-open window as I fumbled to unlock the door. "Hurry up and show me your identification!" All at one time I was reaching for my passport, sliding out of the car, and trying to keep my skirt from riding up indecently. He grabbed my hand out of my purse and shook my arm. "Don't you understand what I'm saying? Identification! Show me your identification!"

Gary answered with more calm than I thought I'd ever feel again. "Here's my passport. We're American. My wife's passport is just inside her purse. She'll have it out in a minute."

The angry man responded well to Gary's calm. "Americans! Well, where are you staying?"

Gary continued to answer for us as I silently thanked God we were not staying with friends whose names we would surely have had to mention. "The Holiday Inn, on Sol Harris."

"If I phone them will they have you registered?"

"Yes. Room 576."

The man's anger gradually subsided, yielding to a sickly solicitousness. "What are you doing here? Don't you know it's dangerous for Europeans to be inside places like this? The laws are meant to protect you. You never know what might happen in one of these places. What are you doing here?"

Out of the corner of my eye I saw Paulos come out of the hall and begin to run in our direction. "We're here to judge the singing competition. You know, from last week's newspaper. A professor at the University of the Natal made the arrangements. The organizer is coming this way right now."

The previous weekend's English-language newspaper had run a large front-page story on the singing competitions. But this man did not read English-language papers. "What are you talking about, singing? I don't know anything about any singing!"

Paulos's presence seemed to enrage him all over again. "Do you have permission for these people to be here? Don't you know it's illegal for Europeans to be here without permission? Don't you kaffirs have any respect for the law? Don't you know I could have you all thrown in jail for this? What do you think you're doing, bringing these people in here without written permission?"

Several uniformed guards had come to stand around the car, and at the white man's angry nod they moved us all into the office. Paulos barely understood English. He shook his head politely, looked at the black guards, and spoke softly. "Zulu please."

One of the guards started translating before the white man began to thunder again. "You'll speak to me or not at all, or I'll have you thrown in jail. Don't you people understand anything? Permission on paper. Black and white. Very simple. Or can't you even understand that?"

Paulos tried to explain. "Every week . . . The superintendent . . ."

The competition at the Dalton Road Hostel had been held every week for something like sixteen years. The hostel superintendent was indebted to Paulos for running things so smoothly. But this angry little demon would hear none of it. Indeed, he would not even permit the translations that might have allowed Paulos to answer effectively. "Do you have the superintendent's signature on paper, in black and white? Do you have these people's names in black and white? Black and white. You must have permission. That's the law. Do you have permission?"

Paulos's gentle face looked unfortunately foolish as he

struggled to master a situation that was increasingly stacked against him. "Permission. Ja. I get it now."

Perhaps it was his apparent helplessness, perhaps his eagerness to please, that fanned the white man's contemptuous fury. "No, not now! That's not how things work in this country! This country has laws that must be obeyed! And the law says you must have permission in black and white, for people to enter these premises! Not permission once they are already inside! You are all breaking the law, and unless you two are out of here in ten minutes I'll have you all thrown in jail!"

With that he turned to attend to the three people, now in handcuffs, whose behavior had apparently triggered the alarm that had brought him out in the first place.

> Go your own way
> Go your own way.

Paulos was sweating profusely. From a few doors down strains of *isicathamiya* drifted into the office. Paulos's dignity had been seriously wounded, and he was battling with himself to transcend the injury and discharge his dual responsibilities, to us and to the competition. Feeling profound empathy for his predicament, we looked at him and hoped that he could read our faces accurately. He touched Gary's arm. "Come. I take you out."

We walked out of the office, looking back for the white man's reaction, but he seemed to have forgotten us. We probably could have walked directly into the singing competition without his knowing, or caring, what had become of us. But Paulos was too responsible to take such risks. The driver was waiting for us. Somehow he and Paulos made us understand that they would drive us outside the compound gate—perhaps fifty yards from where we now stood—where we would be legal. We would wait in the car while Paulos phoned the superintendent to straighten things out.

172

At five o'clock they returned to the car. We understood that they had failed to reach the superintendent and now thought it best to return us to our hotel. We offered to keep waiting, but they refused. Paulos looked absolutely miserable and he kept repeating, "Sorry. Very sorry."

We, too, were very sorry. We were sorry to have occasioned his humiliation. We were sorry to have missed the competition. Gary was leaving the country before we would have a chance to return to Durban, and without him I wasn't sure I wanted to go anywhere near Dalton Road again. We were disappointed. And we were as angry with the little white tyrant as he had been with us. The driver must have understood what we were saying, for as he let us out of the car he said, with quiet venom, "Very sorry that crazy man. Crazy bastard can stop what she want to stop. Just like that."

> Both of us—
> We'll play with you some other time,
> My darling.

Perhaps Gary and I would have learned the real lesson of that night, rehashing it on our own. As it was, we did so over coffee with Wesley Hanforth, at his house a few hours later. He was waiting on his doorstep when we drove up at nine, and he began to bluster as soon as we stepped through the front gate. "What the hell happened over there? Paulos rang me up at around seven, but he was so upset I could barely make out what he was saying. Something about a little white madman threatening you with prison and throwing you off the premises? Who the hell was that, I wonder? And what the hell did he think he was doing? Doesn't he know how much that competition does to keep that bloody place from exploding? And that without Paulos they'd have a bloody riot on their hands every bloody weekend?"

Wesley stopped for air, and he continued a bit more

calmly. "Paulos got through to the superintendent at around six and got things squared away. But it wasn't until nearly seven that they managed to pry some poor bloke out of a pub, to go along and adjudicate. Those chaps warmed up until seven in the morning, and the competition went on as usual. It's probably still running now. Spectacular!"

For the next two hours we explained what had happened, in as much detail as we could remember. Wesley asked questions, and we struggled to provide answers that would allow him to understand just who the little man was, who had caused all the trouble. He finally decided the man must have been an undercover security agent. "The little bastard was new to the night shift, and he obviously didn't know a bloody thing about the hostel, and once he realized he'd made a mistake he didn't know how to back off. The superintendent gave him bloody hell. He may even lose his job for that little display."

Wesley paused before finishing. "And you, my fine American visitors. You've just seen how South Africa really works. You've actually felt it."

And so we had. For a few minutes we had felt the absolute tyranny of petty white officials who, with or without explicit statutory support, can overturn a black person's life in shockingly short order. Black life can be crowded and squalid and crumbling, in ways that photographs never quite seem to capture. But perhaps the biggest burden of black life in South Africa is its essential fragility. For the law of the land is, at core, that the land is white, and its riches and opportunities are white, as well. Blacks enjoy such privileges as urban residence and employment on the basis of special dispensation, or benign white failure to enforce repressive legislation. But these privileges can be revoked in a minute, at the level of Parliament or that of a small, new official who feels the need to flex his muscles. In a single, sudden instant a black man may find himself in prison. In a flash a child may be crippled for life. In a single minute a woman may find herself endorsed out of the township, evicted from her home, and on her way to a homeland she has never seen.

Of course any particular injustice may be fought through lengthy court proceedings. Any particular official may be adjudged to have behaved wrongly. But South Africa is a country where blacks very rarely get second chances. Eventual legal vindication cannot rebuild the shattered structure of a lifetime's care and effort.

King of kings!
Our Creator wipes the tears.

In South Africa black people may have privileges; they have no real rights. For a brief, frightening moment, even with my white skin I was one of them.

WALK
STEALTHILY, BOYS

When I phoned Wesley Hanforth from Johannesburg, he did not sound surprised to be hearing from me again. "So you're still here with us, eh? When are you coming back to catch the competition? Paulos has a permanent certificate now, you know. The superintendent wrote out a formal certificate, a kind of blanket pass, that Paulos can use every week. It's a very official-looking thing. Makes Paulos feel quite proud. So you're really quite safe. Even last time, you know, you probably weren't in any real danger. Bit of a fright, of course, but not any real danger. I can arrange for you to adjudicate on any weekend, you know. This one. Next. Any time we can guarantee a judge it's to their advantage."

Gary had stretched his annual vacation to its limit, but he had finally had to return to California, nearly a month before I was due to follow. I had promised myself that I wouldn't leave the country without returning to Durban to attend one of these all-night competitions. But before phoning Wesley I had also promised myself that however confident and optimistic his words, I would insist on having an English-speaking companion before committing myself. He was not unsympathetic. "You really would be quite safe alone, you know. But in your place, I might feel a bit uneasy as well. The problem is that we're having exams just now, and the students are all writing. I'd be glad to go along myself, but I've been there so many times. They know me too well and I'd just throw the whole thing off."

He phoned back the following day with news that he had found an undergraduate to accompany me. "This chap is so bloody bright that he can easily take the night off. But he wants to be a psychologist and I promised him that if he came to your hotel an hour beforehand, you'd give him the inside story on his chosen profession. I've already confirmed things with Paulos, so we're on for Saturday night. You can give Steven a ring when you get into town. And Gillian and I will expect you for coffee earlier in the evening. Ta."

So Wesley had it all arranged. All I had to do was be there.

Much was familiar about waiting in the lobby of the Holiday Inn as the morning hour neared three. The dark silence of the outside street. The bright silence of the deserted lobby. My mounting anticipation of *isicathamiya*. I knew that tonight was my last chance for this competition, as last time had been Gary's. I was far too excited to have slept earlier. I had visited with Wesley and Gillian until nearly one; Steven had arrived just after two. I had drunk enough coffee to keep Shaka's whole army awake for a week.

When the long black car pulled up to the hotel entrance I nearly sprang through the door. As before, Paulos conveyed an air of earnest responsibility. As before, his driver shook our hands and helped us into the backseat. Both men wore the same clothes I had seen the last time we were together; no one mentioned that night. Paulos explained, once again, that although the choirs would attempt to impress us with their dancing and their clothing, we were to adjudicate on the basis of singing, alone. Once again we drove down Dalton Road and through the open gate of the compound. This time, though, the driver pulled further inside. He parked deep in the shadows on the far side of the recreation hall, out of range of the driveway's bright lights. And after only a minute or two in the car, Steven and I were hurried through a side door into the hall. Under the starless black of the sky, the air felt surprisingly balmy against my cheeks.

Once inside the door we were rushed along one aisle and then another, to be seated in two chairs at a small, wobbly table at the foot of the stage. I had the impression that the room was large and full of people, but we were moved along too quickly for me to see more clearly than that. A tall man carrying a bullhorn strode up to our table and introduced himself as Mr. Maphumulo. Standing to my left he explained the rules in well-practiced English. He would announce each group by number, and they would be expected to enter immediately. Each group would have ten minutes for its onstage performance. He had no idea how many choirs the evening would bring; none of us would know until the last group had sung. Although the groups put a good deal of effort into their clothing and their dance routines, we were to make our judgments on the basis of their singing alone.

Most important, under no circumstances whatsoever were we to turn around and face the back of the hall. I recalled Marcus Nzimande's description of the competitions' insistence on absolute impartiality from the judges, and of performers' suspicions that any form of eye contact constituted an attempt at illegal influence. Even one hasty look toward the rear of the hall would necessitate their finding another adjudicator and starting all over again. Until that moment I had forgotten that last time, when Gary and I were waiting in the car out on Dalton Road, several men in white suits had tried to force a few folded bills through our partially open window. We had laughed and shaken our heads in deliberate misunderstanding. "We just want to hear the singing. We don't want to be paid."

Mr. Maphumulo was continuing. If we wanted anything to drink or if we needed to use the toilet, we must raise our hand while continuing to look straight ahead. The competition would be stopped and our needs satisfied. Although every group would enter the hall from the rear, and although we would hear them coming toward us, and although we might hear audience excitement at their clothing or entrance routine, we ourselves would not see them until they circled our table or began to climb the stage stairs, up in front and to our right. Mr. Maphumulo stood with us as I set up my little tape recorder and camera, stacking extra tapes, film, and batteries in one corner of the table. He remained almost motionless to my left as I pulled a notebook and pen from my purse. I tore out a few pages for Steven.

Glassware or china clinked from behind, and Mr. Maphumulo's hand moved from where it had been hanging by his side, just visible out of the corner of my eye. A black hand emerging from a long-sleeved shirt placed two cups of coffee on the table. Finally Mr. Maphumulo seemed satisfied that we were ready to discharge our adjudicators' duties. I saw his hips turn toward the rear of the hall, and I imagined him raising the bullhorn to his lips.

"Choir Number One. I'm calling Choir Number One."

The audience quieted, and a rough, driving vocal sound took over the hall from outside, recalling old recordings of Zulu war songs in the bush. The singing drew closer, but particularly while I knew the men were still too far back to be seen without turning around, I imagined Shaka's *impis* (regiments) parading before their King. One powerful lead sang out with authority.

You have touched us (*just*)

A thundering chorus of basses answered his authority with their own. A single high voice gave fullness to the group's roar.

You have touched us (*just*)

Deliberate rhythmic stamping added to the feeling of military discipline. The sound suggested perhaps thirty young men, marching barefoot and carrying familiar Zulu full-body shields and the short, stabbing spears called *assegais.*

You have touched the black lions

I imagined black skin shiny with sweat, gleaming in the African sun as this regiment prepared itself for battle.

You have touched the black bull

In Zulu tradition they sang their own praises, likening themselves to the strongest and most fearsome of beasts and predicting victory over the enemy.

You young men

An occasional very high voice shrieked over the group's mounting frenzy.

Raging

A sudden additional stamp decorated the regular pattern, as the warriors leaped and kicked in perfect, disciplined unison.

You will meet your match!

I could feel the vanguard of the army almost upon me as they began to repeat the figure of their song.

You have touched us (*just*)

Suddenly that vanguard was before me, shrieking and leading the rest of the group in circling our very vulnerable table.

You have touched us (*just*)

Although the character of the singing did not change, except perhaps to intensify, my visual image of a full Zulu regiment evaporated in the reality of the young men now singing directly at my microphone. Instead of thirty they were only nine. And instead of Zulu skins they sported the nattiest of Western clothes.

You have touched the green lions

Six of them wore immaculate white trousers and bright blue blazers, double-breasted and ornamented with gleaming silver buttons. Dark blue dress shirts and large, soft white bowties completed their attire. In contrast, the two high singers wore black suits, white shirts, and bright red neckties.

You have touched the green bulls

Isicathamiya leaders conventionally dress differently from the rest of the group, and the powerfully singing leader of the Rovers was no exception. Over beige slacks he had layered a dark brown dress shirt, a maroon dashiki-style shirt trimmed with black fringe, and a splendid white necktie.

You raging young men

Nine pairs of feet stepped precisely in highly polished, black shoes. Nine pairs of hands gestured deliberately in spotless white gloves.

You will meet your match!

The Rovers mounted the stage by a rickety set of stairs, pushed far stage right.

You have touched us (*just*)

The stairs shook and the flimsy, Masonite platform that was the stage echoed their every step.

MIGRANTS

You have touched us (*just*)

Around the stage the walls were of brick, once painted white
but now peeling badly. Cardboard replaced three of six win-
dowpanes. The ceiling's open woodwork exposed a good deal
of mildew and woodrot.

You have touched us—
The black lions
The black bulls

But the Rovers circled around the stage, alternately stealthy
and stamping, continuing to invoke a glory that had nothing
to do with the structural disintegration around us. Finally they
stopped in center stage.

You raging young men

They stood close together, gloved hands clasped before their
chests.

You will meet your match.

"Choir Number One, ten minutes!"
I checked my watch. This group had taken nearly that
long to make it to the stage. In that time they had transformed
the migrant compound into the royal Zulu kraal, rekindling in
each person in that dilapidated hall the raw strength and communal glory that could find no place in Durban's factories. We
had been warned not to judge on the basis of clothing and
dancing. No one had told us how to evaluate a group's power
to transport us through time and space.
"That was Choir Number One. Now I'm giving you Number Two. Choir Number Two!"
Again the singers entered from the rear, their voices grow-

ing louder, step by step, as they approached our table. Again we heard them long before we could see who they were.

"Choir Number Three! Number Three!"

Again and again emissaries from the choirs circled our table, making exaggerated eye contact with Steven and with me before joining the rest of their group in taking the stage for the main body of their performance.

"Choir Number Four!"

The men moved in caricatured imitation of a lion in the wild, after whom this singing style took its name for some years in the late 1930s. That was in response to Solomon Linda's hit song "Mbube" (lion), better known in America as "Wimoweh."

> Go your own way
> Go your own way

"Number Five! Choir Number Five!"

When the NKA Special came into view their blazers were dark green over the brilliant white of their trousers. Each man wore a long strand of beads across his chest. White spats complemented white gloves and ties.

> Go your own way
> Go your own way

They moved in a stalking crouch, knees deeply bent, bodies steady and straight. They sang a combination of Zulu and nonsense.

> Go your own way
> Go your own way

Arms reached forward at shoulder height, elbows slightly bent.

MIGRANTS

Go your own way
Go your own way

In perfect unison with eleven companions, each man lifted his right leg forward and carefully placed it, still bent, on the floor ahead.

Heh heh hey ma
(*Oo hoo*)

Only after his right leg had been firmly planted did a man finally shift his weight to it and, again in unison with his colleagues, repeat the sequence with his left.

Heh heh hey ma
(*Oo hoo*)

Movements were both easy and purposeful.

Heh heh hey ma
(*Oo hoo*)

As a lion stalks its prey with unhurried confidence, so did these singers move toward the stage that was the object of their long, slow march through a sometimes impatient audience.

Heh heh hey ma
(*Oo hoo*)

Hundreds of conversational voices competed with the choir's entrance chant.

Heh heh hey ma
(*Oo hoo*)
Go go

A beer or soda bottle dropped to the floor, momentarily silencing the audience with its ringing bounces.

> **Heh heh hey ma**
> **(*Oo hoo*)**
> **Go go**

Like so many others that evening, this choir took far longer to enter the hall than the distance from door to stage required.

> **Heh heh hey ma**
> **(*Oo hoo*)**
> **Go go**

But with their repetitious chant they succeeded, finally, in engrossing audience and adjudicators in the particular mood they were trying to create.

> **Heh heh hey ma-a-a-a-!**

By the time the singers were positioned in center stage, the audience was in the palms of their outstretched hands.

"Choir Number Six! Ten minutes."

The ten Lucky Stars stood in a row across the back of the stage. They had entered, holding maroon blazers twisted taut between their hands as if they were carrying banjos. Backs to the audience, they donned blazers, arranged beads, and, it appeared, straightened neckties. Through the high stage window the sky had begun to lose its impenetrable blackness. Dawn would break soon, and we had entered that nameless period, so familiar to all-night drivers, when the sky no longer belongs to the night, but has not yet been claimed by the day. The Lucky Stars turned to face the audience, ten faces eerily illuminated, each with its own small red glow. "Ooooh's" and "aaaah's" sounded behind me, and applause rippled through the crowd. When the men moved forward I could see a small flashlight protruding from each breast pocket. Our repeated warnings against being influenced by costumes took on new meaning. I had to fight to keep my attention on this choir's singing and off the otherworldly aura surrounding each face.

"That was Choir Number Six. Now I'm giving you Number Seven."

I am told that choirs do not dance during their ten minutes of official onstage performance. And perhaps at one time in these competitions' long history such restraint was, indeed, the rule. But not tonight.

"Number Eight. Choir Number Eight."

For every choir performed onstage by accompanying their singing with elaborate choreography and carefully coordinated kicks, lifts, and turns.

"Choir Number Nine. Ten minutes, Number Nine!"

Marcus Nzimande had warned that until I became quite familiar with this musical genre, I would hear each new group as better than the last. I might be particularly partial to those who reproduced Western idioms and used English words. Alternatively, I might find myself protectively favoring those who refrained from playing, wholesale, to the white judges. Marcus had noted these consequences of innocent ignorance as major problems associated with even well-meaning white adjudicators. He was right on all counts.

"That was Number Nine. Now I'm giving you Choir Number Ten."

In an effort to develop the necessary familiarity, I had listened to several *isicathamiya* albums before even considering accepting an assignment to adjudicate. And from the beginning of the competition I took careful notes on each performance, hoping, at the event's end, to be able to recall the early groups and compare them to those who had come later.

"Now I'm giving you Choir Number Eleven. Choir Number Eleven!" But for all that, it was not until almost the middle of the competition that I was able to begin to recognize a new choir as less good, on musical grounds, than its predecessors. In one group, the rumbling basses did not sing in precise unison. In another the two highest singers sounded flat.

"Choir Number Twelve!"

Even after I was able to differentiate performances, one from another, my judgments were far more often based on personal taste than on freedom from musical flaw. Every group's singing had something unique and outstanding about it; astonishingly few included any real fault.

"Now I'm giving you Number Thirteen."

Most performances were vocal medleys in which the choir presented songs in such quick succession that it was often impossible to tell where one finished and the next began. Musical genres shifted seamlessly—from the sound of Western hymnody to that of 1950s rock and roll, on to a more identifiably African sound, to gospel, to contemporary country, to American Negro spirituals, and back through them all again. Lyrics shifted in a similarly unannounced fashion. A hymn to the Lord introduced a greeting of the family.

> Oh my Lord,
> Teach us to find,
> And kneel to pray.
> We greet you Father.
> We greet you Mother.
> We greet you Brother.
> We greet you Sister.

"Number Fourteen. I'm giving you Choir Number Fourteen."

A praise of the ancestral spirits became a Christian parable.

In the days of our forefathers
People lived peacefully.
Jesus of Bethlehem
Was born to rule the Israelites.
King Herod killed the children,
Killed them all.

"Now I'm giving you Choir Number Fifteen."
Bitterness at the lonely helplessness of migrant life led
into traditional rural admonitions.

Answer, my child.
We hear them calling you from far away.
My home is not here
But in a distant land.
Repent!
You are an unlucky sinner
Your dowry was a pig,
And you must repent.

"Choir Number Sixteen. Sixteen!"
Seventeen men in black suits stood across the stage and
saluted Steven and me as adjudicators. Their leader, in a white
suit, knelt in front of them and pleaded to us in caricatured
obeisance. This was the largest group of the evening, The Greytown Evening Birds, and their numbers filled the stage with life
when they began to sing.

When you see us here
We are from far away.

Small movements of hip and knee created waves across the
stage.

We come from there,
The place where times are hard.

White gloves moved jauntily up and down, in and out.

> **We are here**
> **We want money.**
> **We are here in this city**
> **Because we are poor.**

This group's upbeat physical performance styles and relentlessly spirited musical references to rock and roll belied the content of their lyrics. Their music came straight from 1950s "American Bandstand," but their words told of a life "American Bandstand" never knew.

> **We have left our parents**
> **And our relations.**

Like choirs throughout the evening, these men used foreign musical idioms to lament the migrant conditions that suffocate them at home. They live in town, far away from friends and family, because times are hard and there is no money to be earned in their enforced rural homes. They are lonely for the loved ones left behind and frightened of the violence of the city that remains, even after years, an alien place. Week after week, year after year, *isicathamiya* choirs sing of these concerns; their pain does not diminish with familiarity. Although migrants are known for a political conservatism born largely of vulnerability and urban naivete, the eloquence of their opposition to apartheid's migrant system cannot be overstated.

> **We want money.**
> **We beseech the Baas,**
> **For we are hungry.**

Lamentation gave way to playfully repeated nonsense syllables, as fourteen bass voices maintained the rock and roll beat.

Weh wah weh wah weh wah weeeh—
Weh wah weh wah weh wah weeeh
She wah wah wah wah wah wah wah
Away tonight.

Finally the group moved to English lyrics.

I love you
Shake my bloomer.
I love you
Shake my Daddy.

And they finished out their ten minutes, fully immersed in the rock and roll that had given form to the whole performance.

Ow! Ay!
My Lordy!
Rock and Roll!

The Greytown Evening Birds sighed an exaggerated sigh. They had worked hard, and it was now time to move on.

Goodbye, Mister
Goodbye, Ma'am
Goodbye I am going now.

"That was Choir Number Sixteen. Now I'm giving you Number Seventeen."

Choirs exited from stage and hall in near-exact reversal of their entrances. Announcing their departure, groups resumed the characteristic *isicathamiya* stalk and moved down off the stage and back through the hall, their singing fading from loud to soft to silent. Some groups sang in musical continuation of their main performance, striving to maintain their hold on the audience for every last moment.

> We are leaving.
> We will play with you another time
> My darling.

"I'm giving you Choir Number Eighteen. Number Eighteen."

Others sang special exit songs, designed as final pleas for the judges' attention. Affecting obsequiousness, they clasped white-gloved hands beneath black chins.

> Oh my Baas
> Please, Baas, don't forget me.

They departed on this note of supplication.

"Now I'm giving you Choir Nineteen. Choir Nineteen!"

The Jabula Home Defenders took a deceptively simple musical leave. Over steadily rhythmic bass, the lead singer appropriated the motif that a higher voice had been repeating as part of the previous song.

> Away. Away.
> Away ——ay ——ay ——ay ——ay ——ay ——ay.

The group moved off the stage in a slow, deliberate stalk.

> Goodbye, Goodbye,
> Goodbye I am going now.

They circled the judges' table, each man looking deep into my eyes and Steven's.

> Goodbye, Goodbye.
> Goodbye I am going now.

Back down the center aisle they went, and they disappeared from our view, two by two. Their voices remained with us, repeating as the men moved toward the back of the hall. They stopped before walking through the door, and, from their sound, turned to face us from behind.

Mmmmmmmmmm.

Mr. Maphumulo was once again standing by my side, bullhorn resting on the table. That had been the last choir. Steven and I must be especially careful not to look around as we deliberated over winners. During these few critical moments we were particularly susceptible to outside influences. Even now, if we made it necessary, they would look for a new adjudicator and reconvene the entire competition.

Sunlight poured through the windows. The day was already hot, and I was suddenly aware of how many hours I had been awake. After having been so wholly involved in each group's performance, it was now almost more than I could manage to look through my pages of notes and discuss them with Steven. In truth, we had been conferring in whispers throughout the competition, choosing early favorites and comparing them to later ones. We agreed easily on the four groups that would win prizes. And we compromised quickly about the order of prizes.

Tens of hands presented themselves for us to shake. Winning groups mounted the stage and sang in triumphant cacophony. Paulos retrieved us from the table and guided us firmly to the car. It was nine o'clock in the morning. The last thing I saw as I looked back into the hall was the numbers of the winning groups listed publicly on Mr. Maphumulo's slate. I remember thinking that the order wasn't quite right. Or was it?

IN
THE
CITY

IN CHORUS

As described earlier for the Venda and the Shangaan, South Africa's indigenous Nguni (Zulu-, Xhosa-, and Swazi-speaking) peoples lived traditional lives that were highly communal and permeated by music. Whether events of social significance concerned the society's recurring cycle of seasons and battles, or the individual's progress past life's expectable milestones, each significant event was marked with its own communal music. Group singing was by far the most highly developed of Nguni musical traditions. Largely unaccompanied by drums or other external instruments, singing has always been inseparable from the dance movements and gestures without which it cannot be artistically whole.[1, 2]

Musicologist David Rycroft describes Nguni choruses in more detail. Songs have at least two voice parts, each singing its own words, in its own time, to its own melody. Imagine the first voice beginning at twelve o'clock on a circle, moving clockwise to complete its first stanza by the time it returns to twelve o'clock, and then starting around again. The second voice does not come in until the first has already reached two or three o'clock. If a third voice is present, it may move along with one of the other two or sing its own text and start at its own entry point. Voices that move together will often create the open-sounding parallel fourth and fifths that Western music students are taught to avoid.

In a two-part call-and-response song, the first voice—often a solo singer—will call out a musical phrase, and the second voice—often a chorus—will respond with a phrase that overlaps the end of the call.

Show us the way to freedom
> (*Show us to freedom now*)

Several overlapping phrase pairs make up a stanza.

Show us to freedom now
> (*Show us the way to freedom*)

The roles of primary and secondary voice get lost as the song proceeds.

Show us the way to freedom
> (*Freedom in South Africa*)

Each part sounds relatively complete by itself, but all parts are seen as absolutely essential to the song as a whole.

Freedom in South Africa
> (*Show us to freedom*)

In fact, precisely as Rycroft insists Nguni singers do, I find that when asked to demonstrate the freedom song transcribed above, I do not sing either the "lead" or the "chorus" all the way through. Rather, I find myself jumping from part to part at each entry point, in an attempt to reproduce the whole interactive work.

Whereas Western song highlights finality by using a dramatic cadence, Nguni song highlights entry and repetition, emphasizing the ever-changing balance among parts. Voices enter and leave, move and hold, but the stanza always comes around again and the singing goes on and on.[3]

(*Show us to freedom*)

Show us the way to freedom
(*Show us to freedom now*)
Show us to freedom now
(*Show us the way to freedom*)
Show us the way to freedom
(*Freedom in South Africa*)
Freedom in South Africa

(*Show us to freedom*)

Today's *makwaya* genre of formal choral singing is one contemporary heir to this Nguni tradition of part singing; David Coplan explains that it also carries the legacy of mission Christianity. Earlier I noted the contradiction inherent in the Church's stimulating black progress and kindling black aspirations, while, at the same time, maintaining black dependence, powerlessness, and economic inferiority. *Makwaya* developed as part of black middle-class, mission culture. Like mission Christianity itself, then, *makwaya* has, over the years, symbolized both advancement and stagnation, both expression and repression.

Makwaya shares with other aspects of black middle-class culture its original, formal introduction as a replacement for the traditional idioms the Church viewed as primitive, heathen, and, by definition, unacceptable. On the basis of their preexisting vocal proficiency, blacks were quick to learn European choral conventions and to perform admirably according to European aesthetic standards. Black composers began to create Western-sounding choral works in African languages. Christian converts translated their custom of musical socializing into congregational singing. But European choral singing had little in common with its African counterpart. In contrast with African independent polyphony, European hymnody prescribes four parts that move together, in harmony dictated by a dominant melody. Unlike Nguni tongues, the languages of Europe are not tonal, and their hymns have no place for the tune-tone relationships that govern Nguni song. So early African choristers found themselves having to violate their own culture, even as they used it as a resource for westernization.

By the end of the nineteenth century, disillusioned mission blacks recognized the fallacy of wholesale westernization. Black nationalist leaders began to advocate the development of politics, religion, and culture that drew on Africa, on Europe, and on the unique experience of urban South Africa. Afro-America became an important resource and inspiration. Particularly as learned from Americans who toured South Africa, and on the African Native Choir's 1893 tour of the United States, black American musical idioms were admired by middle-class black South Africans and readily incorporated into their culture.

Choirs added Negro spirituals to their repertoires. Composers integrated elements of spirituals, minstrelsy, and ragtime into their hitherto Western classical compositions. They also began to arrange traditional Nguni songs for four-part Western choir, and to use features of traditional singing in creating new, syncretic musical forms. Early nationalism influenced *makwaya* in other ways, too. Composers used classical Western idioms in topical songs that warned rural men of the dangers of city life, protested the injustice of new governmental statutes, and lamented such immediate tragedies as disease epidemics. Black choirs abandoned the stiff, immobile stance of their white counterparts, reembracing the rhythmic body movements that integrate traditional song and dance into a unified whole.[4]

Makwaya was bound up with the black middle-class struggle to establish a meaningful identity in South Africa's cities. These people held Victorian whites as their role models, and they disdained the rural and working-class blacks who represented all that they had rejected by embracing Christianity and westernization. On the other hand, they continued to be rejected, excluded, and demeaned by the white establishment, and much of their African heritage remained dormant beneath Christian activity. For these black urbanites, music provided a basis for socializing and for asserting common values and aspirations. Tea-meetings and choir concerts soon came to serve social, cultural, and economic purposes. They brought community members together, presented entertainment, and reinforced developing cultural tastes. Equally important, they raised money for the sponsoring school, church, or individual through an established system of paying for admission and then bidding for refreshments and for particular works of musical entertainment. The bidding system fused economic and social activity, much as beer-drinking functions had done in traditional settings, and it recirculated capital within the black middle class. The repertoires of choirs presented at these regularly scheduled events included Western classical and religious, American popular, and African traditional selections, and syncretic compositions that incorporated them all.

> Let us make blessings,
> Let your path be bright.
> May your work succeed.
> May grace and good fortune
> Follow you everywhere.

By the 1920s and 1930s, the white government had begun to encourage the revival of black tradition as part of its program of confining blacks to rural areas removed from the cities. Middle-class cultural leaders were quite explicit, in these years, about the need for creating an African national culture that incorporated the best of Africa and of the West—a culture that would promote positive black identity, rather than serving the Christian Church or white political supremacy. In view of the importance of music in African life, it should not be surprising that musical performance was central to this evolving culture.

Choir singing remained the most popular and prestigious performance idiom among black urbanites, and regional and national choir competitions were organized to promote vocal excellence. However, even these competitions reflected ongoing tensions between black aspiration and self-expression, on the one hand, and white control on the other. Black crowding and poverty, coupled with government restrictions on black movement and assembly, meant that black music competitions required white sponsorship. Both the Eisteddfod, begun in the 1930s, and the Johannesburg Bantu Music Festival, begun in the late 1940s, initially succeeded on the basis of good will among liberal white sponsors and civic officials, and black leaders and participants. Both events soured as apartheid's contempt and hatred inevitably proved unable to tolerate either black integrity or interracial respect and cooperation.[5] But somehow *makwaya*, the music of a proud, hopeful, and constructively nationalistic middle class, survived.

Go, go well
And be blessed.

OPEN
FOR ME

Outside Uncle Tom's Hall in Soweto's Orlando West district, dustclouds nearly hid the cars skidding in tight figures through the building's unpaved parking lot. Bits of rubbish flew this way and that, finally coming to rest in a concrete corner, protected from the hot, dirty air that swept through the township without bringing any kind of relief. But inside the hall was another world. Although the physical structure bore the grime that coats even the sturdiest of township buildings, the people who moved about within it were creating a kind of paradise. Sunday afternoon was half gone. Church services had been attended; family dinners had been shared. And now, wearing the lightest colors and fabrics of summer, thirty-some members of the Sivo Music Group were rehearsing. They stood in a relaxed group, their mature voices echoing against the room's harsh surfaces and acquiring a mellow fullness bare walls could not explain.

When their director, Similo Mvovo, saw me standing in the doorway he smiled devilishly. He brought the choir to the end of their next phrase, held them there longer than the singers appeared to expect, and ended their long *makwaya* song almost before it had begun. He spoke a word in Xhosa, blew a soft note on his pitchpipe, and the whole tenor section sang out in unison.

Auntie!

The choir's other three sections answered in rich harmony.

Auntie, open for me.
I am getting wet in the rain.

They all turned to face me with a traditional Sotho song.

> **Even if there are two**
> **Even if there are three**
> **I don't have enough cattle**
> **To make a home for a new bride.**

Three times they sang it through, repeating the opening call, varying tempo and strangely spaced silences with subtle control.

> **Auntie,**
> **Auntie, open for me!**

They paused a long pause, singers smiling shyly as Similo spoke in his resonant bass voice. "This is to say hello to you, Helen." Before I could respond they added their final phrase.

> **I am getting wet in the rain.**

A friend later explained that in recent years this, like many African folk songs, has acquired political connotations. The traditional song concerns a young man's struggle to accumulate enough cattle and household goods for *lobola* (bridewealth). However, when sung in contemporary settings, particularly settings including white people, the song takes on an entirely new meaning.

> **Open for me!**
> **I am getting wet in the rain!**

The Sivo Music Group is a Soweto-based choir named after its founder and director, Similo Mvovo. It is one of perhaps hundreds of choirs that coalesce within Soweto's churches, schools, neighborhood organizations, and employee associations, much as neighborhood or company-based sports teams coalesce in America. In the 1950s and early 1960s the group was a church choir, performing for church functions and participating in formal choir competitions. After returning from the Johannesburg Bantu Music Festival with fourteen trophies in hand, they were asked to sing to raise money for the Blind Children's Association. Church officials refused permission. Sivo was a church choir, they said, and as such they were restricted to serving the church.

The principle of mutual assistance is central to black traditional life. As noted earlier, black urbanites transplanted this principle from country to town life, using performance and entertainment to reinforce solidarity, to promote collective goals, and to raise money by recycling capital within the community. Events like tea-meetings, choir concerts, and beer parties have historically served these various purposes. Thus, although government physical and social services to the black townships are notoriously inadequate, entertainment-based fund-raising has allowed communities to finance their own medical clinics, child care, and supports for those with special needs or handicaps.

Similo Mvovo viewed the church's restrictions on his choir as a prohibition against his social responsibility to the black community. He left the church; most of his choir members followed. They re-formed as the independent Sivo Music Group in the mid-1960s, and have been singing to raise money for charitable organizations throughout Soweto ever since. On one of my first Sundays in Soweto, I had seen their name on a flyer in a small Lutheran church. The church was reconstructing its sanctuary and Sivo had scheduled a concert to help their fund-raising effort.

Open for me!
I am getting wet!

The Sivo choir epitomizes the tradition of *makwaya*, and their repertoire expresses the genre's major themes. When I walked in on them they were practicing a work by renowned choral composer Todd Matshikiza. After Similo interrupted their rehearsal to have the choir sing my welcome, he returned them to work. They had a performance in two weeks' time, and the audience would expect selections by Matshikiza and by contemporary Sowetans P. J. Simelane and M. J. Khumalo. The audience would also demand such Western religious classics as "The Lord's Prayer" and "A Mighty Fortress," and segments from Mozart's *Requiem* and Handel's *Messiah*.

In an earlier conversation Similo had explained, "As an African choir it becomes quite prestigious for us to sing the songs which we may be perceived by other people as not being *able* to sing. Like the *Messiah* songs, for instance. Songs which are not perceived as already part of us. Songs which we are perceived as working hard to be able to sing. We are engaged to raise funds because of our prestige, and so we sing what gives us our prestige in these people's eyes." When this choir had won its trophies, their required competition selections had come almost entirely from this Western choral literature and had been judged according to Western aesthetic criteria.

However, these songs do not really touch the choir's soul. "When our choir sings *Messiah*, for instance— Now we'll sing *Messiah* for the music, per se. Not for its message. We will just sing the music, and not really think of the meaning of the words, so to say. So the finesse of the music is lost."

Despite his choir's roots in the Christian Church, Similo seriously questioned the group's personal commitment, today, to Christian hymns of faith and hope. Demonstrating both pride and embarrassment in his cynicism, he echoed my own doubts about Divinity's place in the mortal profanity celebrated without shame throughout the land of apartheid. "I think it is in desperation that a person just looks at God as the ultimate. If everything else has failed, OK. Let me believe that God will save our situation. I have been told that there is a God, and I have failed here and here, and so YES, God must be the answer."

OPEN FOR ME

Thy kingdom come,
Thy will be done.
Forever and ever!
Amen.

The choir shifted passionately to their second musical theme, Negro spirituals. To this African choir, these American songs are perhaps the most meaningful in their repertoire. Similo's voice broke repeatedly as he tried to explain why these slave songs are so important to his choir of middle-class, community-conscious Sowetans. "Because of this country's very great restriction in expression, somehow our music is also confined. We can sing the *Messiah,* and nobody will stop me from doing it. And if we sing a rugged type of song where it's a love song, for instance. OK. Nobody will stop me from doing it. But to sing about some specific event in the township, or some particular hope for the future. Then we have this very great inhibition.

"That is why when my choir sings Negro spirituals, they just change completely. They *really* change. You can see the tears in their eyes.

No more peck of corn for me
No more. No more.

"You can see them taking out the wrath of their local situation. It's really as if they are singing about their own situation. You can see the audience just going mad.

No more pint of salt for me
Many thousands gone.

"Many people are used to Negro spirituals being sung in a glib way, but we try to sing them as perhaps the slaves would have sung them.

No more Mistress call for me
No more. No more.

"We try to give them that spirit. Now all this we can do because they are Negro spirituals, and nobody can say, 'Why do you say this and this about our government?' "

No more hundred lash for me
Many thousands gone.

For these contemporary Africans, Negro spirituals provide a vehicle for self-expression much as they did for their original singers. Slaves could cloak concrete hopes and plans for tomorrow in the language of the Bible, giving secret voice to information and feelings they might speak directly only on pain of death. They could sing safely of following the drinking gourd and of laying down a burden by the riverside; it would have been unthinkable to describe a specific escape route or to announce that a fleeing brother was awaiting supplies in the marshes by the river, where dogs could not trace his scent. In singing the songs of American slaves, South African blacks are, indeed, describing feelings and circumstances quite close to their own. But even before the State of Emergency which is, at the time of this writing, well into its fourth year, a South African song might be banned or a performer jailed for proclaiming a hope that freedom will rise from the flames of destruction; a Negro spiritual simply echoes the words of people who lived long ago and very far away.

Although contemporary choirs and composers are wary of protesting specific apartheid oppressions, Sivo proudly sings one song that would seem to cross safety's ill-defined boundary. "This song tells of all the horrors of one of our jails here, called Modder-Bee, and it is banned at the SABC.

He slept days and days
In that prison of Modder-Bee

"You can't sing it; you can't play it.

My parents did not know his whereabouts
And they looked in different places for him
But there was no trace

"We sing it in public appearances, but many people have been saying, 'Look, you're taking a risk by singing this song.'

Mother was troubled
And Father was troubled, too
They had no more joy

"And each time we sing it there's so much applause, and there are so many requests to sing it again.

And the day my mother's child arrived home
He brought painful news.

"People feel so worked up on this thing, and these are just the types of things we are not supposed to be singing about."

He said that he had seen the picture
Of hell.

It is said that Pretoria is struggling to establish a compliant black middle class, to create a black subpopulation whose daily life and anticipated future are comfortable enough that they will work—and fight—to maintain the status quo. Like appointed homelands officials, certain urban blacks are issued licenses to operate lucrative businesses in closed township markets. Hard-line Marxist rhetoric suggests that the whole black middle class is in treacherous allegiance with Pretoria. However, as I learned again and again, from every one of the South Africans who became my teacher, black and white generalizations are far more likely to reflect oversimplification than to represent complex human reality. Not all black professionals favor their own relative comfort over the long-term well-being of their people as a whole. Not all pursue individual wealth and success at the expense of the community at large. In a land where meaningful protest and effective opposition are extremely dangerous, people manage to use ingenuity and resilience to declare themselves and their values with quiet integrity.[6]

> **In that prison of Modder-Bee**
> **He had seen the picture of hell.**

With the third component of its repertoire, traditional songs of South Africa's black peoples, the Sivo choir celebrates African spirit and strength. Although they may sing spirituals to express their innermost pain, with these African folk songs they demonstrate the liveliness, the vitality, and the pride that are, historically, so important to their identity. They do not sing these songs with voices alone. They sing them, dance them, radiate them—with voice, body, and spirit. And I cannot help thinking that the intense, earthy exultation aroused with the simplest of African lyrics represents perhaps the most powerful protest of all, against Pretoria's attempts at dehumanization.

Sivo concluded their rehearsal with a medley of African songs. From their clustered voice-part groupings they moved into a circle, and the circle began to turn in rhythm. Serious concentration on technique gave way to the sheer effortlessness of becoming their music.

OPEN FOR ME

> The beauty of a man is his cattle
> Don't forget, girl.
> (*Bring my money back*)
> (*Bring my money back*)

Even the large mother who, throughout the rehearsal, had not removed a tiny baby from her breast, swung hips and elbows into the song.

> You must carry yourself nicely
> At your house, girl,
> (*Bring my money back*)
> (*Bring my money back*)

Thirty singers circled as one.

> The beauty of a man is his cattle

Thirty singers, hands in the air, turned in thirty small circles.

> You must carry yourself nicely, girl

Slowly, one by one, thirty singers moved through the door, out of their world of color and back into apartheid's world of black and white.

> (*Bring my money back*)
> (*Bring my money back*)

WHEREVER WE MAKE IT

Iph'indlela

The big soprano Rosie sang out from right behind me. I whirled around, surprised and inexplicably delighted. She put a long, well-manicured finger to her lips, winked, and repeated her call.

Iph'indlela

The carpeted foyer of the "international" restaurant was filled with friends of the Sivo Music Group, gathered to help the choir celebrate its twenty-fifth birthday. Sipping from cocktail glasses, guests formed and re-formed themselves into clusters that were, even in this multiracial gathering, either all white or all black. Similo Mvovo is one of few South Africans I met who seems comfortable in both the white world and the black. He holds a high-level management position in one of the country's large conglomerates, having moved into this job when people still hoped that appointments like his were a sign of meaningful change and real opportunity, rather than of tokenism and entrenchment. For years Similo has had white colleagues and subordinates at work, and it was not surprising that at least some of them had accepted the invitation to his choir's party. Neither was it surprising that they did not find themselves mingling, or vice versa, with the schoolteachers, composers, and nurses who were the choir's black guests.

> Where is the way?
> Wherever we make it,
> My love

From the stairwell the choir answered Rosie's call. As a group they all danced their way among the milling guests and through a doorway into a small auditorium.

> Wherever we make it,
> My love

Black hips and shoulders took up the rhythm around the room, and when the last choir member moved through the door, the black guests danced after him as if on cue. We whites moved along in stiff, self-conscious imitation.

> Wherever we make it,
> My love

I had long before learned that the Sivo choir opens all its performances with this traditional Zulu wedding song. They habitually arrive at a venue along with members of the audience, and they seat themselves, individually, among the audience. When it is time for the concert, Rosie simply sings her opening phrase and from their places throughout the hall the choir's other members join in. They rise without hurrying. Relaxed, enjoying themselves, they make their separate ways across each row to the center aisle, and they dance up onto the stage, singing all the while.

I had heard this song five or six times in rehearsal, and I had listened to it on tape so often that I knew every phrase of the overlapping calls and responses. Rosie is a large woman with a powerful voice. I had frequently wondered at the reaction of whoever it was that she happened to be sitting next to when, without warning, she sounded her opening call.

Iph'indlela

Where is the way?

AT HOME
IN SOWETO

Robert Mokoena and I were driving through Soweto when we found ourselves following a small, open truck piled high with furniture. In the jumble of legs and cushions tied behind the battered green cab I could make out a headboard, table, dresser, and several chairs. Up ahead, cars honked and drove close on one another's bumpers. Robert chuckled. This was, he said, a wedding procession, and the truck was carrying the couple's wedding gifts to their new home. If they were lucky enough to have a place of their own, the furniture they had been given would constitute their household goods. If, as was more likely, they would be living with one or another set of parents, this truckful of goods would be added to the belongings that undoubtedly already filled the home. Perhaps the parents had a storage shed that could house the newlyweds in a semblance of privacy. Perhaps between house and outdoor lavatory there were a few feet of dusty yard which could be walled in and roofed over to approximate an additional room. I suddenly thought back to Samuel and Elisabeth Kgapola, the young Anglican couple in the Transvaal. These two had wanted the simple dignity of privacy; for it they had had to accept citizenship in the independent homeland of Bophuthatswana.

My first image of Soweto's oppressiveness had been of its tiny matchbox houses, crammed together in the dust. Less visible than the physical deficiencies of existing buildings, however, was the grossly inadequate number of homes altogether. Housing in South Africa's black townships has always been in short supply, related to underlying administrative conviction that black people belong in the rural bantustans, that urban townships must be tightly restricted, and that blacks who live in the townships do so as a matter of special and often temporary privilege. Only in 1986 did legislation acknowledge some blacks as legitimate township residents, that is, as permanent residents of white South Africa.[7] And subsequent legislation indicates ongoing official ambivalence toward even the limited black urbanization currently in effect.

When I was in South Africa in 1984, long-standing laws of Influx Control granted legal township residency only to blacks who met specific criteria; different criteria determined different residency privileges. Men with residence rights (assigned on the basis of ten or fifteen years' continuous, registered employment) were not necessarily entitled to have their families live with them. Men with permission to bring their families needed to produce proof of approved housing;[8] it was for these last that the housing shortage was harshest. A man who had persevered to earn residency rights in Soweto might find himself added to the tens of thousands of families who had already been on that township's official housing waiting list for years.[9]

The international media cheered when, in 1986, the pass laws were scrapped and the Abolition of Influx Control Act repealed or amended thirty-seven separate laws that had controlled blacks' presence in the urban areas.[10] Supporters argue that the Act has freed black South Africans to live where they choose and to move about the country at will. Critics charge that rather than implementing the Act in such a way as to enhance black urbanization, the government has simply manipulated housing shortages and relied on other, unrepealed, employment and urbanization laws, to continue to enforce de facto influx control and to retain its iron hand on the development of black urban communities.[11]

I thought back to the home I had visited with Peter Mabotho on an earlier Sunday; the two rooms of that tiny structure had housed at least eight people. The Urban Foundation estimated roughly seven million "informal urban settlers," nationwide, in mid-1988. In the country's gold-producing, industrialized midsection as many as 2.4 million people were thought to be staying illegally in the townships, living in backyard shacks, garages, and squatter camps,[12] in preference to enduring landless, hopeless starvation in a homeland. To these people, taking shelter in a packing crate in an urban squatter settlement represents initiative and promise; crowding in a Soweto matchbox must seem luxurious.

As if reading my thoughts, Robert began to talk. "You know, when we begin to consider ourselves lucky to have a two-room house without electricity or running water, and when we fight one another for the privilege of living in such rubbish, then we are lost. People are approved for housing, and still they can wait on a list for ten years, fifteen years, without getting a house. And when the government goes to build houses they say, 'Ach, two, three rooms is all these people need. See how they live already. Plumbing? Electricity? They are already getting along without.' As if we *like* to live with ten or fifteen people in three rooms. As if we *like* to have our toilets and taps outside and be choking from the smoke all winter long."

He echoed an already familiar refrain as he continued. "People are fond of saying that in this country we have the First World and the Third World very close together. They imply that we like being Third World, and that we wouldn't know how to live in a First World situation, and that we would like to bring the white First World part of South Africa into the Third World. When it is the Third World that must be done away with altogether. Men who have no permission to live with their families have something to complain about. Men who have permission to live with their families but no house to bring them to live in have something to complain about. And men who live with ten people in two rooms have something to complain about. All of them! The laws are made so that we cannot live a clean, calm family life. And then they say they cannot change the laws because we do not live as they do."

We pulled up to the home of Robert's friend Deborah, bright and clean in midday's direct light, and somewhat larger than its neighbors on either side. Inside, Deborah's small living room had an inexplicable feeling of spaciousness. Seated around the periphery were five or six people Robert had wanted me to meet. Middle-aged and extremely articulate in English, they had all been well schooled by missionaries before the 1950s policy of Bantu Education eliminated this crucial alternative to the government's deliberately inferior curriculum for black students. Each guest held a leadership position in a sector of community life. Race relations. Religion. Culture. Trade unionism. These men and women were all friends of Robert's, but except for a few individual pairings they did not know one another. At first conversations reflected preexisting connections. Two women discussed a mutual relative, two colleagues a series of lectures.

Trade unionist Edward Jabulani sat down to my right and discoursed on South Africa's black unions and the government's efforts to eliminate and coopt them. Deborah interrupted, calling our attention to an opulent buffet arranged on the table. Uniformed in white shirts and black skirt or slacks, a young man and woman moved softly around the room, offering wine and other drinks. He sliced from a pork roast and a duck. She served from bowls of colorful salad and vegetables. I complimented Deborah on the elegance of her home and her luncheon, and she murmured appreciation. By the hand she led me down a short hallway—the first hallway I had seen in a township house—to the home's three small bedrooms and two baths, past the modern kitchen, back through the living room again, and out the front door. She told me, "I am glad you like our lovely home. We have worked hard to make it this way from the original two-room matchbox. Of course we have eight of us living here, and most often a guest or two. But you see, we have used the entire lot. We have extended the walls right up to the borders, and we have no room for a garden, or even for a single blade of grass."

In my mind's eye I searched through the rooms I had just visited, for the side-by-side kitchen and bedroom that must have constituted the original structure. I tried to fathom the amounts of imagination and persistence required to transform that matchbox into this gracious home. Until Deborah had mentioned it, I had not noticed that outdoor planting was confined to window boxes, or that a scant half inch separated the house wall from the fence that marked the lot line. But she was still speaking.

"Even in Soweto we can make our own elegance." She laughed. "Of course one must have children who will put their books aside to make bricks and apply whitewash." She winked. "And those children must also be willing to work on Sunday, to assist when their mother entertains."

When we returned to the luncheon, conversational groups had shifted. I took my plate of food and looked for an empty seat. Jonathan, a choral composer, beckoned. He spoke eagerly of his struggle to write in a traditional vein, to use traditional Zulu pentatonic and hexatonic scales, but with enough sophistication to please urban choristers and their audiences. His tone was commanding, and it drew everyone else into our discussion. In this particular gathering only Robert and Jonathan readily identified themselves as singers; Edward had, early on, denied interest in any songs but those of his union. Still, everyone had an opinion about black music and musicians, and everyone, it seemed, shared a common treasury of songs.

Jonathan and Robert debated a musical point while the others smiled indulgence. Robert cited a particular English hymn as an example. Suddenly the women interrupted his argument with the hymn itself.

Tell the love

Without hesitation Robert and Jonathan abandoned their debate to echo the women's call and continue with the response line.

(*Tell the love*)
Of Jesus

The women called again.

By the hills

Edward reinforced Robert's bass, belying his earlier disclaimer of musical inclination.

(*By the hills*)
And waters.

In four parts these six Christians (only two of whom were singers) filled the room with richness, invoking the God who had, until now, been largely absent from this gathering on His Sabbath.

**God bless Africa
And her sons and daughters.**

Song completed, Robert and Jonathan resumed their debate while the others continued to eat and listen. When Deborah spoke it was to broach the overall problem of integrating African folk idioms with inevitable westernization, in such a way as to permit traditional African culture to remain vital and alive, to continue to grow and develop. One to another, these erstwhile strangers lamented the detrimental influences of today's outside authorities on their own music.

"They encourage certain kinds of African singing that suit their own political purposes."

"They insist that we must sing our own music in a style that existed a hundred years ago. So that style becomes locked in time. It cannot grow. It cannot change. Although this style may be very lively, it is at the same time absolutely dead. They have killed it. Fossilized, really."

"They insist that we are from several tribes and that we must speak in our own languages and live in our own bantustans. In the cities, man, if they would leave us alone, all of these different languages would by now be only two languages, one from the Nguni languages and one from the Sotho."

"Ye! It suits *them* that we must speak in many different languages. It doesn't suit us!"

"It's *their* problem, not our problem. They just make it more complicated."

"They insist on being involved where they have no business to be involved in the first place."

"Ye!"

Again without discernible introduction someone launched a song, this time in Zulu.

I will never return to Zululand

They all knew of my interest in singing, and Deborah grinned at me as their impromptu choir finished the short song's second line.

That is where my father died.

They repeated. A moment before they had been talking about issues concerning a culture they all shared. The topic had not really changed. Although their interaction was now sung rather than spoken, they were still considering their culture, affirming with every note their participation and involvement in its on-going meaning.

**I will never return to Zululand
That is where my father died.**

Spoken conversation resumed.

"They claim to be experts about our singing. And they talk such rubbish. In writing, too, they talk rubbish."

"They may be experts in the grammar and syntax of our languages. But they simply don't understand the idioms. How could they? The idioms are so deeply embedded in our culture that if you just translate them you wind up with a completely wrong impression. But they translate them nevertheless."

"And then they may even claim that we sing about nothing, when it's their mistake. Sometimes I'm so cross with them!"

A voice sang out again. This time the song leader was Jonathan, the language Sotho.

**Hey motsoala!
Hey motsoala!**

**Oh my cousin!
Oh my cousin!**

This song was clearly a favorite among them all. Jonathan repeated words and inserted nonsense syllables, dissolving the women into helpless giggles.

**Oh my cousin!
Oh my cousin! (*My cousin! Cous— Cousin!*)**

Voices faded in and out as individuals reacted to Jonathan's musical antics and then tried to smother their laughter with food or drink.

AT HOME IN SOWETO

Auntie went to Pretoria
She went with an iron wrench

Cutlery clinked against china.

A bicycle wrench.
I stamped and signed (*My cousin!*)

Cups clattered softly in saucers.

Oh my cousin!
Oh my cousin!

Although my outsider's presence and my explicit interest in singing might have prompted the first or even the second song, by now these middle-aged, middle-class Africans were singing for themselves and for each other.

I signed and stamped.
I stamped and signed.

They had been strangers an hour or two ago, but now they looked at one another in brotherhood.

Oh my cousin!
Oh my cousin!

Face to face to face they gazed. Out of nothing more concrete than a shared experience of having been black in South Africa's urban townships for the past half century, they were creating a sound as lovely as any I had ever heard. No longer were they decrying their circumstances, no more derogating white authority. Now they were celebrating themselves with a richness even they had not quite anticipated.

IN THE CITY

Oh my cousin!
Oh my cousin!

Every time Jonathan began the song again, the others produced new variations on their harmonies. They had all sung the song before—probably many, many times—but they had never sung it quite like this and would never sing it just this way again.

Kopse!

Jonathan finished with a sudden squeal. Everyone laughed, delighted, except me, whose delight at that moment was not of the laughing kind.

For a few moments we ate without speaking. When I asked what the song had meant, everyone had an answer.

"That's a very common song. It's one of the commonest."

"Ye! It's a wedding song."

"It's not actually sung at the wedding, but it's about a marriage."

"It's an old song."

"Not so old."

"But not so recent."

"It's from the time of that old bicycle with the big, big wheel in front and the small one in back. And this chap was carrying . . ."

"In those days all marriages were registered in Pretoria. It didn't matter where you came from. You had to register in Pretoria. So that guy takes his bicycle and he carries his girl at the back. And he goes cycling. I can just imagine even cycling from Johannesburg to Pretoria, and obviously this chap went further than that. And he keeps talking to the bicycle to give himself the courage. 'That bicycle must carry me until I get to the Registry.'"

"But where does that *motsoala* come in, Johnny?"

"The long and short is that when they get to the Registry he suddenly realizes the pride of it! The height of it! The clerk there has placed the stamp, and then he signs. The bride and bridegroom sign, to show that now they are truly married. So that's the climax of the song."

"But where is that *motsoala?*"

I tried to envision a similar conversation among my friends at home.

" 'Ring Around a Rosie' " is a very old song."

"It's about flowers. About roses and posies."

"But where do those ashes come in?"

"Johnny, you've got it wrong. You know what happens, she was accompanying them, that cousin. But see, she wasn't used to this new contraption, and so she was dead scared as they were going along! Ye!"

The image of one poor bridegroom peddling himself and his new bride *and* her terrified cousin for miles on an old-fashioned bicycle was more than anyone's seriousness could bear. Again the room was filled with laughter.

Jonathan stood up to say goodbye. He was writing a doctoral thesis and had promised himself at least a few hours at his desk this afternoon. But before he could reach the door the women were singing again, in Zulu.

The beauty of a man is his cattle

Sheepish at complying so easily, Jonathan joined in and began to dance.

(*Bring my money back*)
(*Bring my money back*)

Robert and the others put aside their plates, rose, and continued the song in body as well as voice.

(Bring my money back)
(Bring my money back)

Deborah's children ran in from the kitchen, dish towels snapping high as slim hips swayed low.

Don't forget, girl,
You must carry yourself nicely

Though Jonathan looked guiltily at the door, he made no move toward it. Everyone would soon be leaving but he could not bring himself to be the first to break the delicately spun, magical thread that had, without our noticing, wound around us all. Edward danced over to my side, grinning, and he spoke as the others continued to sing.

"I was wrong to say I sing only with the union, but you have seen that already. I think you may understand something very important about us with our singing. Something that perhaps we have not yet thought to understand for ourselves."

You must carry yourself nicely
At your house, girl!

TOWNSHIP
JIVE

On the international music scene the most widely popularized of all South African forms is the syncretic, jazz-based township jive known as *mbaqanga*, named after traditional maize- or mealie-bread. Dominated more by instrumental than vocal sounds, *mbaqanga* developed largely among professional performers, created by the best to entertain everyone else. This book highlights singing and its importance in the ordinary, everyday experience of being black in South Africa. Nonetheless, the driving instrumental bass, upbeat melodies, and relentless vibrance of *mbaqanga* are so much a part of black urban life that any discussion of South African music would be incomplete without it.

With each section of this book I have illustrated ways that in black South Africa singing is inseparable from life. And life is, in turn, inseparable from the country's history, from the religious, political, economic, and social currents that have washed the land ever since whites laid claim to that which blacks do not believe can be owned. Broadly speaking, traditional music has remained a rural idiom. It is practiced without deliberate modification by those blacks who stayed in the countryside, refused Christian missionization, and, insofar as possible, continued to practice African tradition. Among middle-class Christians in town and, to a lesser extent, on rural mission stations, *makwaya* became the music of choice. *Mbube* or *isicathamiya* developed as the music of the migrants. Though they work in town for most of the year, their lives are engineered explicitly to prevent them from becoming westernized or urbanized as real community members. Still, they are no longer truly rural. *Mbube* reflects this dilemma. And among the ever-expanding urban working class, among those unschooled blacks who defied prohibition to settle in the urban areas apart from formal structures of permission and employment, a succession of vocal-and-instrumental jazz forms came to dominate social music. Today these forms emerge as *mbaqanga*, the genre that inspired Paul Simon's *Graceland*, and captivated Broadway in Mbongeni Ngema's *Sarafina!*.

In his authoritative volume *In Township Tonight!* David Coplan traces the development of black urban music in South Africa. He identifies *mbaqanga*'s roots in the slumyards that proliferated in the black urban locations (more recently designated "townships") between the two world wars. Impoverished location residents assisted newcomers and capitalized on the housing shortage by renting living space to those who needed it. A room, a bed, half a garage, ground under a tarp stretched between shed and fence. All of these spaces might be rented—and then subdivided and sublet—to house the families who sought opportunity in the urban areas the government was trying so rigidly to control. Municipal facilities never kept pace with the population. Physical structures could not withstand egregious overuse. Initially ill-planned locations quickly deteriorated into slums that were always overcrowded, often squalid and dangerous, and never, ever sleepy or without palpable vibrance.

Remember that like all black South Africans, these unschooled, newly urban blacks came from a tradition of communality in which individual life derives meaning from its group context. Community social life and culture are far more than diversions from the daily struggle to survive; for these people they are essential to survival itself. Much of social life in the unruly slumyards came to revolve around the now-legendary shebeens. These places were illegal beer halls, run primarily by women and trading in a wide variety of home-brewed and European alcoholic beverages. Often operated in hostesses' homes, shebeens offered weekend-long parties of drinking, dancing, and music. Entertainment was originally provided by the guests themselves. But by the 1920s hostesses were hiring musicians whose performance expressed the blend of city and country with which patrons were anxious to identify.

Like middle-class tea-meetings and choir concerts, working-class shebeens were often organized on African principles of reciprocity and recirculating capital. Hostesses took turns sponsoring shebeens. They assisted one another in fermenting "native beer" and in hiding drums of home brew during official raids. Neighbors cared for displaced children while homes were transformed into centers for drunken partying. Thus, shebeens allowed struggling urbanites to translate traditional social principles into new, town-based structures. They allowed people to demonstrate community self-help at the same time as they encouraged socialization and recreation.

A new class of semiprofessional musicians blossomed in the twenties. Their playing synthesized diverse musical forms— vocal and instrumental, religious and secular, African, European, and American—into the syncretic urban idiom of *marabi*. Not only did this term denote a musical genre; it soon came to apply to a style of wild partying and to the practitioners of that style, as well. Coplan describes *marabi* as having a distinctive rhythm and the individually entering parts of African polyphony, structured within a Western I, IV, V harmonic system. The music conveys a sense of perpetual motion, due largely to the near-endless repetition of identifiable segments, patterned after the repeating strophes of traditional part singing. *Marabi* parties were boisterously unrestrained, highly sexualized, and, in time, frequented by violent location gangs. The middle class regarded the whole genre as misguided westernization. They felt that it incorporated the worst of both Europe and Africa, and that with it the proletarians were threatening the "civilization" the elite had tried so hard to cultivate.

Marabi musicians were paid to entertain. In addition to demonstrating virtuosity and endurance, they were required to perform elements of the various musical styles demanded by their patrons: African traditional singing. Mission-popularized brass bands. European hymnody. Western Dixieland, ragtime, and jazz. In the hands of less-westernized performers, *marabi* drew heavily on traditional melody and part structure. More westernized musicians emphasized ragtime and jazz. Regardless, the diverse genre of *marabi* represented a vehicle for developing a self-concept that would allow unschooled urban blacks to differentiate themselves, proudly, from their rural countrypeople, on one side, and from the educated middle class, on the other.

Marabi bands acquired devoted followings, and their music soon moved beyond the shebeens. In the late twenties and thirties, promoters incorporated *marabi* into variety concerts, and they eventually programmed evening events to conclude with several hours of dance music by the band. Through the early fifties at least a few Johannesburg concert halls were open to nonracial audiences, allowing black township music to develop some following within the liberal white community. Jazz musicianship thrived. Depending on the band and its audience, a given evening's music incorporated more or less African sound, more or less township-based frenzy, more or less Western polish. The era from the thirties through the fifties saw the stardom of township music legends Solomon "Zulu Boy" Cele, Wilson "King Force" Silgee, Zakes Nkosi, the Merry Blackbirds, the Jazz Maniacs, and the Manhattan Brothers. These last are the same bands that gave rise to such contemporary exiled musical greats as Miriam Makeba, Dollar Brand, Hugh Masekela, and Jonas Gwangwa.

Coplan points out that street music had been a part of Johannesburg's popular culture since the establishment of black locations. Paralleling the development of shebeen and concert bands, street performance remained a focus of black urban life. Nowhere was this truer than in Sophiatown, the mixed-race Johannesburg location that served, until the government removed it in 1955, as the center of black culture. Sophiatown nurtured musicians and journalists, playwrights and poets. And in its unruly, overcrowded atmosphere of violence and vitality, young boys playing pennywhistles created the music that would, in the 1950s, take the name of *kwela* (climb on). (The name comes from the sound made by police vans against whom the boys played their whistles as a warning and a kind of general camouflage.) The whistle itself was a six-holed German metal flageolet, initially adopted to substitute for the traditional reed flute. In the hands of young black urbanites, these simple whistles imitated mission brass bands, European pipe and drum bands, and the brass and reed sounds of *marabi* virtuosos. Location youngsters paired pennywhistling with a highly vocal style of jazz improvisation, and it was this whole genre of street music that became known as *kwela*.

An integral part of the life and values it expressed, *marabi* inevitably developed and changed as it took root in mixed-race concert halls outside the slums where it had been spawned. Formal concerts and late-night dancing were often followed by still later-night jamming. For these all-night sessions, bands put aside their written orchestrations of Count Basie to play a freer, more eclectic kind of music. Coplan explains, "These late-night 'do or die' sessions helped forge [African melody], *marabi*, *kwela*, and American jazz into *mbaqanga*, the people's own jazz, an expression and celebration of their new cultural identity."[13]

Mbaqanga was immediately popularized by the South African recording industry, and the new term initially referred to a broad spectrum of commercially successful, Africanized jazz. At one end of this spectrum were such robust, unique talents as Miriam Makeba and the Manhattan Brothers. At the other were pickup musicians hired cheaply by studios to record repetitious licks to duplicate a given label's last big hit. It is this end of the spectrum, under white control, that African music writer John Collins holds responsible for the genre's name. He translates *mbaqanga* as "quickly made, steamed mealie porridge," and he identifies it with music that is nondescript and manufactured quickly and cheaply.[14] By the 1960s *mbaqanga* had incorporated electric instruments. Today's bands may include vocals, guitar, bass, drums and percussion, keyboard, accordion, violin, saxophone, whistle, flute, trumpet, and trombone.

Like so much of black life and culture in South Africa, *mbaqanga* is intertwined with white manipulation and control, and with black resilience in response. *Mbaqanga* arose as an urban art form, a hybrid of idioms culled from black America, African tradition, European colonialists, and street-inspired ingenuity. It developed at the hands of the white-owned recording industry, meeting the musical specifications of white executives and rewarding black musicians with a financial pittance. But outside the recording studio, in the black community itself, *mbaqanga* continues to reflect the musical tastes and talents of the townships. In the grip of apartheid, this urban music embodies a whole set of late-twentieth-century blacks' aspirations, and with every beat it sounds their indestructible determination.

> **Bring back
> Nelson Mandela!
> Bring him back home
> To South Africa!
> I want to see him walking down the streets
> Of Soweto!
> Tomorrow!**[15]

IMAGES
OF HOME

The KwaMashu house of Jonas and Suzy Mphahlela always reminded me more of a community center than a family home. Considerably larger than the surrounding matchboxes, this structure gains an additional feeling of spaciousness from a tiled front patio that runs the length of the house and reaches almost to the street. The last time I visited, an *mbaqanga* band was jamming in one room, a girls' dance group was practicing on the front patio, and the three members of a girls' singing group were ironing their costumes in the kitchen. My friend Thandi, Jonas and Suzy's second daughter, was in a bedroom having a lesson on the traditional Zulu *ugubu* bow.

Outside the house a sign announced the sale of ice and cold drinks within. The front door stayed open, and all afternoon children walked barefoot through the cramped living room, eyes straight ahead, parents' money clutched in dirty fists. One little boy had no right eye, and he walked with his right jaw tucked deep into his shoulder, as if to hide that whole side of his face. One child limped badly on a leg that seemed to have no foot. Another had a bit of shriveled gristle for an ear, still another two stiff fingers in place of a hand. Perhaps these children's physical deformities indicated simply that fuller-bodied siblings were too busy on Saturday afternoon to run errands for their parents. Perhaps such errands were the excuse these children needed if they were to leave their homes and expose themselves to strangers at all. Perhaps, instead, the deformities reflected the appalling lack of medical services in the townships. How many were birth defects that prenatal care could have prevented or good postnatal care corrected? How many the legacies of untreated injuries suffered in the township violence that engulfs even the tiniest bystanders?

Jonas was listening to records and talking on the telephone in the living room. He called out playfully to each child, but most were single-minded in their reason for being in his home. With few exceptions they barely acknowledged him. In the kitchen Suzy gently coaxed from each small messenger the object of his or her visit. The singers' ironing board rested on the large chest-style freezer, so for each purchase of ice or soda the flatiron was returned to the oven, the costume draped over a chair, and the board and its padding upended while Suzy rummaged through the freezer. I joined Jonas in the living room to watch the township pass through. He laughed his now familiar lament. "I tell you, Helen, man, I don't even know whose home this is!" But he liked being at the center of things.

The girls in the kitchen called their group Black Blessing. Like nearly all township children they had grown up singing everything they heard around them. They were equally proficient in makwaya, reggae, disco, and mbaqanga. Durban's KwaMashu township is administratively part of the KwaZulu homeland; the urban location is geographically close to traditional rural villages. So these very stylish, westernized youth were also schooled in the traditional Zulu song and dance of their people. They had an important gig at a community hall that evening. Their costumes were slinky, one-strap dresses of blue and black, cut to highlight subtle curves and to shimmer with gentle hints of movement. Wrinkles would destroy the desired fluidity, and they fought to keep the flatiron at a temperature that would press the gowns without scorching. As one girl ironed, a second worked the short hair of the third into hundreds of long, slender braids, using extensions of natural hair. Their Zulu conversation was punctuated with phrases of song. The girl with the braids, Mara, sang a breathy alto lead, and the other two harmonized high. The hair styling had taken several hours and was completed as I watched. After studying a mirror from every possible angle, Mara squealed with delight. She ran through the house, collecting compliments and squeezes in every room. She returned to the kitchen, but before taking over the iron she had Black Blessing run through a whole song.

Awu, my Father

They moved arms and ground hips in stereotypic Motown gestures,

You created me, Lord

competing valiantly with the instrumentals that blared from every other room.

Lord King of Kings

The sound of *mbaqanga* and the moves of staged seductiveness gave no hint of their song's Christian content.

You put me in this garden

They shook their breasts in the frank, confident African sexuality that westernized performers manipulate so flirtatiously.

Because You love me so much

Abruptly Mara walked away from the song, tossing her new shoulder-length braids, each ornamented with bright beads at the end. "There is too much noise. And we must finish our dresses." She took up the iron, leaving her two friends to style each other's short hair in intricate patterned parts and close, flat braids.

A tiny girl in a black leotard had been standing by my

chair in the living room, watching Black Blessing through the doorway to the kitchen. Her large almond-shaped eyes were still wide when, as they went back to grooming, she took my hand. "Thandi says you must come see."

Every time I visited this house, Thandi seemed to be rehearsing a different group of girls. One time it was singers. One time traditional dancers. Today it was modern dancers—four statuesque adolescents and the sprite who held my hand. A tape player blasted from a windowsill. Clad in leotards and knitted leg warmers, the five girls stalked and slinked about the large front patio in time with the disco music on cassette. Although Thandi herself was having a bow lesson, she ran out every five or ten minutes to critique the girls' performance and make suggestions. They had been working for weeks on a rather conventional modern dance routine for an upcoming community competition. Moonwalking à la Michael Jackson was popular at the time, and over Thandi's laughing objection they had decided to incorporate this fad into their routine.

Twenty or thirty people crowded at one end of the patio to watch, their numbers continually swelling as passersby peeked through the gate and did not continue on their way. Thandi had choreographed the original routine to feature each dancer as soloist for a section of the music. One girl emphasized extensions, a second leaps, a third turns. All five moved in unison toward a center point and then out from it. Four stretched in shifting pairs while the fifth darted among them. The routine ended with the four folded in on themselves like springtime flowers after dark. The fifth stood just behind, fully extended and poised, ambiguously, to pounce or to protect. The dancers' expressions were serious, their concentration high. This was much more a rehearsal than a run-through, and their faces reflected more effort than enjoyment.

They held position through a few seconds of silence. When the music started up again the break dancing began. The pickup audience abandoned quiet curiosity to clap in rhythm.

Traditional bow player in KwaZulu.
Gary Gardner

Shangaan women pause between songs, Gazankulu.
Helen Q. Kivnick.

Venda rondavels and countryside.
Gary Gardner

Venda countryside.
Gary Gardner

Venda woman drums on a plastic barrel while other women dance
and the rest of the village looks on.
Gary Gardner

Impromptu choir performance at teacher training college, KwaZulu.

Gary Gardner

High school choir performance, KwaZulu.

Gary Gardner

Girls' gumboot dance, middle school, KwaZulu.
Gary Gardner

Boys' gumboot dance, middle school, KwaZulu.
Gary Gardner

Bridal party at hillside wedding in KwaZulu.
Helen Q. Kivnick

Outdoor kitchen at hillside wedding in KwaZulu.
Gary Gardner

Dancing in the streets at township wedding, Atteridgeville.
Helen Q. Kivnick

Guests at township wedding, Atteridgeville.
Helen Q. Kivnick.

Women in Shembe service, Ekuphakameni.
Helen Q. Kivnick

Squatter shack outside KwaMashu, Natal.
Gary Gardner

First the girls turned stiff, probing the effects of rigid knees, rigid elbows, rigid neck and shoulders, on otherwise graceful dance steps. Then they turned liquid, abandoning initiative of movement and giving their bodies over to waves that flowed from head to toe, from toe to head. As a line and a circle joined only by the touch of fingertips, they transmitted their waves through a continuous circuit of blossoming womanhood. They concluded with a sensual display of acrobatics, slithering around one another's bodies in astonishing defiance of gravity. The audience had grown quiet. Almost without breathing they absorbed the performance that was, for the earnest concentration of the dancers, a magnificent and naive exploration of the body.

Thandi was prouder than she could say. Discouraged by the dearth of opportunity for township youngsters to get ongoing training in the arts of song and dance, she has instructed the children in her community, at home, for years. "If they can go to school at all, they must live with this bloody Bantu Education that teaches them very little in the first place, except it teaches them that they are stupid and not as good as someone else. And singing and dancing are taken over by these political cultural organizations that take away your own mind and pour in the mind of the organization. Where can these children just learn and grow, to discover who they are in this world? Where can they receive practice and training in activities they can do on their own, to make themselves feel strong and good? I love working with them, and so they know they are welcome to come to me. And they come, and they come, and they come. They are always coming! Sometimes I feel so bad when I must be away for my own work, that I am not here to work with them. They come even when I am not here, you know, and they practice here even without me. They learn from one another and from the discipline of working regularly, whether I am here or not."

She giggled. "Soon they will outgrow me and they won't even need me anymore."

How can I go back
How How
To the beauty that I had?

Thandi walked me out into the street to ask a favor. She was learning to play the *ugubu* bow, the Zulu version of the generic musical bow found among each of South Africa's indigenous peoples. Professor Percival Kirby suggests that the musical bow developed from the hunting bow, inspired by the twang of a bowstring released after tension.[16] The musical bow is traditionally played by tapping the taut string with a thin stick. In some variants the musician's mouth serves as a resonator; one end of the bow is held in or against the mouth during playing. In other variants a resonator is added by fastening a gourd or, after the Europeans, a tin can, to the bow. Thandi needed to play this instrument in a film she was shooting at the time. Although special effects might easily have concealed her ignorance, she had chosen, instead, to seize the opportunity to learn this bit of dying Zulu tradition. Today's lesson was finished, but her teacher's arthritis was quite painful and she really needed a ride home. It wasn't very far. It wouldn't take very long. Could I? Would I?

As long as Thandi came along to translate and navigate, I was quite willing to drive any place my rented Corolla would take us.

I smiled and extended my hand when I was introduced to Mrs. Ngwenyana, a large, soft woman with an ageless face. But she giggled and looked away, wiping dark hands on a darker dress. Thandi slid into the backseat; Mrs. Ngwenyana eased herself into the passenger's seat, the large *ugubu* bow by her side. Thandi leaned forward, hands on the corner of my seat back. With alternating exchanges in Zulu and English she managed to attend to both her respected elder and her American visitor. Almost immediately we left KwaMashu's well-defined streets and crowded, brick-walled houses behind. Dirt roads became tire tracks as we drove into the variegated green hills that cradled the township. Tall, coarse, light-colored grasses scratched against the bottom of the car; farther away, the next hill looked a bit greener. Soon even the tire tracks disappeared. Thandi suggested that we leave the car at this point and walk the rest of the way as she does when she drives here with her father. Willing to risk Budget's car where Jonas might well try to protect his own, I declined her offer.

The driving was easier when the grass gave out entirely, for then we could see the stones and ruts. Finally our path became a trail of dirty rocks, and we had to park after all. Mrs. Ngwenyana tried to hurry ahead. Thandi whispered that she felt ashamed in the company of a modern white woman, and that she had further embarrassed herself at her earlier awkwardness. We made a production of rolling up the car windows and making sure the doors and trunk were locked, so that even with her arthritis Mrs. Ngwenyana might move ahead alone. We stepped carefully around the biggest, sharpest rocks. Patches of green growth and bare gray-brown covered the hillside like the hide of a mangy cow.

Just over the next rise a small, mud shack crouched in a gentle furrow. Its rear wall was sided with packing crates, stamped TOYOTA and 11 and CKD in different directions as eight large segments of crate were overlapped and stuck in the mud wall against harsh weather. Pieces of metal and plastic sheeting covered over the top, held in place with large rocks. Some distance away we saw another shack, more imaginatively shaped than the first. Made from rusting pieces of corrugated iron propped against one another and held together with wire, its walls were no more regular than the sizes and shapes of their metal sections. A large yellow bucket was tucked under a curling flap of iron. To one side a small garden struggled for life.

Thandi explained that this hillside was a squatter area. Most people earned some kind of living from the city. Since the area was not an administratively organized location, it had no utilities at all; the shacks themselves might be demolished by the authorities at any moment. This uncertainty was the primary reason people had not built permanent rondavels of mud and thatch as their ancestors might have done in this spot. Water was carried from the township far below, in plastic buckets balanced on women's heads and girls'. I thought back to the distance we had come by car, before even beginning to walk. In the dry season it might take all of a woman's waking hours just to carry water for her family and the garden that fed them.

> **The cock, Mama.**
> **It is dawn**
> **There is no water**

Mrs. Ngwenyana lived with her son Bhoyi in a two-room hut built of milk cartons that had been filled with sand and, in some places, smeared solid with mud and dung. One wall held a four-paned window, the entryway a door that closed. A few scrawny mealies had grown as high as the flat, sectioned roof. In the small anteroom Bhoyi sat at a table, studying by kerosene lamp. Thandi introduced us, and he smiled at me like a firefly. He answered her questions in soft monosyllables. He was studying an economics text, preparing for an exam in the correspondence course that was all the education he could manage. She promised we would leave him alone as soon as she had concluded her business with his mother.

Eventually Mrs. Ngwenyana pushed aside the dark blanket that separated the two rooms, emerging with a new bow she presented to Thandi. A single string stretched, taut, from end to end of a slender, light-colored wooden bow. It stood four or five feet high. Midway between the ends an open calabash was tied, lightly cushioned, to the convex side of the wooden arc. Along with the instrument itself went the slender, slightly roughened stick used for playing. The large woman belched softly. Thandi whispered that her teacher had been drinking from the pot of traditional beer always brewing in the hut's darkness. She would probably be relaxed now, and she might even be persuaded to play for us on the new bow. For all her shyness around people both western and Zulu, she was, after Chief Minister Buthelezi's mother, perhaps the greatest living player of the *ugubu* bow. If there had been even a chance she would agree to being taped, Thandi would have suggested that I bring my recorder along.

We three women walked slowly back to the car. Thandi handed me the bow. I took it and looked to her teacher for assistance; we all laughed at my clumsiness. Mrs. Ngwenyana reclaimed the instrument. With the fingers of her left hand she held the wooden bow at the calabash, positioning the hollow gourd against her fleshy bosom. With her right hand she tapped the long string, producing a lonely sound much in keeping with the surrounding landscape. Her left thumb moved up and down the string, changing its pitch to produce a haunting sound that was, at first hearing, too foreign for me to recognize as a melody. She moved the gourd to and from her breast, varying resonance and sustaining tone. The afternoon wind blew through her ragged, loose dress. Her body was the body of the hills, her melody the song of this wind. As I had so often before, I wondered again how South Africa's whites could pretend, for even a moment, that the country's blacks were not of this land, of *all* of this land. From the beginning to the end of time.

> My love
> Let us to go the mountains
> And stay in those mountains.

Outside the Mphahlela house I prepared to return to the city. Thandi rehearsed me again and again in the directions for driving out of KwaMashu and back onto North Coast Road, that would become Umgeni Road, that would take me south into Durban. Although I was not unfamiliar with the drive the unmarked, unpaved township streets always twisted my sense of direction like a pretzel, leaving my safe return to the city in the hands of the spirits.

In a few minutes Thandi would be leaving with Black Blessing for their performance. She had agreed to go along and use their sound check as a time to vet their act. "And then I must come home and listen carefully to this tape. I must decide what we can do with these wonderful songs."

She pulled a cassette out of her pocket. Earlier in the afternoon I had given her a tape of some newly written American anti-apartheid songs, the last of which was one of my own. We listened through the tape together, and I watched her face closely. These songs were far from the earthy idiom that was her element, and I had no idea what she would think of them. I needn't have worried.

"These are wonderful! We cannot write such songs in this country, and we certainly cannot sing them on radio. So it is very good that you are singing about our situation over there across the ocean. Now this last one especially could become a real disco hit." She had laughed at our inside joke. "I know you dislike disco, but even you must admit that it could be wonderful for this song!"

Thandi held up the tape as she knocked playfully on my car and waved goodbye. "You know, if I could sing these songs here as I would like to, there would be no need for them."

TAKING
A WIFE

"We have a traditional belief in our Zulu religion that if you marry in a way that leaves the parents unhappy, then your marriage won't be happy. And to make parents happy you must open marriage negotiations in the traditional way, by offering your prospective father-in-law *lobola* (bridewealth). I did it myself." Edward Khanyile laughed broadly. This young man holds the highest law degrees South Africa awards. His designer clothes are cut from fine, imported cloth. His office reflects Western elegance. But the elements of tradition in this young professor's life are far more pervasive than his professional persona leads whites to expect.

While describing *lobola* negotiations in contemporary Zulu tradition he slid in and out of delight, self-mockery, and annoyed impatience. "You can't simply go to a man and say, 'I'm asking for the hand of your daughter in marriage.' You would be insulting him in a serious manner, and you would be lucky if you didn't get hurt in the process. The traditional way of opening marriage negotiations is to send messengers. They are supposed to stand at the entrance and shout in metaphoric language. 'You of so and so! He of so and so has sent us for a good relative, to kindle your fire. We are saying this through so many cattle. You may count them by their color,' and so on.

"And then the father will simply chase them away. He wouldn't even talk to them! And they would come on another day, and they would stand there and shout and shout. And after an hour or two the father would instruct someone in his household to invite them in. So they would be shown to a particular hut—or a room if it is a modern house—where they would wait for the father to come and ask them what they are looking for. Then they would start telling their story in that long-winded traditional way we Zulus have. And the father might interrupt them repeatedly. 'No, I can't even speak to you. My mouth is tight.' And they would have to pay something to open his mouth. 'I can't speak to you now because I'm up in the tree.' And they would have to pay something to bring him down.

"Finally they would be ready to start negotiating *lobola* and the very first thing, he would send them away. 'No. You go away and come back on another day. I must inform my brothers and my relatives.' So they go away and come back again, and this time there is serious negotiating about how much they have to pay. All the close relatives become involved. The brothers of the father. The aunts. Everyone. How much livestock. How much cash. Usually it is both cattle and cash. It's quite amazing in 1984! Eh?

The beauty of a man
Is his cattle

"Actually there is also a rule providing that no marriage can be celebrated unless the woman publicly declares it to be her own free will. So when the messengers first come in, the father will call his daughter and ask if she knows them. And if she says 'No,' then those men will be chased away, and they may be beaten. In fact, today the messengers won't even be sent unless the man and the woman have already agreed to marry each other."

Girl, you must carry yourself nicely
At your house

Lobola is not merely a purchase price; it is also part of a social contract that binds two clans. Traditional marriage signifies the bride's separation from her own clan and her membership in that of her husband. In an economy based on subsistence agriculture, *lobola* compensated the bride's father for the loss of his daughter's labor. It also demonstrated the groom's respect for the bride and her family. Today's *lobola* retains some of its traditional connotations; its very existence brings to mind the tradition from which it comes. But particularly in urban areas it is most widely regarded as a commercial transaction prerequisite to marriage.

Bring my money back!
Bring my money back!

Edward Khanyile himself bypassed some of the roundabout negotiation ritual. "Myself, I didn't follow the strict, formal traditional way of standing at the entrance and shouting. Or of having messengers speak for me. I phoned my wife-to-be, who informed her mother, who informed the father that I would be coming on such and such a day. I gave them plenty of advance notice. Of course I couldn't just go by myself. So I asked a particular man to go with me. And when the day arrived, that man just didn't turn up. I had to get a substitute, so I went together with my mother. We didn't stand at the entrance. We simply went in, sat down, and started chatting.

"My wife-to-be was waiting in another room, and when the time came she was called in and asked 'Do you know these people?' And she said 'Yes,' and then she left again. The negotiations were carried out by the parents. My in-laws were quite understanding and sympathetic. I had just completed my degree, just finished writing the examination. I had borrowed money from here and there and there, and I think I had managed to get together two hundred fifty rands. That was the price of only one or two head of cattle, and at that time people were paying ten head of cattle. But they appreciated my circumstances and they did not take the pitiful amount as an insult."

IN THE CITY

That was in the mid-1970s. Since then, Edward Khanyile has climbed high up the ladder of academic success. The couple's three children are all in school, and his wife is working on her own university degree. His mother has brought his seven younger siblings from the bush to live in Edward's home and reap the benefits of their older brother's westernization and ambition.

**Remember girl,
You must carry yourself nicely.**

WED
IN TRADITION

Weddings have always called for major celebrations among the Zulu. Lasting for days, outdoors, and held at both the bride's and the groom's family kraal, a traditional wedding is a public festivity with an open invitation to everyone in the surrounding areas. The whole community is involved in an elaborate series of proceedings, all revolving around song and dance. Anthropologist Elkin Sithole describes the events preceding the final marriage ceremony, as practiced in the 1960s. Weeks ahead, a conductor of singing is invited by each of the two clans to prepare them for the competitive singing that will dominate the celebration. The conductor recruits whole families of singers from the clan. Special songs may be written for the occasion, and special arrangements will be practiced.

A few days before the wedding, the bride's singers come to stay with her immediate family. They clean, cook, brew beer, practice their repertoire, and otherwise assist with final preparations. The groom's people arrive on the eve of the wedding, singing and offering payment for acceptance into the bride's home. Ritualized hostility is part of the tradition, and the groom's people are initially denied. Finally someone from the bride's family accepts their payment, and the celebration is under way. Once food has been served the bride's and groom's parties may mingle. Although everyone must conserve strength for the next day's singing, Sithole describes this night as long and festive, full of friendship, lovemaking, and song.

They were jolly,
They were singing and making music.

245

The next morning the groom's family washes and dresses at a nearby river, first the girls and women, and then the boys and men. They sing en route to and from the kraal. First, they are practicing for the day's events. Later, at midday, it will be the responsibility of the men in the groom's family to sing their declaration that the wedding has begun. They retreat to bring their women from the river, and they return to the kraal, led by the groom. As the groom's people sing and dance, the bride's people come forward and the competition begins.

The two parties are led by their respective conductors, and they perform simultaneously—with different songs. Throughout the afternoon spectators pay careful attention to the singing, rewarding individuals who stand out by presenting them with such small articles as mirrors, handkerchiefs, scarves, and umbrellas. By day's end the strongest singers may find themselves heavily laden with these tokens of admiration, most of which are eventually returned to their owners. On one level, spectators try hard to listen to each group and to the individual singers within them. On another level, they may be more interested in the romantic opportunities posed by this ritual demonstration of admiration. Some men refuse to take back the items they have given. Others present gifts on the basis of attraction rather than singing; they know that in attempting to return articles, a woman will have to make contact with the man who gave it.

At the beginning of the competition the bride sings with her own party.

You are making me leave my parents

Later in the afternoon she is led to join the groom's people.

My heart melts with joy

This is her first opportunity to prove that she belongs with them.

They were jolly

Participating in their singing and dancing, she must perform well even on songs she has never sung and dances she has never danced before.

They were singing and making music

The singing and accompanying dancing persist, ever louder and more energetic, until the crowds disperse at sunset.

But today the fist is sounding.

Only now, after a whole day's efforts, are the singers free to eat. Immediately after the meal, the groom's party stands near the bride's house and sings their summons for her to follow them. Both parties use the night to travel to the groom's kraal for the next day's events.[17]

Bride, come!
Our home is far away!

Drama scholar Peter Larlham observed festivities at the groom's kraal, at a traditional wedding in Zululand in 1980, nearly twenty years after the celebrations characterized by Sithole. The bride and her party prepared themselves just outside the kraal. Meanwhile, the young men of the district gathered a bit farther off for the *umgangela,* the ritualized stick fighting that gave rise, under other circumstances, to migrant team dancing. Armed with fighting sticks and small cowhide shields, the young men formed teams and took turns displaying traditional warrior skills. One by one each youth rushed forward, leaping, kicking, and beating his shield with his stick. All the while his comrades accompanied his performance by shouting the clan's praise names in fast, raucous rhythm.

> Sons of my father
> Sons of my father,
> Today the fist is sounding.

In the middle of the afternoon the assembled bride's party moved to the kraal. Men first, women last, they sandwiched the bride between them and concealed her beneath an umbrella. Slowly, rhythmically they walked. Solemnly they sang their clan's anthem, indicating the bride's respect for her family and her sadness at leaving them. Finally they positioned themselves across from the groom's already waiting party, and the community guests gathered behind.

> Take care of this orphan.
> Tomorrow you may call her a thief or a witch.
> You may call her a liar.
> Take care of this orphan.

The traditional wedding itself has three main dances: that of the groom's party, that of the bride's party, and the final combined dance. All are accompanied by singing. Throughout the afternoon, sex-segregated groups from the two clans moved forward to perform long, precision dances. First one clan and then the other took over the open space between them. The young women punctuated these formal row dances with individual displays of agility and strength, analogous, in some ways, to the young men's *umgangela*. Individual dancers were accompanied by shrill whistles, sharp cries, and piercing ululation from the older women stationed behind. Like the marathon singing described earlier, this day's dancing provided an occasion for young people to give one another small gifts and initiate new courtships.[18]

It's boys!
It's girls!

As the long afternoon drew to a close, the bride's father stepped forward and delivered a speech to the groom, praising his daughter and praying for the ancestors to bless the marriage. The groom touched the bride lightly and then performed his own vigorous display of dancing, accompanied by loud shouts and praises from his party. The bride responded by breaking out of formation and leading the members of her own party in wild, individual dancing. The bride's party re-formed a long line to perform a final, excited dance, still facing the groom's party. Both clans maintained line formation and proceeded to the cattle enclosure for the combined dance that was the day's climax.

I swear, Mama,
It's true!

Inevitably, contact with Western customs influences the development of ongoing African tradition. Even people who practice a "traditional" life find themselves assimilating bits of the West into African tradition, at the same time as they accommodate tradition to aspects of westernization. Thus what is described as traditional at one point in time may differ substantially from a later era's view of the same tradition. And what is once adopted as Western may subsequently come to incorporate aspects of African tradition. Each of South Africa's indigenous peoples has its own specific wedding traditions. But as the products of Africa they have much in common. All involve communality and individual virtuosity. All revolve around singing and dancing. All take place in the open air, out on the land that is never meaningfully separate from the life of the people of Africa.

A PLACE
TO SMILE

In my rented Toyota I followed Robert Mokoena through the maze that was Pretoria's Atteridgeville township. Peter Mabotho's son Lukas was marrying long-time sweetheart Lucinda, and the Mabotho family celebration would last all day long. Knowing that I would never find his house on my own, Peter had sent Robert to meet me at the township's entrance and lead me to Ramakatsane Street. At the first corner the roads turned to dust and stone, and I was lost. We wound between matchboxes of brick and stucco, creeping along to protect our tires. Before we reached Peter's house, we came to a huge, double-peaked green tent towering over a tightly parked row of cars. We squeezed our two Toyotas up against the canvas. People were gathering at the Mabotho house, nearly a block away. It seemed that this celebration would soon take over the whole street, and Robert murmured that Peter had surely arranged for someone to protect all our cars from local *tsotsis*.

The tent was pitched in the middle of a corner intersection, where the dirt road was wide enough to accommodate it and still permit cars to pass, one at a time. I ducked in, under a green flap, as we walked by. Homemade ornaments of tinsel and sequins glittered from the support wires, with carefully lettered signs, bell-shaped, dangling among them.

WELCOME LUCY!

HELLO LUKAS!

GOD BLESS BOTH OF YOU!

Colorful paper chains stretched from corner to corner and snaked their way along the tables, between bowls of salads and sweets, and plates piled high with biscuits and cheese. Banquet tables were set with linen and silver, enough for perhaps a hundred people. But already more than that were milling around outside Peter's house, and things were not yet really under way. I recalled the serial seating Jocelyn had described when we were celebrating Elisabeth Kgapola's robing into the Mothers' Union, months before. Robert now said more about the township feasts that are, like so much of black city life, urban adaptations of traditions developed in the bush.

"Hospitality is our way, and when we have a celebration the whole community is invited to take part. Peter Mabotho is an important man in Atteridgeville, so there will be many, many people who will come to share this happiness in his family. And he has many friends from elsewhere, like yourself, that he has invited for this occasion. I happen to know that they have slaughtered an ox and a sheep as well, for this feast, and the women have been cooking all week for this day. My wife is among them, and our own kitchen has also been drafted for this purpose."

His smile faded. "In these days of economic trouble, such a feast can present a big problem for a family. It is our tradition to share our happiness and our food with everyone. But the expense is very great. And there are many families that simply cannot afford it. There are neighbors who will come to eat, and we know that they will not have a good meal like this again for a very, very long time. So they eat not just to celebrate but really to survive. And there are neighbors who will not afford such a feast when their own families must celebrate, so they cannot give back what they accept from others. This tradition is our way. It is not well suited to this life in the city, in these times of difficulty, but we lose ourselves when we think of behaving in some other way."

Robert tossed a plump raisin into the air and caught it in

his mouth. "But these are not concerns for the wedding day of Lukas Mabotho. Peter has arranged for a big, big feast, with many tables. Today everyone will be satisfied. This is not a time for talking of such problems."

He pushed me gently through the people crowding in and around the Mabotho house. "We must show Peter that you have arrived safely."

But we were sidetracked in the kitchen. Robert stopped to squeeze his wife, who was supervising final preparation of the traditional Sotho sour porridge. And I found myself caught in Jocelyn's warm embrace as she whirled around from the vat of custard that would soon be part of the afternoon's trifle. Peter appeared in the doorway and his resonant voice boomed. "Helen, I'm so pleased you made it! And I see you are at home in my home even without me. Please make yourself welcome."

He engulfed Jocelyn and me in his big arms and, switching to Sotho, quickly moved off to greet newer arrivals. Jocelyn shooed me out of the kitchen, teasing. "You are wearing the wrong dress to be working in the kitchen, so you must go out to enjoy the party."

Only then did I notice that the women in the kitchen all wore matching dresses, tailored from a black and white print featuring geometric rondavels. Jocelyn giggled that Peter's many women friends had had quite a time agreeing on fabric and pattern in time for them all to make up their dresses for the occasion. She laughed again. "But here we are in black and white, and you are in blue that will show every little drip and splash. Go out, and I will come and find you just now." So I went.

At the back of Peter's house stood a jacaranda tree, blooming in glorious purple. He had once explained that when they were enlarging their house, they found the tree so lovely that they bricked a patio around it rather than cut it down to build an enclosed room. Today this patio was haven for the elders who sat in a circle, sometimes talking, sometimes silent, while younger generations celebrated everywhere else. In traditional weddings the elders have responsibilities within their clans' activities. But in contemporary urban African-Christian hybrids, the elders are often more comfortable sitting together to one side, listening for traditional songs and waiting for their progeny to come by and pay appropriate respect.

It was back here that I met Peter's mother, a spry-looking woman near eighty, wearing a patterned head scarf and the black and white dress of the women running the feast. Her husband had been a *sangoma*, and her own face was tattooed with a thin, dark stripe from her hairline to the tip of her nose, indicating completion, long ago, of her own traditional initiation. I knew that Peter's parents had not easily accepted their son's mission Christianity and Western education. Although I could see his gentle, serious face reflected in his mother's more severe features, I could also see in her eyes the gulf that continued to separate her from her son.

I stood by the corner of the house, trying to imagine what these elders must be thinking of the changing generations sired since their own turn-of-the-century childhoods. But before I could imagine very much, I found myself swept up in the procession of guests that was singing and dancing its way around the house.

> **It is love**
> **It is love**

This procession had much in common with the one Joyce had led in Mabopane, at the robing celebration. People sang with voice, with body, and with soul. But today their numbers were larger and their pitch more fevered.

> **It is love when it is burning**

Singing was punctuated with high, sharp shrieks and with the ululation that is the traditional responsibility of old women.

To kiss my wife

Whistles blew. Voices imitated birds and wild animals. Everyone ululated.

Is the feeling of love

Arms were raised and lowered as crowd space permitted. Feet stepped high and light in rhythm. And along with all the movement the song repeated as if it would never stop.

To kiss my wife
Is the feeling of love

Around and around and around the house we marched, hundreds of guests moving with irrepressible excitement.

It is love
It is love

Lukas had managed to drive off a short while ago, to fetch Lucinda and her entourage. When they returned the real celebration would begin. Until then people were just practicing.

It is love when it is burning

As the procession moved past a pile of bricks by the front gate I noticed Robert standing alone. I would be leaving the country soon, and I joined him outside the merrymaking for what might be our last opportunity for serious talk. Together we watched the river of guests flow by—old and young, fancy and plain, clean and dirty. A slender white woman bobbed along on the current. In Afrikaans-accented English she had told me that she was an old friend of the Mabotho family and had been particularly close to Peter's late wife, Eleanor. Responding to my curiosity about her own family she had also explained, uncomfortably, that she was here alone because her husband did not enjoy eating or otherwise socializing with black people.

At the sight of her, Robert launched into a quiet tirade. He held a glass of wine. Like all of us, he had already had enough to drink that his usual reserve had begun to melt away. "Ach, Helen, those Afrikaners are such bloody liars! In church they are such religious people. They believe in one God. They believe in all of us being the created ones of God. But as soon as they step out of the church doors they will go into another vista which completely negates everything they have been saying."

Robert is an intellectual, and his involvement in music has brought him into contact with many of South Africa's artists, white and black. So I thought he might be interested in a description I had just read in André Brink's *Writing in a State of Siege*, of the two faces of Afrikaner identity. "You know, Brink says that as Afrikaners developed a sense of themselves as a people, their national identity had two sides. One carried the earthiness, ingenuity, and endurance that enabled them to survive the Great Trek. And a warmth and compassion went along with all that, and a sense of justice. But the other side carried a sense of being superior to everyone else, of being chosen, and of being RIGHT, with everyone else being wrong.

"For a while the two sides stayed together. But when the Afrikaners won power in 1948 they wanted to set themselves apart from anybody else who had ever held power or lived in this region. Those first qualities—ingenuity, resilience, and justice—really characterized everyone who had managed to survive the harsh conditions of the land. The only thing that set the Afrikaners apart was their sense of superiority, of being RIGHT. And so they adopted the one prickly, really despicable side of their identity and discarded the kinder, more compassionate side. Of course without the kindness, the self-righteousness is absolutely intolerable."[19]

I stopped for air and continued with a thought that had been prowling around my mind for weeks, but that I had not before heard myself put into words. "Brink's essay helps me understand how these people can be such liars. With such straight faces. How they can sign accords they have no intention of obeying, how they can steal territory and say they didn't, how they can use words like 'separate development' when what they really mean is kicking everyone who isn't white out of South Africa altogether. If they really believe that they, alone, are 'chosen,' then whatever they say or do is RIGHT, simply because they are the ones saying or doing. What constitutes lying for everyone else is, for them, just enacting God's divine will."

Robert took my thought and ran with it. "You are right! And the way they throw words around! You know, most of them haven't got a clue about what communism is all about, but if you are self-assertive, if you differ from me, if your opinion is different from mine, then you are a communist. Most of us blacks know how to rub the white man the right way. I mean you can't be fifty-five in this country and not know how to do that. And they are so arrogant that they think what we show them of ourselves is what we really are. They see a black man smiling and saying 'Yes, Baas' and they think this chap really loves his white master, loves working like a slave and obeying like a dog. They see some black men laughing and singing and they think 'Hey, these chaps must be happy with the way things are. Just look at them singing and laughing.' "

Robert laughed at the ridiculous caricature he had drawn, but his mirth did not last long. "You know, each of them will say, 'I grew up with a black man. We used to play together. We used to make clay oxen together. His mother was my nanny. We were brothers. We spoke the same language. I understand these people.' And maybe he did, back then. But somewhere along the line that bond broke and that understanding got lost, and that black boy who was that white boy's brother became an untouchable. You know the husband of that Afrikaner woman we saw a moment ago. He and I served on a committee together once, for a children's center, and after a meeting he put his arm on my shoulder and confided in me. He said to me, 'You know, Robert, you black people can't really feel love. You don't really love. Not *real* love the way we feel love.' It's like, if I pinch you, you don't really feel pain."

We had been wandering away from the house as we talked. Fundamentally opposing black and white assumptions about human decency and honorable relations clashed with nearly audible force. Suddenly, from behind the tent, we heard the real honking of car horns. Lukas and Lucy had returned! In a golden car decked with ribbons and dragging streamers in the dust, bride and groom were driven slowly past the guests who quickly lined the street, crowding in on them from both sides. They waved like royalty from behind windows open just a crack for air, rounded the corner, and were gone. Robert and I hurried back toward the house.

By the tent cars were arriving, honking playfully, and disgorging the tens of young people who had accompanied Lukas and Lucinda from her parents' home. They all remained by the tent until bride and groom returned. When Lukas and Lucinda stepped from their car people cheered along the whole length of the block. Old men and young boys, large women and small girls ran down to the tent to lead the bridal procession that was about to begin today's formal wedding.

News is for two, alone

The singing rose up from all around me.

News is for two, alone

People clapped and kicked in place.

News is for two, alone

Robert's wife had appeared beside us. She reached up to place her hand, fingers extended, on the top of her husband's head. Arms bent, shoulders bumping forward and back, he turned around and around under her touch. All around me, couples were doing the same.

When the two are in love
(*When they are in love*)

Down the center of the dusty street the bridal procession came toward us, led by two men in work clothes stepping in *mbube*'s exaggerated crouch.

Talkers are left behind

Knees bent, hips still, they stalked with the silent grace of a lion.

Talkers are left behind

The first wore what looked like a long, blue lab coat that opened with each step forward and fanned out around the leg that remained behind. The second wore the stained coverall that signifies the array of dirty jobs South Africa reserves for its black laborers.

A PLACE TO SMILE

Talkers are left behind

Arms reached up, forward, and down, hands shaking, fingers spread and stiff, palms parallel to the street.

When two are in love
(*When they are in love*)

The Western-looking bridal party followed behind these two, doused with handfuls of confetti from every direction. Lukas wore a tailored suit with a pale pink rose in his lapel; Lucinda's gown and veil were floor-length and white. Lukas's face is very dark and, like his father's, quite round. He walks with his father's dignity. Lucy's face is lighter than his, and, although she is slender, also quite round. She is very pretty, and her smile is shy, radiant, and lovely.

Appear!
And let them see the stars!

The couple's friends were young and bold and bright, walking smartly on the rocky street with a confidence that was almost cocky.

Stars, stars
Let them see the stars!

As they approached the house, a tape from inside suddenly blared pop tunes and drowned out the singing of the crowd.

I want ya, Babe

The young people's feet turned, their hips ground with the movements of pop that differed, if not in substance then certainly in subtlety, from the traditional dance movements of the procession.

Forever, Babe

The amassed singers did not yield to the tape without a struggle. They resumed their song more loudly than before, and they danced in place, refusing to turn their backs on the competition.

Stars, stars
Let them see the stars!

For some time the two musical forms battled one another,

My Baby mine
Stars, stars

and I found myself thinking back to the singing competition Gary and I had seen at a wedding on a KwaDlangezwa hillside in Zululand.

Forever, Babe
Let them see the stars!

That particular district was close enough to Empangeni and Durban that our host laughingly described its people as "westernized traditionals." Both bride's family and groom's had been practicing their songs for weeks. In the tall, wet grasses the groom's family had stood at the top of a hill, singing one song after another, their full harmony carrying down the hill and out across the green of the countryside. Then the bride and her family made their move. Handmaids holding her parasol and lifting her long, white train above the grass, the bride's party sang with a volume the groom's people could not match. The bride made her way slowly up the hill, each family singing louder and louder in an attempt to overpower the other. At one point the groom's people seemed to win, and the bride and her party retreated, in silence, to the bottom. But the bride's people were more numerous, and they were louder, and finally, after several hours, the groom and his family gave way, disappearing over the far side of the hill.

> Stars, stars
> Stars, stars

Today the young people seemed surprised that their elders were persisting, and when someone silenced the pop tape they readily joined in the traditional singing and dancing that ruled the day.

> Stars, stars
> Let them see the stars!

Now I stayed behind, watching Lukas and Lucy lead the head of the long procession out from behind the far side of the house before its tail had left the street.

Through loudspeakers an organ sounded Mendelssohn's "Wedding March," accompanied for the first few measures by earsplitting ululation up and down the block. A short ceremony was conducted in Sotho, in front of the house. A priest read from the Bible to solemnize the Christianity of this occasion. A woman ululated and declaimed, waving a hand broom high in the air—a traditional symbol of Lucinda's obligation to work at maintaining cleanliness in her new home.

IN THE CITY

God's love is wonderful every day
Hallelujah
Amen

Robert explained that in order to include essential elements from the traditions of Africa, Christianity, and South African secular law, a township wedding has many separate components. The marriage in church. The marriage before the magistrate. The celebration at the home of the bride. Finally there is the celebration at the home of the groom, welcoming the bride, the *makoti* from her own clan, into the groom's family. He added that in Sotho tradition, after the groom pays *lobola* the two families bring bride and groom together to be counseled by family members in the responsibilities, skills, and pitfalls of married life. When instruction, celebration, and family singing are completed, the bridal couple retire to quarters in the home of the groom's family, where they will live while the bride proves to her new family that she is worthy to have married their son.

Today's celebration constituted the final component of this marriage, the official welcoming of Lucinda into the Mabotho family.

She awakens
And tidies the house
While her in-laws are still asleep.

Although formal counseling and instruction are no longer practiced in township weddings, their essence is retained in the choruses that weave through modern celebrations.

You said you love him.
Now can you tolerate his demands
In marriage?

From many African tongues, choruses find their way into a common culture shared by black urbanites throughout the country.

> Now you are married.
> Will you still be loving,
> As you were in courtship?

As the first round of guests were seated in the tent, several hundred others continued to sing and dance outside.

> Behind a closed door
> Stands the table
> Where problems and faults are settled.

Friends and relatives toasted the couple with the wine we had all carried in from outside and with traditional grain beer that had been brewed for the occasion and ladled from a huge clay pot three men had struggled to carry from the house. Champagne bottles popped at each table. First people spoke to welcome Lucinda. She had chosen a kind man from a very good family. The family was lucky to have her. She was a hard worker and her ready smile was a source of joy to them all. She should not think of herself as *makoti*, from another clan; from now on she was as much a Mabotho as anyone could be.

Then people moved on to speak of Peter's late wife, Eleanor, dead of a heart attack at an hour when traveling through township streets, even to the hospital, was too dangerous to be risked. In voices both choked and joyful they recounted the warmth they had all felt for her, her love for her family, her hope that Lukas and Lucinda would one day be married. The family had visited her grave the preceding day and again that morning, to report on the wedding proceedings. She was with them in spirit all the time, but especially on this day everyone who had known her could feel her presence.

Throughout these testimonials, I could not silence the burning words Robert had been forced to accept from his Afrikaner colleague. "You black people can't really feel love. Not real love."

Peter made the last toast. He spoke of his family with pride and affection, and he reminded the assembled guests that he thought of his community—their community—with feelings that were much the same. "I want to assure you that no matter what else you may see all around you, Atteridgeville is still a place to live in. It may be a place we cry. But it's still a place to smile, a place to laugh and to smile."

It's true
It's true
I swear, Mama,
It's true!

VI

IN
PROTEST

LET FREEDOM SING

HOUSE OF PEACE

AN INJURY TO ONE IS AN INJURY TO ALL

A SONG FOR ONE IS A SONG FOR ALL

INSIDE IN PRETORIA

SENTENCED FOR SINGING

NONYAMEZELO: ENDURING WITH DIGNITY

SINGING AND SPIRIT IN SOUTH AFRICA

NKOSI SIKELEL'I AFRIKA

LET
FREEDOM SING

Although daily activities reflect a perpetually shifting balance between westernization and African tradition, a strong culture of community remains the birthright of every black South African. In urban townships, rural villages, resettlement areas, and squatter camps, the cultural conventions that underlie all proper behavior reflect a uniquely communal resolution of inevitable interpersonal tensions between cooperation and conflict, group preference and individuality, harmony and discord. It is in this context that musician and scholar Andrew Tracey describes South African singing, first and foremost, as a form of cooperation.[1] Where singing in other cultures emphasizes product, singing in South Africa emphasizes the coactive process of performing—the group relationships enacted as people call and respond, as parts enter and move around one another, as qualities of tone and physical movement vary over time.

We have seen that black urbanization in South Africa developed entirely as a consequence of white domination. For the past century formal political resistance to such domination has been primarily an urban phenomenon. As such it has been characterized by the cultural forms that evolved in the black locations as waves of new urbanites struggled to define emerging relationships with one another, with white institutions inside South Africa, and with black and white constituencies outside South Africa's borders. *Marabi. Makwaya. Mbube.* All these can serve as musical windows on the social and political realities of their singers' lives. Each represents a unique way of expressing relationships among singers, and between singers and the world outside.

In the West we recognize politics as a primary system for regulating ongoing relations within and between social groups. In South African tradition, this political approach is inextricably intertwined with the musical; both concern people's struggle to live and work together.

> **We do not care, even if we are arrested.**
> **We are prepared for freedom.**

In 1912, a cadre of mission-educated, middle-class black South Africans organized in political opposition to increasing repression. As the South African Native National Congress, parent to today's African National Congress (ANC), they adopted a "civilized," middle-class strategy of formal petitioning and eloquent protestation. Where earlier black fighters had waged bloody battles, the Congress used reason and persuasion. Where earlier black liberationists had fought over territory, the Congress fought over freedom. Patiently they protested new legislation that steadily eroded the limited rights and privileges black people had managed to retain while the English and the Afrikaners were battling each other for control of the land. The ANC did not cast their struggle in Western terms of "rulers" and "the ruled." Rather, they sought peaceful coexistence among equals. In the words of one-time ANC president and Nobel laureate Albert Luthuli, this group's goal has always been " '. . . not that Congress shall rule South Africa, but that all Africans shall fully participate in ownership and government.' "[2] For thirty years ANC tactics were moderate, their progress minimal, and their membership disappointingly small in number and elitist in character.

A second generation of black liberationists founded the ANC Youth League in 1944. Nelson Mandela. Oliver Tambo. Walter Sisulu. Under their leadership, the League moved to transcend the Congress's major weaknesses. They sought to expand the group's appeal beyond the small black middle class.

They articulated the universal black pride and confidence that have characterized the liberation movement ever since. After the Nationalists' electoral victory in 1948, the Youth League shifted the Congress from a deferential policy of petitioning to a vigorous program of civil disobedience.[3] It is the essential messages of these Youth League founders—indeed, their very voices—that continue to underlie the mainstream of black opposition, now more than forty years later.

> They are all in KwaNonqonqo prison.
> Here is Mandela—in prison.
> Here is Sisulu—in prison.[4]

From the outset, we have discussed mission Christianity as responsible for the mixed blessing of South Africa's black westernization. The tapestry of traditional life unraveled as wefts of Western religion, economics, education, and politics wove themselves imperfectly on the incompatible cultural warps of Africa and the West. We have seen how the color bar in mission church hierarchies catalyzed the formation of black separatist churches. At the same time, we must acknowledge that mission Christianity has both directly and indirectly nurtured the politics of black liberation. Until quite recently many of the blacks who became political leaders were educated in mission schools; their Western values and aspirations were part of Christian socialization. Critically, the pacifism that dominated the liberation movement's first half century was also born of Christian ideology.

Consistent political failure did not easily dissuade the movement from its calm, dignified commitment to nonviolent brotherhood. For fifty years reasoned petitions and peaceful civil disobedience were met with government-sponsored aggression and statutory repression. Still Congress liberationists turned the other Christian cheek until, in March 1960, government troops massacred unarmed, peacefully demonstrating civilians at Sharpeville.[5] Elsewhere throughout the country black demonstrations were attacked with batons, tear gas, diving aircraft, and shooting. Only after the ANC was actually banned did it relinquish its policy of nonviolence; late 1961 saw the formation of its military arm, Umkhonto We Sizwe (Spear of the Nation). And even this new group limited their violence to sabotaging property such as power pylons and other symbols of the State.

Thus liberation activism emerged in the missionized black locations, spearheaded by the educated black elite, and weaned on an ideology of Christian brotherhood. For these reasons the movement's early singing was primarily in the hybrid *makwaya* idiom. *Makwaya* was an integral part of the overall urbanization of mission blacks, superimposing Western hymnody on indigenous, unaccompanied, rhythmic part singing. As white rejection led mission blacks to a conscious effort at cultural self-definition, *makwaya* embodied their commitment to both Africa and the West, to both their people and their God. Still today, this idiom constitutes an important current in the powerful stream of protest song.[6]

Rolihlahla Mandela
Mandela says "Freedom now"
Now we say "Away with slavery,"
In our land of Africa.

Contemporary links between singing for freedom and singing for Christ are pragmatic as well as historical and ideological. Even before the State of Emergency in effect at the time of this writing, written permission was required for almost any black gathering, and South African law provided for the banning of any assembly the authorities judged likely to endanger public complacency. Church services have remained at least partially exempt from these prohibitive restrictions. Particularly after sweeping bans imposed in February 1988, on eighteen important anti-apartheid organizations, today's mission churches stand nearly alone as institutions whose legally permitted activities explicitly contradict apartheid's oppression. It is far from co-incidental that anti-apartheid rhetoric echoes from church pulpits while the authorities strain to keep political platforms empty. Thus, local black churches play a newly revitalized role in township social and political life. Wesleyan hymns give meaningful voice to the love and justice that are the ideological taproot of both Christian church and black liberation. As such, these hymns may be sung without alteration in religious and secular gatherings, alike.

God, give us strength to endure.

With only minor modifications many hymns can be made politically explicit.

God, give us strength to endure their oppression.

With the unexpected appearance of the police they can once again become generalized expressions of faith.

God, give us courage to stand firm
When we are threatened.

Industrialization at the turn of the century introduced a working-class element to hitherto largely middle-class black urban populations. Musicologist Veit Erlmann notes that these new black urbanites accepted the Western-sounding *makwaya* as an appropriate idiom for protest against living and working conditions they soon found intolerable. However their personal distance from Western education and the immediacy of their rural traditions led these workers to add rural musical forms to the repertoire of political song. Erlmann identifies traditional war songs, hunting songs, clan anthems, and work songs as frequent models for musical protest. Each of these forms heightened group solidarity and raised energy and excitement in its specific rural setting; all functioned similarly in the city. Today's freedom songs continue to draw on these diverse musical idioms. In addition, they reflect the new musical trends that emerge as freedom fighters struggle to interpret the last decades of the twentieth century, and to find their place within it.[7]

In South Africa today, even such routine activities as going to work and attending school are, for blacks, regulated by law and relentlessly monitored by armed representatives of the State. Blacks have no official input into the laws that constrain every aspect of daily life. Organized protest is marginally legal at best, and all but a small handful of leaders are dead or numbered among the thousands locked, for months or years on end, in prison.[8] Even children under the age of ten may be detained without charge or subject to unexpected bursts of gunfire. Indeed, under the State of Emergency armed authorities may use beatings and bullets to enforce their personal interpretations of the law, free from accountability to court or quarry.[9]

Songs allow people to give voice to that which may not be publicly spoken. Some of this allowance is inherent in the imagery and the symbolism that enrich all poetry. For example, an explicit threat to overthrow the government would constitute a criminal offense under South African law. In contrast, a poem or a song may suggest or seem to suggest, without making bald statements that would render their lyrics illegal and their singers imprisonable. A protest song permits black people to express both anger and pride. However, its place within African traditions of praise-poetry and self-delectation allows it to carry several additional layers of meaning that enhance both its richness and the protection it offers.

Here is a black man, Botha!
You take care! Here is a black man!
Botha, take care the black man!

Is this a plea? An exclamation of pride? A warning? An expression of self-comfort or mutual encouragement?

Take care the black man!

For urban blacks, singing in protest against oppression is just one of many threads in a tightly woven, highly variegated fabric of vocal response to the circumstances of daily life. We have seen that their musical heritage places particular emphasis on group singing. Be their conditions celebrated or excoriated, be their reactions joyful, mournful, or angry, South African blacks are likely to comment in song. And the power of their singing lies as much in its process of solidifying relationships—between people, across distance, over time—as in the manifest meaning of words. As important to a gathering as the message of any lyric is the unified community created simply through the process of becoming a chorus. Singing together lets individuals know that however small each one may be, they are all part of something that is large and strong. Singing transforms an assemblage into a community, and it ties this new community to a movement that is larger, still. Singing allows a group to voice despair, and, at the same time, it begins to relieve that despair and replace it with the will to persevere. Singing can galvanize to action; it can calm to patience and reason. Singing is both an expression of spirit and a source of that spirit's essential renewal.

The burden is heavy
But we children of Africa,
We are prepared for freedom.

HOUSE
OF PEACE

Shortly after midnight, August 31, 1988, a large bomb rocked Khotso House, the Johannesburg building housing many of the country's nonviolent, nonracial, anti-apartheid organizations. South African Council of Churches. Interchurch Media Programme. Detainee Parents Support Committee. Black Sash. United Democratic Front. And more. The government had banned some of these groups from all activities six months earlier; others had continued to function. The bomb was apparently planted in the basement, and it blew concrete right through the roof, six floors above. The heavy front doors of Khotso House flew through walls and windows of flats across the street. The whole block of DeVilliers Street was cordoned off, Khotso House condemned. Only after several days were the occupants permitted to make their way through the destruction to their offices. By then the rains had come, and materials that might have survived the explosion had been soaked by the storm.

When I was in South Africa, now-Archbishop Desmond Tutu was serving as General Secretary of the South African Council of Churches. Just after the 1988 explosion he came to revisit his old office. The street was still cordoned off, and public gatherings of any kind certainly remained illegal. Nonetheless as the archbishop entered the building, dozens of blacks assembled amidst the rubble in the street, and they danced and sang. While he remained inside, their numbers swelled to hundreds. Hands on each other's shoulders, they spiraled round and round. Every minute the spiral grew larger, their collective voice stronger. But their song did not cry in anguish or call for war.

Instead it rang with vitality, with dignity, and with determination. What had been taken from these people was priceless and irreplaceable; what the enemy had not been able to take was even more precious.

Where is the way?
The way is wherever we make it.

AN INJURY TO ONE IS AN INJURY TO ALL

For most of this century, South Africa's system of industrial relations excluded black workers, keeping their wages artificially low and "reserving" explicitly skilled, high-paying jobs for whites. As early as 1920 blacks organized into unregistered unions, but statutory obstacles and employer hostility contributed to their early decline. Legislation following a violent mine strike in 1922 provided for industrial councils formed jointly by companies and registered employees' trade unions. But black workers were excluded from the definition of "employee" and therefore from these councils and their jurisdiction. White workers were empowered to organize on behalf of their own advancement and working conditions. Because blacks were not similarly empowered, management was free to accede to the demands of white unions at the expense of nonunionized black labor.

World War II saw an enduring resurgence of extra-legal black organization. Finally, legislation in 1979 identified workers of all races as "employees," and independent black trade unions proliferated. Statutes also legislated unfair labor practices, leading to substantial union victories over management in the Industrial Court.

Through the mid-1980s South Africa's black trade unions existed in uneasy tension with apartheid laws. The unions effectively increased black people's power by winning higher wages and improved working conditions; in so doing they placed themselves in direct opposition to apartheid's unspoken policy of protecting white interests through black subordination. The State has relentlessly demonstrated its power to detain union leaders, harass members, prohibit meetings, and legislate to render specific actions illegal. In spite of such ongoing government obstruction, tremendous black industrial mobilization took place through the late 1980s.[10, 11]

Singing is as natural a part of trade unionism as of any form of urban organization. For singing requires people to cooperate with discipline and energy, producing something that, in turn, satisfies those who gave it life. Similarly, trade unionism has historically required members to work together within specific structures, uniting around issues, acting together, and producing results which are of benefit to all. David Coplan notes that within the early, unregistered labor organizations music was quite consciously used as a way to unify middle-class leaders and working-class members. Volunteer choirs performed middle-class *makwaya* and working-class *ingomabusuku*. Unionists created songs in both genres, using existing melodies and writing new lyrics in praise of particular leaders and organizations, and the union movement as a whole. Like other union activity, music gave people from different backgrounds an opportunity to work together around common interests, toward common goals. The early dominance of the *makwaya* idiom emphasized the westernized African demand for full participation in urban society, based on merit, hard work, and good-faith promises.[12]

> We children of Africa
> We are prepared for freedom!

Late 1985 saw thirty-three unions and federations, representing over 500,000 workers,[13] unite to launch the Congress of South African Trade Unions (COSATU); membership rose to an estimated 650,000–800,000 over the next twenty-four months.[14,15] After years of debate among the unions that eventually affiliated, COSATU proclaimed that workers' struggles on the shop floor could no longer be viewed as distinct from the community struggle in the black townships. Unions' demands for promotion of black workers into high-level managerial positions were inseparable from students' demands for education that would prepare them for such positions. Union efforts to secure workplace conditions conducive to self-respect could not be detached from community efforts toward similar conditions at home. The unions' policy of a democratically mandated leadership was substantively one with the black community's ever-louder call for a government democratically mandated by all members of South Africa's population. By definition, the trade unions are primarily working-class organizations. An expanding union presence in hitherto strictly "political" arenas reflects the extent to which the political struggle has, particularly in the past decade, effectively integrated its middle-class founders with their working-class countrypeople.

In the mid-1980s widening restrictions on gathering and dissenting left the black unions and churches among very few black organizations with legal permission to assemble as part of their ongoing activity. And the unions found themselves the only organizations with even a quasi-legal mandate to work for what might be called effective opposition to the white power structure. They took this privileged position as a responsibility to struggle for the rights of black workers both in the workplace and outside it. COSATU condemned apartheid and set time limits for the implementation of significant change, clearly identifying itself as a dominant force in black liberation. As the strengths and goals of the labor movement merge with those of the wider movement for liberation, labor songs merge with the freedom songs that have characterized the liberation struggle since its inception. So, too, does government action against political opposition merge with action against the unions.

> A black man is being dragged by a chain.
> A black dog.
> These dogs are being killed.
> For what?

From the moment of COSATU's founding, the unions have alleged State and State-sponsored harassment. One National Union of Mineworkers strike buckled early when telephones went out of order, simultaneously, at NUM offices throughout the country. A subsequent successful NUM strike was settled in a way that appeared to threaten the unions' very ability to strike. Black trade unions were made financially liable for company losses caused by strike actions not directly related to work issues.[16] On May 7, 1987, two bombs shattered the foundations of COSATU House in the biggest explosion Johannesburg has ever seen.[17] Foreshadowing the next year's explosion at Khotso House, equipment and records were destroyed; the building was declared unusable; the perpetrators were never found.

February 24, 1988, saw Pretoria's most sweeping crackdown on nonviolent anti-apartheid opposition since 1960's banning of the ANC and 1977's clampdown on black-consciousness organizations. COSATU was ordered to confine its activities to labor affairs. Relevance to labor and industrial relations notwithstanding, the following activities were prohibited: calling for the release of detained unionists or other individuals; calling for the restoration of unlawful organizations like the ANC; calling for election boycotts or other anti-government publicity campaigns; commemorating the incidents of public violence that mark anti-apartheid history.[18, 19] In late September 1988, the government served a last-minute ban on a COSATU-sponsored conference scheduled to forge a new alliance among remaining fragments of anti-apartheid opposition. COSATU officials called the ban " 'a recipe for disaster,' " tantamount to a government declaration " 'that there can be no peaceful solutions to South Africa's problems.' "[20, 21]

A SONG FOR ONE
IS A SONG FOR ALL

After several scheduling conflicts and changes of plans—mine and those of union leader Duma Jabulani—I was finally in town and able to accept his long-standing invitation to a meeting of his shop stewards. I arrived at the hall and was accosted by a slender young woman with hair elaborately braided and ornamented. Duma had been called away for emergency negotiations. However, my attendance at this meeting had been approved, and I was to feel welcome.

Knowing no one I sat by myself, off to one side of the large room. Arriving members glanced in my direction, acknowledging the presence of a white stranger, but no one approached me. The meeting came to order under the chairmanship of a bearded young man wearing a dark warm-up suit. From behind a small table at the front of the room he spoke softly in English and Xhosa. I struggled to follow at least his English words, but I was taken completely by surprise when everyone in the room turned toward me, smiling and singing, and began to applaud.

> **We are here. The organized workers.**
> **Workers, unite!**

He announced, "Helen, you have been introduced and we are glad to welcome you." He continued to speak, louder now, his voice rising and falling in the cadences of a preacher. And suddenly, without having broken stride, his speech had become a song, and the two hundred assembled shop stewards had become a chorus, answering him in powerful open harmony.

IN PROTEST

> **We are going!   GO!**
> **We are going   GO!**

He sang out and the chorus answered.

> **We are (*Go*) going (*Go!*)**

Call and response thundered back and forth

> **We are (*Go*) going (*Go!*)**
> **We move (*Go*) onward (*Go!*)**

until, just as suddenly as it had begun, the singing stopped.

> **No mind of fear.**

In the space of a single line the chairman was once again speaking and the rest of the membership were once again listening.

This unselfconscious interchange between singing and declaiming repeated itself all afternoon. Sometimes the singing appeared to run the course of a whole song. Sometimes it was no more than a phrase or two, offered by everyone in support of a point made by one speaker or another. Sometimes it was paired with one of the responsive chants that are another part of black South Africans' traditional repertoire of vocal expression. Sometimes the singing stood alone. Always it unified the meeting. Particularly after prolonged, potentially divisive discussion, members seemed both eager and relieved to sing together. These workers were not always in agreement about the best strategy for achieving agreed-upon goals. The day was hot; tempers were short. But long before any conflict escalated beyond the expression of different opinions, a song reminded everyone of all they held in common. Singing together united the two hundred people in that room in creating a few moments of glorious sound, and it functioned as a metaphor for the larger cooperation their work together would continue to demand.

It's been a long time working for the Boers;
Workers, let us unite!

My introduction to Duma Jabulani had been arranged by his brother Edward, whom I had met at the home of one of their friends in Soweto. Over the telephone Duma and I acknowledged having been told about one another, and we agreed to meet early one Monday morning. Edward's easy smile and his eagerness to talk about issues confronting the unions had led me to expect a similar gregariousness in his brother. Instead I found Duma to be solemn, with little time for pleasantries. A muscular, bearded man, he greeted me with an expansive yawn and explained that he had spent all night driving back from a meeting of the leadership in the Northern Transvaal. He would normally have spent the morning sleeping off his exhaustion. But his brother had been quite intrigued with my notion that singing makes a valuable contribution to trade unionism, and he was eager to talk with "the little white American with the big respect for black singing."

He began without preamble. "I am taken with what you have told my brother, that you have seen music as a contributing factor to human life. You are right, you know. But this singing is something that we take for granted, and perhaps we do not appreciate it to its fullest."

He paused. I did not interrupt, and after a moment he continued. "You are also right that this singing is something we don't have to pay for. It is something that is free, but something that means so much. For instance, yesterday we were coming from the North, many of us driving in the car on a gravel road. It's a very shaky ride on that road, and you are not sure to avoid a puncture. And as soon as we got up to the tarred road that means you are approaching a major city, one chap just started a song. We did not know this song, but we were harmonizing to give us strength for our long journey and to give gratitude to God and to one another. That is what our singing is, you know."

As workers we have come to a better surface.
Uncertain of our car, we have traveled on dirt and gravel.
Our workers wait for us at home.
The workers in the North rely on us
To carry their message.
In unity our union has survived the test.

On one level this improvised song was one of hundreds that must ring out each day as black people sing, spontaneously, about whatever is on their minds. Mothers sing about mothering their young; trade unionists on the road sing about traveling and trade unionism. On another level this song was a thinly disguised ode to the progress of the unions and the overall black struggle. As such it was, at the time, a legally acceptable proclamation of a sentiment that was itself barely within the law.

For all that it is arguably illegal to organize and protest in cooperation with respected opposition leaders, for all that certain songs may be forbidden, even in South Africa it is not yet altogether illegal to sing. We have seen that singing is a masterfully developed, indigenous mode of expression. And, at least in part, singing has enabled the people of the black community to draw a measure of strength from the very oppression they are fighting. Observers generally agree that through years of slow, steady progress, black unionism has taken advantage of the tiny, winking loopholes of opportunity that South African law has left open for black advancement. And singing has always contributed to the spirit and the undauntable resolve of the union movement.

> You, Boers, have undertaken the impossible.
> You will persist until your strength fails
> And then you will surrender

Singing enhances the movement's unity in various ways. Although it is certainly true that songs are written for one union, one shop, or one strike, the movement as a whole has developed a body of songs that are sung throughout the country. For workers who may speak different languages, live in different regions, and endure different conditions in different industries, these songs represent a common reserve that is important in helping diverse people transcend their differences.

At regional and national gatherings, strangers who see one another singing the same songs are, in a moment, no longer the same strangers. At mass rallies, singing together transforms thousands of individuals into a cohesive group that demonstrates an ongoing capacity to cooperate in the creation of something beautiful and strong. Even at the local level, singing together can function to remind workers in a single shop or a single organization that people can work together regardless of their differences, contributing personal skills and talents to produce something that is valuable for them all.

Singing also serves trade unionists as a source of inner strength, of morale. As Duma suggested, singing together allows workers to boost their own spirits, to cheer one another on in the face of danger and discouragement. It also allows them to offer praise and gratitude to their leaders and to the union as a whole, for giving substance to otherwise vague aspirations. Especially with today's restrictions, singing helps to remind unionists, each and all, that while they are persevering as individuals and as family units, they must also depend on one another. Across superficial divisions, they must be responsible for one another as one national family. Only united can they win the freedom that will be their prize.

It is alleged that in attempting to discredit and fragment the unions, employers practice illegal intimidation, harassment, and dismissal of unionists. It is also alleged that the police assist in intimidation and harassment. And of course union leaders have been detained by the government, and, like Dr. Neil Aggett, have died in detention. Particularly under these harsh circumstances it is crucial that the unions preserve internal solidarity. It is essential that they maintain high morale among members while leaders are detained, high morale among unemployed workers while strikes are in progress and while legal action against unfair dismissal is pending.

A 1982 incident illustrates the extent to which singing can support just such spirit and solidarity. The Metal and Allied Workers' Union (MAWU) had organized employees of the B&S Steelbrite Furniture Company in the Transvaal city of Brits. Newly elected representatives approached management about negotiating such issues as safety gloves and masks, and sick leave. Management's response was to dismiss the chairman of the shop stewards and, when the others questioned his dismissal, to fire the entire labor force.

The dismissed union members spent a full year out of work, trying to take B&S to the Industrial Court on grounds of unfair dismissal. The local Roman Catholic church donated the use of its hall, and the workers met there every day for that year.

Don't be afraid

They sang. They chanted. They sang. They discussed their case. They sang.

Don't be afraid

They received no unemployment compensation. They had no income. They were harassed by the security police—arrested for putative pass violations and taken for interrogation.

Don't be afraid

Living on the edge of poverty when they had been employed, they shared resources and supplies throughout that year of amplified scarcity. They borrowed from friends and families. They sold their belongings. They defaulted on rents. They could pay no school fees; their children were forced to leave school.

Don't be afraid
Workers

But every day they came together. They encouraged one another and they heartened themselves. Always they sang.

Workers
The day we were talking about is here

They did not allow one another to drift off into despair. The group did not dissolve in undisciplined depression. They met in the church with the same regularity that had governed attendance at work. They stayed together, convincing one another, day after day, that justice would be done in the end and the court would find in their favor.

Sociologist Georgina Jaffee has documented this extraordinary incident on film and she told me, "I'm convinced that singing played an incredible part in that struggle. They made up songs for that particular struggle, and they also called on songs that were familiar within the trade union movement as a whole. There was so much singing, it rang through the church walls."

> We are going
> We are going
> We are going
> Even if it's terrible

They sang about their own struggle, and they sang about unionization throughout the country. They sang to master their own immediate challenges, and they sang to assert membership in the community of black workers, at large. They sang to remain unified, and they sang to retain spirit. And after a year, just before the case was to come to court, B&S settled with the union and the workers were all reinstated with back pay.

> We are going
> We are going
> We are going
> To freedom!

The authorities are far from oblivious to the power of union singing. Unionists acknowledge that companies regularly employ informers, *impimpis*, to attend meetings and report on the proceedings, including the songs sung. In the written records of an interdict filed by the Goldfields Mining Group against NUM in early 1984, one *impimpi* documents what he claims is a union leader's incitement to violence through song. "I attended a meeting for the National Union of Mineworkers at the Number Two compound. The meeting was . . . opened by Medulla [the organizer] leading the crowd with the warrior song, 'It's a long time that we've been working for the Dutch people for nothing. We are now tired; we are now tired.' "[22] Singing is clearly regarded as an important enough activity that in an affidavit sworn before the court, with the explicit purpose of discrediting the union, the company's undercover representative saw fit to quote the lyrics of a song as evidence of incitement to violence.

A SONG FOR ONE IS A SONG FOR ALL

**It's been a long time working for the Boers
Workers, let us unite!**

Duma Jabulani had been detained in the government's 1981 sweep of union leaders and anti-apartheid activists. I knew that his ten months in isolation had been painful; he had alluded to unhealed psychological wounds. From his discussion of the close ties between workplace and community, I also gathered that his everyday activities flirted with the illegal, and that the extent of his success in trade unionism paralleled the extent to which Pretoria saw him as a threat. I could not keep from asking how, despite his own past experience, he continued to court detention.

His face and voice were grave. "I have better things to think of than detention." His answer moved quickly from the personal to the collective. "It isn't on our minds. Not one bit. Otherwise it's going to scare us away from our work." He assumed a rather tense bravado as he continued. "So you don't bother thinking about 'are we going to be detained?' I mean, you are not breaking any law by organizing workers into the union, and by negotiating for the workers' rights."

I pushed a bit harder, in that pre-Emergency era when laws at least appeared to restrain the State. "But with all of the laws against engendering dissatisfaction with the government or embarrassing any group in power, are you really not breaking any laws? Couldn't they call some of what you are doing or saying illegal?"

Duma laughed a big laugh, his muscular chest straining his union T-shirt and his smile showing the space, halfway back on the right, where two teeth were missing. His answer was both gentle and determined. "My dear, in South Africa it is illegal for a black person to do anything other than breathe, and *that* only under certain circumstances. So the law gives me two choices. I can breathe when the law says I may do so, and hold my breath until I die. Or I can join the struggle for the rights of the workers who make the whites in this country such very rich people. The choice is really very simple."

> We don't care
> Even if we get arrested.
> We children of Africa
> We are prepared for freedom.

I had made clear to the shop stewards that I would have to leave their meeting at a certain hour. Had Duma been present I would have relied on him to advise my exit. But I was on my own, and when the time came and the meeting showed no sign of drawing to a close, I tried to slip out unobtrusively. The chairman stopped me with a characteristic demonstration of graciousness and community pride. "Helen, I know you must leave us now, but if you are interested in our singing we cannot let you go before we sing our national anthem. Comrades! 'Nkosi Sikelel'i!' "

Everyone rose. From somewhere in the room a woman's voice sounded the first line alone, before the powerful chorus took over.

> Nkosi sikelel'i Afrika.
>
> God bless Africa.

Fists were raised on bent arms. Faces were solemn.

> Rise up spirit!
> Arise! Arise! Arise!
> Rise up spirit!
> Arise! Arise! Arise!
> Rise up, spirit of the people.
> God bless our people.

A SONG FOR ONE IS A SONG FOR ALL

The song became a chant.

Power!	IS OURS!
Power!	IS OURS!

I started to thank the group for their hospitality, but the chairman's voice overpowered mine. "Comrades, that was very good for warming up but you know we can sing better than that. Let's do it once again!"

INSIDE
IN PRETORIA

It takes less than an hour to drive from Johannesburg, South Africa's commercial center, to Pretoria, the administrative capital. From downtown Johannesburg, the M-1 heads north through the city. It passes affluent white communities with meticulously manicured grounds and homes that range from comfortable to spacious, and from spacious to palatial. Finally the road leaves city and suburbs behind, becoming the Ben Schoeman Highway across the high, Witwatersrand plateau.

Just before reaching Pretoria, the Ben Schoeman Highway and Old Pretoria Road merge at the Voortrekker Monument, Afrikanerdom's testament to its own glory. In a land of symbols subtle and overt, this sentimental monument extols three themes of Afrikaner freedom: Independence from British rule; Domination over indigenous black peoples; Devotion to the land and the God whose divine will the "volk" claim to enact. Roughly a mile farther north Pretoria Central Prison abuts the road on the left, standing in concrete testimony to the role of incarceration in ensuring the administration of Afrikaner dominion. Inside this massive compound is the notorious "maximum jail," where Pretoria locks the nation's white male political prisoners. Here, too, are death row, where the black condemned wait, and the gallows, where they receive their country's final justice.

South Africa's black condemned do not confront the end in silence. As blacks sing together throughout life, affirming community, humanity, and richness of spirit that apartheid cannot strangle, so they sing together at the very last. When ANC supporter Benjamin Moloise was hanged in October 1985, for a murder he insisted he did not commit, his mother told reporters that her son would go to his death singing a hymn of praise. However metaphorical her words might have sounded to the international community, South Africans recognized them as literal. For singing—a great deal of singing of all kinds— is widely recognized as a common feature of black prison life, particularly in anticipation of an execution. When Wellington Mielies and Moses Jantjies were hanged in September 1987, for murders committed as part of the violence that had been sweeping black townships for at least three years, newswires noted black prisoners' practice of singing through the night to give the condemned men courage.[23] For all prisoners this singing becomes an indelible part of the experience "inside" that remains with them after they have been released.

Anti-apartheid poet Jeremy Cronin was jailed for seven years under the Terrorism Act; his wife died unexpectedly during his sentence. Eighteen months after being released his face was gentle, his manner calm, his voice surprisingly without rancor. He told me about apartheid in prison and about the voices that transcended the apartness. "There was a small group of white political prisoners held pretty much in racial segregation. The prison is constructed with thick stone walls, so you can't see the other sections, but you can hear. We'd be seventeen hours in single cells each day, and then seven hours of being together as a small community, in our case six, seven, eight people. During the day there's a lot of noise, and we would be involved in activities like cleaning, or in a workshop, or eating together, so we wouldn't hear the noise from the black sections. And also during the day there are two shifts of warders on simultaneously."

But night's dark silence lets white prisoners hear the voices of their black brothers through walls of concrete and stone. "At night there is only one shift of warders so the surveillance is less strict. At night things also quieten down a bit, and then you can actually hear the other sections. There's something like two hundred people on death row at any one time, and in the evenings there's a tremendous amount of singing. Very mournful hymn and chorale-type singing and call-and-response-type singing. The singing one gets in African churches. But obviously with a rather sad feel to it."

The Lord is my shepherd
I shall not want

Those who were going to be hanged would hear three days beforehand of their imminent execution. "They tend to hang two, three, or four people simultaneously. As many as seven. They would get messages saying, 'You, Prisoner so and so, are due to be hanged at seven o'clock sharp on such and such a morning.' Signed, 'Greetings, the Sheriff of Pretoria.' And then the singing would really start up. Pretty much all two hundred sitting on death row would begin to sing, and it would go three days, three nights, virtually nonstop."

He makes me lie down in green pastures
He restores my soul

Two hundred men would seek to comfort their condemned brothers. To come to terms with the fate that might overtake any one of them at any moment. To *do* something more than sit. To assert themselves as black men who, despite apartheid, believe in God, in justice, and in Africa. "Right through that long vigil they would sing up to the actual hanging."

Though I walk through the valley of the shadow of Death
I will not fear evil

My Lord is with me

The jail is shaped so that a black prisoner must walk down a long corridor and around to the back in order to reach the gallows. "It's a very, very eerie thing. You can't see the prisoner walking to his execution, but you hear him as he walks by.

My Lord's rod and staff will comfort me
Surely His mercy will follow me all the days of my life
And I will dwell in the house of my Lord

"On the appointed morning, just before seven o'clock, we would hear some detached voices break away from the large group and come down the passage which adjoined our section. The gallows were right opposite where we were being held, so we would hear two, three, four voices coming down the passage, singing in a much more constricted fashion now, but still trying to sing. And then we'd hear the gallows dropping. *Duf. Duf. Duf.* And the singing would have stopped."

Forever.

To Jeremy Cronin, these vigils for the doomed told a heartening story of solace, faith, and brotherhood in the face of the most essential of all aloneness. For other whites the mournful hymns continue, years later, to toll eternal damnation. Attorney Ernest Wentzel, dead of cancer in 1986, was one of these others.

The unique tensions and pressures of contemporary South Africa bring forth the worst and best in the country's people. From those who embrace the self-serving view of any single group, the society elicits bigotry and hatred at rare levels of virulence. But there are, in the same country, those who rejoice in its diversity and who struggle with every day of their lives to demonstrate human decency and achieve true justice. In a land where the smallest personal behaviors are the subject of national statute there are people of all races who refuse to become inured to the immorality of daily life. Cognizant of the society's complexities and of the enormous difficulty of making meaningful progress, these people reject narrow political ideologies. Instead, they devote their life's efforts to nonracial justice and universal morality. Inevitably these heroic few demonstrate humanity and integrity as extraordinary as the bigotry about which we hear so much more.

Ernie Wentzel was one of the heroes. A commercial lawyer by trade, he also served in the cadre of eminent attorneys who defend political cases against the State. In 1977 he worked as a barrister for the Biko family, in the much publicized inquest into Steve Biko's death in detention. Also in the late 1970s he successfully defended already jailed poet Breyten Breytenbach on capital charges of treason. Possessed of sharp tongue and sharper wit, Ernie exercised an exceptional capacity for mirth; Breytenbach writes affectionately of his attorney's Sisyphean willingness to mount impossible defenses and, for just a moment, reduce the mountain to so much rubble with his gleeful, gurgling giggle.[24] I never saw Ernie Wentzel in court. Rather, I knew him at home with his wife, relaxing outside over tea and biscuits and laughing with helpless anger at the mess to which their exuberant, muddy puppy was reducing all our clothing. Ernie saw no easy solution to South Africa's problems, but he was unwaveringly committed to trying. He dismissed dogma on the right and left, fought daunting odds with his principles as means and end, and remained, somehow, optimistic.

In South Africa people like Ernie Wentzel are imprisoned without charge, while outside, the government tolerates the murders of anti-apartheid activists and authorizes soldiers to shoot black children in the streets. Ernie was detained twice in the 1960s—once during the Emergency declared immediately after the Sharpeville massacre, and again after the passage of new security detention legislation. Both times he was held in solitary confinement, just a few walls away from death row. Both times the singing of the doomed chilled his very soul.

"It's an awful experience in the jail for the condemned, especially for prisoners who are not condemned. As a condemned man you're coming to terms. But every person in that jail, condemned or not, is affected by the fact that it is an abattoir. It's the quality of being at a funeral parlor, and the only difference is that you're in a funeral parlor where the dead have not yet been declared dead. They're waiting for the privilege of being so. And then the fact of the singing simply raises that onto a very high emotional pitch. It's amazing that people can respond with such self-possession, even to the knowledge of execution coming."

> Until I hide in the wound of Jesus
> In that blood

Prisoners with finite sentences and uncharged detainees recognize the likelihood of new trials and sentences, the danger of fatal "accidents," and the possibility of unpremeditated death at the hands of torturing interrogators. Still, for them time inside is primarily a challenge to affirm life in the bosom of unnatural death. They struggle to maintain sanity in a place where the most basic of physical and emotional needs are violated. In this battle for survival, death remains an enemy to be kept at bay.

Hymn singing for the condemned battled Wentzel's private hold on sanity and life. "The singing is quite deathly, and a lot of people can't sleep at night or have devastating nightmares because of it."

> Let me be purified
> For I have nothing.

Singing is also part of the feverish violence that rages in cells where too many people are held for too long in too little space. "In the very old jails, the ones going back seventy or eighty years, you tend to have twenty or thirty men in one cell. And in a place like that you have a great deal of singing, and a *great* deal of violence. Homosexuality and violence, and then what often goes with violence is a maudlin singing of hymns."

> **I am naked, Lord,**
> **Before Your cross**

Some attribute the maudlin hymns to a sentimentality inherent in this particular form of group violence, as if raping or stabbing a cellmate somehow confronts prisoners with their terrifying inhumanity, and they find themselves suddenly impelled to do exaggerated penance. In America, group cells echo with the din of individual radios and tape recorders. In South Africa, rather than expiate inhumanity with silent prayer or electronic cacophony, prisoners try to drown their internal demons in communal song.

Breyten Breytenbach glimpsed a still darker, more chilling underside to the singing that accompanies violence among warehoused prisoners. In his *True Confessions of an Albino Terrorist* he describes a van transporting a load of men from one jail to another, with songs both mawkish and militant echoing from inside.

> **The cross**
> **Of the crucifixion**

When the van arrived at its destination and its doors were unlocked, the just-severed head of an accused informer was rolled out to greet the authorities.[25]

> **Impimpi!**
> **Hayiiiiiiiii!**

Ex-prisoners do not dwell only on the mournful singing their fellows used to reconcile themselves with eternity, not only on the choruses used to mask or absolve hideous violence. In addition, when political prisoners leave behind the grim walls of confinement, the voices they carry with them sing of freedom.

Inside, freedom songs serve to invoke solidarity in a place where breaking the human spirit has been refined to a science. Outside, recalling prison's anthems of liberation rekindles the flame for whose fanning these men were jailed in the first place. For Jeremy Cronin these freedom songs inspired faith, and he describes how, even among the condemned, they came to take over the prison.

"We had been inside for nearly three years, and even though we were among the few privileged prisoners who knew that more than likely we would be going out the front door on our two feet—maybe after a long, long time but on our feet out the front, rather than in a wooden box out the back—still we felt very sorry for ourselves. We had heard a hanging in the morning. That night we heard some voices from quite far away, singing what was clearly not a mournful kind of singing.

Mayibuye i' Afrika!

Africa will be returned to us!

"In the next nights more and more voices took up the song. They were singing freedom songs now, and shouting freedom slogans.

Oliver!   Tambo!
Oliver!   Tambo!

"And after about a fortnight the numbers singing those songs, and shouting those call-and-response slogans, as opposed to the mournful hymns, had risen to virtually the full complement of the people on death row."

Amandla!   Ngawethu!

Amandla!   Ngawethu!

Amandla!   Ngawethu! Ngawethu! Ngawethu!

What had happened was that three young ANC guerrillas had arrived on death row. Far from being dispirited, they had begun to sing freedom songs, to unify and raise consciousness in all the other prisoners around them. "It was as if they were telling the others, 'Look, we are all victims of apartheid. Even if you are a murderer or a rapist, we are all part of a larger struggle. Although we few may die, the cause we're struggling for and the reasons *why* we ended up in this place have to do with the system. The cause we're struggling for will live on.'"

You, Benjamin Moloise, have strength.

You, Wellington Mielies, have courage.

You, Moses Jantjies, be calm.

There were always a few who used common songs to sow the seeds of encouragement among them all. And when it was the turn of these few to need heartening, their seeds had blossomed and borne fruit.

You, my brothers,

Have strength

Have courage

Be calm.

"We never saw those black political prisoners. And often they would be separated one from the other, and they would be moved around to keep them disoriented and to prevent them from organizing. But they would shout in the evenings, and sing to each other. Back and forth. It is very difficult to shout messages unless you are quite close to each other. Singing carries more easily." Even when its words are lost in stone walls and iron bars.

For Cronin, the songs echoing inside also occasioned an expression of the comradeship that had, all along, been the essence of his struggle. "After something like four months these ANC chaps were suddenly moved down to our section. And now that they were close, it was possible for us to shout and to sing back and forth. Soon another three joined them. Particularly on commemoration days, like the June 16 anniversary of the Soweto uprising, we would have special programs which we would sing and chant back and forth.

We shall forever remember Oliver Tambo!
Long live Oliver Tambo!

"They would also sing to Denis Goldberg, who was sentenced in the early 1960s. It was very nice that they knew of him, because he was the major symbolic white political prisoner still inside.

We shall forever remember Denis Goldberg!
Long live Denis Goldberg!

"Of course we whities—Our singing wasn't exactly very great, but we tried what we could. We knew the national anthem, 'Nkosi Sikelel'i Afrika.' You see, there were two generations in the white complement. There were people like Denis, who'd come through that period of mass political mobilization of the 1950s; they knew the African freedom songs, but they'd gone a bit rusty. And then there was the younger generation. Our period of political activism was basically between 1964 and

1976, when the mass, nonracial movements had more or less been wiped out. During our period the kinds of meetings you see again today just didn't happen, so it was only inside that we got to learn some more of their songs. Mostly we found ourselves singing 'We Shall Overcome,' and other North American protest songs, which I knew rather better than the African songs."

We shall overcome
We shall overcome

Even the thickest walls could not enforce apartness between these men who had declared themselves, together, the children of Africa.

We shall overcome someday

"A very classical version of 'We Shall Overcome' came back to us several months later. They'd obviously been practicing it, and they sang it back to us. I mention this because when three of those guerrillas were finally hanged—on the eve of their execution their lawyers got to see them. They sent us a message which said, 'We are going to die, but we shall overcome.' "

Deep in my heart
I do believe
We shall overcome someday.

Pretoria Central. The Voortrekker Monument. Strains of freedom and its opposite mark the entrance to Pretoria.

SENTENCED
FOR SINGING

In the fall of 1984 the authorities began to raid videotape archives at services for international news and national media. All of these agencies had covered such anti-apartheid events as the 1983 launch of the United Democratic Front and the 1982 funeral of labor leader Dr. Neil Aggett, after his death in detention. Sometimes confiscated materials would be returned unharmed. Other times, tapes would be magnetically erased before being returned, or they would not be returned at all.

At first these raids were interpreted simply as harassment of agencies that made black opposition real with their documentation. If visual images of anti-apartheid opposition were destroyed, so the interpretation went, perhaps the opposition itself could more easily be ignored. At least agencies that were raided would think twice before spending the money to record opposition events in the future. Agency personnel suffered repeated government-sponsored violations of property and mission. They lived with day-to-day unpredictability, and they struggled to sustain professional purpose and efficacy. Nonetheless, these people were unfailingly gracious to me. Agencies with intact archives simply allowed me to come in and view their materials at leisure; several made staff available to identify participants, translate speeches, and explain context for me. Some offices had defended against anticipated raids by storing their tapes, in ones and twos, in places throughout the city; with a few days' notice their materials were assembled for me. Agencies that had survived raids were perhaps the most generous of all. All encouraged me to dub whatever sound tracks I wanted, perhaps at some level aware that in time my dubs might be all that remained of their efforts.

Soon it was suggested that the authorities were attempting to use raided tapes as a basis for bringing legal charges that anti-apartheid activists were advocating the causes of banned organizations. Publicly leading a song in praise of Oliver Tambo or Nelson Mandela, for example, could be presented as evidence for support of the outlawed ANC—perhaps as evidence for the capital crime of high treason.

> **Rolihlahla Mandela**
> **Mandela says, "Freedom now!"**
> **Now we say away with slavery**
> **In our land of Africa**

Using singing as evidence of links to banned organizations is not new to the South African government, although the widespread use of high-quality, portable video equipment has certainly added sophistication to these efforts. Ernie Wentzel described one such attempt in less-high-tech times. "When people are on their way to trial in police transport, you get a great deal of singing. The policemen who run the transport will often comment on how beautifully the men are singing, although it absolutely drives the senior authorities crackers."

Ernie began to chuckle. "Once I saw the attorney general of Natal—he's the head prosecutor for the province—running with a portable tape recorder and microphone behind a big truck, where the chaps inside were charged with treason and were singing away. The truck was picking up speed and he was running behind, faster, faster, faster, his arm stuck way out in front of him, in order to record this, to try and use it in evidence, as proof of their membership in the ANC."

Ernie's chuckling had become irrepressible laughter by the end of the account. His belly shook and he wiped his eyes. I, too, might have found the image delightful, if it hadn't violated something so precious. But Ernie relished humor wherever he found it. He did not dwell on this story before moving on to another. "You know, you just reminded me of a different case where, in a crazy sort of way, one could almost say that the man who was sentenced to death got sentenced for singing."

Amandla!   Ngawethu! Ngawethu! Ngawethu!

As in all black community life, singing is an expectable component of black political trials in South Africa. Outside the courthouse people assemble and sing to encourage those on trial within. They sing to affirm their own unity with the defendants. And they sing to demonstrate at least passive mastery of a legal process over which they can exert no active control. Inside the courtroom, as well, singing is an expectable part of the proceedings. While waiting for the trial to begin, supporters of the accused sing in solidarity with the struggle for liberation—until the judge enters and quiets the court.

In this particular case eleven prisoners were charged with a number of acts of violence, as members of the ANC. A large security dock had been constructed in the court, to accommodate all eleven accused. The men would walk up into the dock with the clenched-fist black power salute, and they would be singing.

This load is heavy

Prisoner number eleven would enter first,

It needs men

followed by numbers ten, nine, and so on, down through number one.

IN PROTEST

We don't care even if we get arrested

"So the first man that the judge saw every morning and every tea and every afternoon and every adjournment was the eleventh accused. And the eleventh accused, therefore, had the appearance of being the leader of the singing. How the judge hated that singing!"

We are ready for freedom

South African trials do not involve juries. It is the judge who determines guilt and innocence. This trial was particularly confrontational, and tension mounted week after week after week.

Freedom
We don't have freedom

"Talking only somewhat metaphorically, I think that the tension built around the eleventh accused in the mind of that Court because his image was the most prominent, by reasons of the singing."

We children of Africa

Alone among these prisoners, the eleventh accused was sentenced to death.

We are prepared for freedom.

Anti-apartheid activists suggest that the authorities are not really concerned with banning this song or that. They are not really angered at these particular lyrics or those. What enrages them—and I think it frightens them as well—is the unquenchable spirit that all freedom singing conveys. When they hear the singing, the authorities are forced to recognize that far from being broken or dominated into docility, the spirit of South Africa's black majority is vibrant and pulsing and driving relentlessly toward freedom.

Amandla! NGAWETHU!

Ilizwe! AWETHU!

INKULULEKO!

NONYAMEZELO: ENDURING WITH DIGNITY

The desk of Durban attorney Victoria Nonyamezelo Mxenge was buried in papers. Telephones rang and inter-office buzzers sounded incessantly. Clerks hurried in and out of her office, removing books and folders from well-ordered shelves, and replacing them in disheveled piles wherever there was space. Mountainously silhouetted against a window onto the early-afternoon glare, Victoria herself seemed to confirm the white stereotype of black South African women as large, sluggish, and hopelessly weary.

She dispelled derogatory racial stereotypes as soon as she moved out of silhouette. An imposing woman of forty-three, she wore the tailored suit and simple jewelry that are a female attorney's accustomed uniform. She answered questions in a voice both confident and direct. Effortlessly she located letters and files in the office's apparent chaos. She spoke with respect to colleagues, clients, and employees alike. There was an unassailable air of dignity about her.

She was involved in representing sixteen members of the UDF (United Democratic Front) who were about to stand trial for treason. I had heard this organization variously described as "reasonable and optimistic," as "heir to ANC and Black Consciousness struggles," and as "radical," "communist-inclined," and "anti-American." People who praised the UDF's principles wondered how long Pretoria would allow it to exist; critics decried the government's tolerance. I had met several UDF figures, but always under hurried, public circumstances conducive to posturing and rhetoric. I was eager to learn more about this group that people I respected were calling South Africa's best—and perhaps last—hope for a just, nonracial democracy. What did the Front really stand for? What kinds of people were its members? When a mutual friend suggested that UDF personage Victoria Mxenge and I might enjoy one another, I phoned her immediately.

Although she was pressed for time, Victoria seemed almost relieved to put papers aside for our meeting. She stared at me with a calm, somewhat amused challenge, prolonging the initial silence in which we took each other's measure. And then, before I could ask anything in particular, she began to talk about her life as a black woman in South Africa. Her words revealed a woman's traditional concern for those who need help, her openness a woman's capacity for warmth and humor in a context of intuitively assessed woman-to-woman trust. Victoria was a lawyer, a mother, a widow, an aunt, a friend. Perhaps more than any of these, she was a caring, conscientious member of the black community, devoted to improving the present and securing the future of her people.

As she spoke her voice rose in pitch, reaching its peak as she made each point she insisted I understand. "What is your life, if you are black in this country? You must live in a black area that is far from the white city where your job is. It is not easy to find housing in that black area so you must rent whatever little place you can find. And you must pay whatever they are charging. They do not ask if you can afford a rent increase. They just increase the rent and you are not supposed to object. If you cannot pay, then you are thrown out of even that miserable little place. Every day you must ride the bus into the city. It is a long and crowded ride, but the city is where the work is. And when they increase the bus fare you must pay the increase. You have no other way to get to work. You are not allowed to object. You are not even allowed to organize to boycott the buses. And when they raise the price of bread you are not allowed to stand with a placard that says you can no longer afford to feed your children."

"Well, how *are* you supposed to object?"

"But, of course, you are not *supposed* to object at all! You are not *allowed* to protest."

In black South Africa you are not allowed to voice objection to conditions that cripple and kill your life, even when those conditions are the product of laws into whose formulation you have been permitted absolutely no input. Families are broken, children are starved, minds are stunted, and it is illegal for blacks to demonstrate anything except docility. This, in a country whose government our own persistently recognizes as a democracy. This from a people who firmly believe God Almighty chose them to share His covenant. This in a land that is proud to call itself a Christian theocracy.[26]

In this constricted environment, singing continues to function as a quasi-legal way to voice anger and frustration. It may be illegal to carry placards in opposition to unaffordable rent hikes.

> **There shall be houses and security for all.**
> **Forward we march.**

It may be illegal to protest rises in the cost of the bread that may be all a family can afford to eat.

> **There shall be food and comfort for all.**
> **Forward we march.**

But it is not quite illegal to *sing* about casting off these burdens.

Forward we march
To the government of the people.

In discussing the UDF and her hopes for the future of South Africa, Victoria echoed Duma Jabulani's assertion that even when mass protest is illegal, people organize and protest, nonetheless. Raised—white, American, middle class—to believe that laws are for the good of society as a whole, and that breaking the law is to be avoided as a matter of principle, I continually found myself brought up short in South Africa. Laws are passed by the white minority for their own good, and theirs alone. Particularly to the black, "Colored," and Asian opposition, breaking these laws in the struggle for freedom seems to be almost a matter of course. Breaking oppressive laws is to be avoided, if at all, in order to escape authorized punishment as harsh as indefinite detention in solitary confinement, and unauthorized punishment that may be even worse. I found myself playing with the phrases Victoria used to describe the circumstances faced by many of her clients. Legal but inhuman. Illegal but human. Humane, though illegal. This was black life in South Africa.

"Of course there is the question of what is the solution. It's a difficult question because people have been forming themselves into anti-apartheid groups and trying to bring about peaceful change, and since 1912 they have been ignored or destroyed. But still today we are trying for peaceful change. Obviously the whole political constitution must be changed; there is no way in which you can modify apartheid. It's only in this country and nowhere else in the world that people are discriminated *in law* because of the color of their skin."

Momentary desperation threatened. "It's a terrible situation! And why? Why must it be impossible for us to share this country together?"

With characteristic mastery, Victoria quickly bypassed

personal despair by turning to conditions more sweeping than her own. "But where to start? Politics in South Africa is not like politics anywhere else. Political activity organized in opposition to apartheid is an indictable offense. You can be indicted for treason." Treason is punishable by death.

She continued. "You know, there are very few political organizations which are not banned. At the present moment we have an umbrella organization called the United Democratic Front. It was formed to oppose the new constitution, mostly by people who were not even permitted to vote on it."

She explained that the country's new constitution had been approved in 1983 by 66 percent of the white voters, the only racial group eligible to vote on the matter. It added to the existing, and still dominant, white Parliament a "Colored" house and an Asian/Indian house, each having limited authority over the internal affairs of its own racial group. It left the country's black people, twenty-eight million as this book goes to press, constitutionally excluded from any national government role. The UDF coalesced in nonracial opposition to the new constitution; it also opposed other new legislation that further entrenched apartheid, politically divided Indian, "Colored," and black constituencies, and definitively disenfranchised the country's black majority.

The UDF has never been a party with card-carrying members or a formal lobby with a detailed national program of action. Rather, Victoria described it as a kind of umbrella under which hundreds of local, grass-roots organizations around the country have united in calling for a just, non-racial South Africa. Civic associations work for community improvements. Residents' associations oppose oppressive rent increases and peremptory administrative relocation of black townships into the bantustans. Student groups demand input into their own education. Each local grievance is part of apartheid's overall injustice; all that these local organizations share is a fundamental commitment to universal justice and self-determination.

Since the 1986 imposition of a long-term, national State of Emergency, most of the UDF's national and local leaders have found themselves on trial, in detention, or in hiding. On February 24, 1988, the organization itself, along with sixteen other nonviolent anti-apartheid groups, was prohibited from "carrying on or performing any activities or acts whatsoever."[27]

As it united people from all colors, classes, and regions in dignity around a common goal, the UDF was inherently threatening to a State that imposes apartness, contempt, and fragmentation. The Nationalist government controls the country by means of a visible structure of laws and personnel, and a less-visible network of militaristic-sounding secret societies, informers, and violent intimidations. Together these controls reach, like a fast-growing mold, throughout the society's organic substrate.[28, 29] From the outset such a government must have feared the UDF's ability to engage community members without benefit of title or ritual, without offering anything more—or less—than a commitment to empowering people to work together to solve their own problems. Even more, the authorities must have feared the Front's ability to inspire people of different races, backgrounds, and circumstances, around the entire country, to make common cause and understand that the process of just, nonracial democracy was the solution for them all.

The government had battled the UDF from the very first. As early as 1984, national leaders were detained without charge or imprisoned for long stretches before coming to trial; either way, they were removed from the community for months or even years at a stretch. Offices and family homes have been raided and vandalized. Local leaders and their families have been objects of constant police surveillance. Even suspected sympathizers have been held in detention. And, as illustrated by the never-solved June 1985 murders of Eastern Cape organizers Matthew Goniwe, Fort Calata, Sparrow Mkhonto, and Sicelo Mhlawuli, particularly effective grass-roots leaders are, in Victoria Mxenge's words, "simply done away with."

Her voice after the deaths of these four close friends and colleagues sounded unshaken determination. "We cannot just be sent away. We are South Africans. We belong to the same South Africa, and we want to share the fruits of South Africa with the whites of this country. We are not saying they must go to the sea or some such thing. We are *all* South Africans. South Africa belongs to us, black, yellow, white, irrespective of color or creed, and we have got as much right to the fruits of the country as anybody else. We have got as much right. We are *all* South Africans!"

UDF UNITES!
APARTHEID DIVIDES!

The UDF was always suspected of being a front for the banned ANC; in this capacity alone, it has stood, almost from its inception, on the brink of its own banning. On and off, for four and a half years, local affiliates were banned or legally restricted. On and off, restrictions forbade wearing a UDF T-shirt or displaying a UDF poster. The final 1988 prohibitions must be viewed as a testament to the Front's astounding endurance. It might well have been expected to crumble long before. And even after twenty months of prohibitions, the organization remains a powerful force inside the country.[30]

UDF demands for a united, unfragmented South Africa inevitably recall similar demands from earlier eras, spoken in voices the government has sought desperately to silence. Nelson Mandela. Steve Biko. The ANC mobilized in the 1950s and was outlawed in 1960. Black Consciousness emerged from the political desolation of the 1960s to catalyze the 1970s. In each era the government tried to eliminate effective opposition by snuffing out leaders and banning organizations. And regardless of its technical independence, the spirit of unified liberation kindled by the UDF has never been truly separable from the spirit of earlier organizations or the aspirations of contemporary political exiles.

In the face of expectations that have not been met since Soweto's students rose up in 1976, a body of freedom songs has emerged that are increasingly explicit in describing the struggle for liberation. Earlier songs anticipated vaguely defined victory; mass singing now quite openly acknowledges the young people who have left South Africa since 1976, to train as guerrillas and to bring their people a freedom that decades of reasoning have not achieved. Reflecting the diversity of its membership, UDF freedom songs draw on musical traditions of the educated and the working class, city and country, church and battlefield, present and past.

> The Boers.
> Where do they get the gall
> To take our South Africa as their own?
> We will enter John Vorster Prison and free our comrades.
> Tambo! Lead us to reclaim our home.

The South African government has long encouraged black singing and dancing in preference to the intellectual or technological pursuits it regards as white domains. However, the authorities are coming to recognize that black singing is more than a rural people's expression of joy or sadness at the size of a herd of cattle. They are realizing that singing is not necessarily an expression of contentment, not simply an emotional outlet for the urban black people whose labor assures white affluence while perpetuating their own poverty.

Victoria spoke proudly of her people's ingenious use of the singing Pretoria has tried to co-opt. "We black people speak in many ways, and music is one of them. It is part and parcel of life. For years black people would sing right under their noses, and they would never care to know what was being said. Now they are realizing that they must take us seriously in every way. Even our singing."

Government responses to its realizations are varied. Occasional songs are banned. Occasional singers are charged with furthering the aims of banned organizations. Shortly after a State of Emergency was declared in July 1985, the singing of freedom songs was prohibited at funerals of the victims of the escalating violence; a similar prohibition had been imposed during the Soweto riots of the previous decade. Over transatlantic telephone, South African friends commented on the new musical restrictions.

"Our people will never stop to think, 'This we can sing, and this we cannot sing.' No. We sing what we want to sing."

"The authorities are always complaining about anything. Even if we could just sit still and not do anything, it would not please them."

"One cannot say that it is the singing that irritates them. Our very *existence* irritates them. Now we are not going to fade out of this country because they do not want us to be here. They have to know that we are here to stay. And when we are here, we are going to be singing."

Attorney Victoria Mxenge laughed in prescient contempt of government attempts to restrict the deeply rooted, personal voice of song. "Particularly for those who die from political reasons, we believe people shouldn't cry when they are at graveside. So even at a funeral, freedom songs will be sung with jubilation. I don't know of any funeral where there have been restrictions, where freedom songs were *not* sung. You know, people become angry about these restrictions. And if the person who is being buried was a freedom fighter, the people feel they wouldn't have accorded that person the honor he deserves if freedom songs are not sung at his funeral. They recognize what the government feels about it. They may heed every other restriction. No posters. No banners. No flags. The coffin should not be draped in the colors of unlawful organizations. People shouldn't walk; they should go in buses and cars. Coffins shouldn't be carried on shoulders. They can keep all of these. But freedom songs—you'll always hear them."

> Freedom shines before us
> Freedom is in our hand.
> Now we say away with slavery
> In our land of Africa.

Late in the day on August 1, 1985, newswire accounts of ongoing racial unrest in South Africa reported the brutal murder of attorney Victoria Nonyamezelo Mxenge. Witnesses said she was shot and then hacked to pieces when a friend dropped her off outside her home in Durban's Umlazi township. They said the murderers were masked blacks who disappeared into the township.

Police suggested no motive for her slaying; official reports used the catchall description "black on black violence" as if it were some kind of explanation. Black activists accused the police of complicity in the killing; allegations arose of government authorized or protected hit squads. Although Durban's black townships had, until then, remained free of the unrest that had claimed hundreds of black lives over the previous year, Umlazi was suddenly engulfed in riots. Over sixty people were reported killed in the next few days, allowing the government to deplore continuing black on black violence. Concrete reports of investigation into Victoria's murder remained—and have remained to the present day—conspicuously absent.[31]

SINGING AND SPIRIT IN SOUTH AFRICA

In every setting, every genre, singing gives form to the spirit of black South Africa. Traditional part-singing expresses co-operation and playfulness among individuals, each working hard to excel in a way that complements and enhances the efforts of all the others. Call-and-response patterns reenact the dynamic, mutual responsibility between leader and community. Hymn-style singing represents the Christian values introduced by missionaries as indigenous people's salvation. It recalls blacks' good-faith adaptability, their willingness to move beyond traditional horizons; it also highlights the irony of Christianity's broken promises. As the music of working-class migrants, *mbube* embodies proud adjustment to a life that is neither urban nor rural, neither modern nor traditional, neither permanent nor temporary. And ever-changing hybrid idioms reflect the musical initiative with which South African blacks attempt to control their own lives and fashion their own identities. Since the first white presence, this fundamental black self-determination has been challenged.

> What have we done?
> What have we done?
> Our only sin is that we are black.

As these people struggle to survive each day's oppression, singing constitutes an invaluable internal resource. Costing nothing and offering priceless rewards, singing is like spinning straw into gold. It allows blacks to create a continuity from day to day, backward and forward into history. In singing they assert their own identity, rejecting Pretoria's contempt and domination. With their songs they reclaim their heritage, confirming essential unity across linguistic and regional differences. South African law declares blacks to be dull and incompetent; singing affirms their ingenious, resilient skillfulness. Statutes shatter black families, preventing parents and spouses from caring for those they love most; with their tradition of singing, these people provide one another spiritual nurturance. Through its own lens, apartheid has tried to see black people as units of labor to be exploited, or units of opposition to be destroyed. But blacks have relentlessly refused to see themselves as anything less than human; their singing proclaims indestructible integrity.

Traditional black life is rooted in relationships. Within any group, between each group and its leader, relationships of dynamic cooperation give meaning to each individual's participation. Nowhere are these relationships more apparent than in singing, where people work together to create something that is satisfying to them all. It is this principle of cooperation that is, perhaps, at the root of South Africa's historical conflicts. Assuming fundamental cooperation, blacks have consistently accepted white promises; taking their own supremacy for granted, whites never intended to honor the assumptions they invoked.

As exiled anthropologist John Blacking observes, the political relationship of mutual responsibility between leader and community is blatantly violated by the whites who rule this black country.[32] Organized anti-apartheid protest quite explicitly opposes this violation; singing is integral to such protest. Quite separate from the lyrics of particular songs, their musical style—the very process of their singing—constitutes protest. In singing together, these people are enacting their own way of being together. Almost by definition, their singing is a protest against circumstances that make this African way of being human either impossible or illegal. But singing is more than protest against the intolerable. Most important of all, singing is an enactment of the cooperative, honorable, democratic relationships that are the birthright these people are demanding.

We are the children of Africa
We are ready for freedom.

In the small Eastern Cape university city of Grahamstown, I chatted for an hour or so with a black schoolteacher studying Teaching English as a Second Language. Like many others, he was initially amused at my earnest interest in black singing; his early tone was one of condescension. Eventually he relaxed, and although at that point we were discussing his concerns about teaching blacks in the homelands versus in the townships, his comments somehow returned to singing. "Singing is what we do. We don't think about why. We don't sit down and learn how. We just do it, from when we are small, small, until we are dead. If we wouldn't sing, how would we be ourselves? Without our singing we would probably be someone else!"

He laughed, and his expression was startled. But although his last statement almost seemed to take him by surprise, it was absolutely true. In ways superficial and profound, simple and complex, direct and symbolic, singing is who these people are. White Westerners may laugh at the seeming preposterousness of this notion, but we must not ignore it. Today we are called upon to support black South Africans' struggle for liberation; someday we will be negotiating with them as the official leaders of their nation. Our effectiveness now and then—both abroad and right here, with our own multiracial population at home—will depend on our abilities to understand people quite different from ourselves, to see something of ourselves in them, and, with great respect, to cooperate.

NKOSI SIKELEL'I AFRIKA

The South African Council of Churches (SACC) Interchurch Media Programme had been raided shortly before I phoned them. By the time we could arrange an appointment, some of their materials had been returned and staff were trying to inventory the remains of their archive. It was with both generosity and weary indifference that they invited me to view whatever might be of interest.

Film crews walked in and out of the viewing room, removing and returning equipment, asking no one in particular whether one tape or another was in their possession. On my video monitor images were dissolving in and out of magnetic snow, and seconds of sound were broken by silent intervals that rendered whole tapes virtually meaningless. Suddenly I heard the familiar voice of Dr. Alan Boesak, president of the World Alliance of Reformed Churches, addressing a crowd. Even after twenty—thirty—forty seconds, voice and image were uninterrupted. The label on the video cassette identified this as the rally that had launched the UDF in August 1983.

Friends and acquaintances in Capetown had told me that Dr. Boesak had become a principal player on South Africa's political stage with little apparent preparation in the wings. A young Capetown minister of negligible national standing, he had spent several years studying in Holland and returned home with little fanfare. Shortly after his return, he simply appeared in the cafeteria of the University of Cape Town, jumped onto a table, and delivered a speech that overpowered the other voices in the room and won him the admiration of everyone within earshot. Almost instantaneously he became a major public figure.

Alan Boesak is a small, cherubic-looking man whose ideas are clear, words articulate, and delivery mesmerizing. Out of all proportion to his physical stature or the actual volume of his voice, his words boom and crash, shattering complacency and inspiring the will to righteousness. The burning bush. The still, small voice. The thunder on Mount Sinai. Alan Boesak is somehow all of these.

The UDF was launched in a conference at Mitchells Plain, outside Capetown, attended by 1,000 delegates representing some 575 organizations. After the conference, over 10,000 people rallied at the Mitchells Plain Civic Center to support the new Front and hear Dr. Boesak speak of its aims. It was this speech I found myself watching on video. For nearly an hour Dr. Boesak held 10,000 people all but silent with his explanation of the goals of the explicitly nonracial UDF.

> We are here to say that what we are working for is one undivided South Africa which shall belong to all of its people. The time has come for white people in this country to realize that their destiny is inextricably bound with our destiny, that they shall never be free until we are free. . . . They will never be free as long as they have to kill our children in order to safeguard their overprivileged positions. They will never be free as long as they have to lie awake at night worrying whether a black government will one day do to them as they are doing to us . . .

He carried his massive audience to a climactic reminder of

> three little words that express so eloquently our seriousness in this struggle. You do not need to have a vast vocabulary to understand them. You do not need a philosophical bent to grasp them. They are just three little words.

And the first word is the word "all." We want *all* of

our rights, not just some rights. We want not just a few token handouts here and there, that the government sees fit to give. We want *all* of our rights. And we want *all* of South Africa's people to have their rights—not just a selected few, not just the few so-called "Coloreds" or "Indians," after they have been made honorary whites. We want all of our rights for all of South Africa's people, including those whose citizenship has already been stripped away by this government.

The second word is the word "here." We want all of our rights, and we want them *here,* in a united, undivided South Africa. We do not want them in impoverished homelands. We do not want them in our separate little group areas. We want them *here* in this land which one day we shall once again call our own.

And the third word is the word "now." We want *all* of our rights, and we want them *here,* and we want them *now.*[33]

Dr. Boesak did not conclude with these three, oh so powerful words. Instead he exhorted the 10,000 representatives of his countrypeople to sing their hymn of freedom, "Nkosi Sikelel'i Afrika," actively uniting them around the demands he had just articulated. Of different colors and classes, these people had come to Capetown from all over the country. In this final song they were proclaiming popular commitment to the ideals voiced by individual speakers and leaders. They were proclaiming their unity with one another, across differences the government had tried to pose as insurmountable. They were invigorating themselves for the inevitably difficult and dangerous struggle they had undertaken. With theatrical brilliance, Dr. Boesak delivered the final minutes of his speech over their anthem.

NKOSI SIKELEL'I AFRIKA
Lord bless Africa.

Nowhere are the links between South African liberation and the Christian church more pronounced than in the anthem of freedom, "Nkosi Sikelel'i Afrika," that rings from union meeting to freedom rally, from church to stadium, from home to school to cemetery. This anthem was part of the first church service I attended in Soweto, my first Sunday in South Africa; it was part of the last meeting I observed in Johannesburg, just before leaving for the airport to catch my last flight home. I heard it, or reference to it, no matter where in the black community I was, nearly every day in between.

The song was written as a hymn in 1897 by Enoch Sontonga and first sung publicly two years later, at a clerical ordination.

> **Lord bless Africa**
> **Bless our chiefs;**
> **May they fear and revere their Creator**
> **That He may bless them.**

Sontonga taught in a Methodist mission school in a black Johannesburg location that is part of present-day Soweto. Nearly a century ago, he wrote his hymn to voice the despair of urban blacks, that their living and working conditions were poor, that equality based on westernization remained elusive, and that white authorities deceived and abused them far more often than behaving with honor.

> **Bless the ministers,**
> **Bless the public men and the youth**
> **That they may carry the land with patience.**

Today black living and working conditions remain poor, and State deception and abuse of black people are enshrined in statute. Black equality based on westernization is no longer even suggested. The white government makes black progress impossible and protest against slow strangulation illegal. And it explains its own involvement in daily acts of physical violence—daily murder and maiming of black people, both random and intended—as essential to keeping the peace.

**Bless our efforts
Of education and mutual understanding.**

"Nkosi Sikelel'i Afrika" was first popularized by the children's choirs that flourished in the mission schools of Sontonga's time. Later it was adopted by the African National Congress, then still a wholly peaceful organization of blacks who, like Sontonga, relied on and were betrayed by the powers of reason, persuasion, and religious decency. It became a benediction for Congress meetings.

**Bless our efforts
Of union and self-uplifting.**

The song came to assume this same role for black gatherings of all kinds, over the years relinquishing Christian specificity in favor of a more general, all-inclusive outpouring from human beings to their God. It has now become the recognized anthem of black South Africa at large.

Lord bless Africa

This hymn is beautiful when performed by choirs in concert. But it is incomparably stirring when sung by more informal congregations, directly voicing the pain and the hope that have characterized black South Africans as long as whites have ruled their land. "Nkosi Sikelel'i" is a hymn. A benediction. A freedom song. An anthem. But it is not quite any of these, and more than them all.

Although the song uses conventional Western religious

idioms for music and text, it elicits ongoing discomfort and confusion among white members of South Africa's theocracy. I met an Afrikaner businessman in a Malay restaurant in Capetown. While the resident Cape Malay choir was taking a break, the businessman and I talked about singing in his country.

"You're really on to something when you say that singing is important to any people. Back when we Boers were what you might call an oppressed minority, I know how much our own songs and dances meant to us. That's what helped keep our culture alive. What kept us together as a people so that one day we could win power. And those old songs still remind us of where we come from. They are part of our soul. Now this choir we have just heard. I don't think it's beautiful, but it's good for these people to be able to sing their own songs. And the blacks, as you call them. Of course they sing beautifully. But you have to watch them. Do you know this song they sing all the time?" He hummed the first few bars of "Nkosi Sikelel'i." "That song whips them up to drive the whites into the sea. It should be banned. The government is trying to ban it, you know. They shouldn't be allowed to sing a song like that."

"I thought that song was just calling for God to bless Africa."

"It doesn't really matter what the words say, you know." I tried to keep my expression impassive but I felt my eyebrows knit, involuntarily eliciting the explanation that had become, for me, an Afrikaner litany.

"I know these people. I grew up with them. We played together as children." He smiled the familiar Afrikaner smile of patronizing self-assurance. "I understand these Natives. I love them, and I understand them. When they sing about the Lord, they are really singing about taking over our land and getting rid of the rest of us. A song like that, a song they all sing . . . That kind of song should be banned."

"If they should be banned from praying for God's blessing, what should they be permitted to sing about?" I risked a rare moment of sarcasm. "Or maybe they shouldn't be permitted to sing at all."

He responded thoughtfully, nodding slowly. "Ja, maybe they shouldn't be permitted to sing at all."

For an instant he seemed to see his world through my lens, to hear his last words as they might have fallen on my ears. Perhaps he had caught a hint of the vicious inhumanity— and futility—of his suggestion. Perhaps he had glimpsed the incongruity in asserting love for "these Natives" while calling for them quite literally to be muzzled. He resumed his accustomed world view after only a second or two, and his hasty conclusion was all too predictable. "I can't expect an American like you to understand. You mean well, but you don't understand these people at all. You don't understand what we are up against."

Lord, bless Africa.
Bless our efforts of mutual understanding

Victoria Mxenge had struggled to describe this song's peculiar power. "It's a very mild freedom song, if you were to call it a freedom song at all. It's basically a hymn. It's supposed to be sung as a solemn prayer for blessing and dignity to be part and parcel of our struggle. You know, you've been at a rally listening to people singing other freedom songs. Most of them are sung with jubilation and the people will be dancing. But when it comes to 'Nkosi Sikelel'i' the facial expressions will change. There will not be any dancing, and there will be the raising of fists and perhaps looking up, actually looking up at God to bless Africa."

Lord, bless Africa.
Blot out its wickedness
Its sins and transgressions
And bless Africa.

IN PROTEST

Many months after my return home, Rounder Records, an American label with an anti-apartheid history, expressed interest in Gary and me producing a record album of the field recordings we had made in South Africa. We were still sorting through our nearly one hundred recorded hours of black singing. But regardless of what else impressed us on any particular day, the massed singing of "Nkosi Sikelel'i" at the UDF launch continued to echo with the incomparable sounds of the humanness and vitality we had found infusing all of South Africa's black communities; it continued to burn with the fire of these people to be free. It had not been rehearsed. It was not a performance. Rather, it was a massed declaration, presented in the idiom that conveys the people's spirit more fully than any other. Nothing could be a more fitting conclusion for the musical statement we wanted our album to make about South Africa, than this particular singing of "Nkosi Sikelel'i Afrika."

I contacted the SACC, asking permission to use this segment of their tape on our album, and also requesting a production-quality copy of their recording. I had dubbed the soundtrack during viewing, but the jack that had been available had eliminated one track, my tape had run out roughly a minute before the speech was over, and, all in all, my dub was acoustically useless. Permission was granted without hesitation. The tape itself, however, was another matter. The SACC's original recording had been confiscated in a subsequent raid. The UDF had been raided. Afroscope had been raided. The staff member on the other end of the line thought out loud for someone who might have made a production-quality recording of the event and succeeded in holding on to it, intact. We laughed that my lousy, incomplete dub might be the best that existed anywhere. Perhaps I should duplicate it right away.

Although no promises were made, I was assured that if any original recording could be found I would receive a copy. So I waited. And waited. And, of necessity, considered alternatives for the final cut on the album. One day a small, unmarked packet arrived from South Africa, containing an apparently unused cassette. The first side played forty-five minutes of silence. The second side, too, began with silence. But after fifteen minutes Dr. Boesak's commanding voice rang clear, through my speakers:

> And as we struggle on, let us continue to sing that wonderful hymn of freedom, that hymn that has sustained us through all these years and shall sustain us for the years to come. Let us continue to sing "Nkosi Sikelel'i Afrika."
>
> We, the freedom-loving people of South Africa, say with one voice to the whole world that we cherish the vision of a united, democratic South Africa, based on the will of the people.

NKOSI SIKELEL'I AFRIKA
God bless Africa

We will strive for the unity of all our people, through united action against the evils of apartheid—economic and all other forms of exploitation. And in our march to a free and just South Africa we are guided by these noble ideals.

Let the voice of the people be heard

We stand for the creation of a true democracy in which all South Africans will participate in the government of our country. We stand for a single, nonracial, unfragmented South Africa.

God bless our people

A South Africa free of bantustans and Group Areas. We say all forms of oppression and exploitation must end.

IN PROTEST

NKOSI SIKELEL'I AFRIKA
MALUPHAKANYISW'UPHONDO LWAYO
YIZWA IMITHANDAZO YETHU
NKOSI SIKELELA—
NKOSI SIKELELA / THINA LUSAPHO LWAYO

In accordance with these noble ideals and on this twentieth day of August, nineteen hundred and eighty-three, in the Civic Centre, Mitchells Plain, we join hands as community, women's, students', religious, sporting, and other organizations and trade unions.

WOZA MOYA
Rise up, Spirit

We say "No!" to apartheid.

Rise up, spirit of the people

We say "No!" to the Republic of South Africa Constitution Bill, a bill which will create yet another undemocratic constitution in the country of our birth.

God bless our people

We say "No!" to the Koornhof Bills which will deprive more and more African people of their birthright.

WOZA MOYA
WOZA MOYA, OYINGCWELE
NKOSI SIKELELA
THINA LUSAPHO LWAYO

We say "Yes!" to the birth of the United Democratic Front on this historic day.

NKOSI SIKELEL'I AFRIKA

MORENA BOLOKA SECHABA SA HESO
God bless our nation

We know that the government is determined to break the unity of our people.

End the war and misery

We commit ourselves to uniting all our people, wherever they may be—in the cities and countrysides, the factories and the mines, schools and colleges, universities, housing and sports fields, churches and mosques and temples—to fight for our freedom. We therefore resolve to stand shoulder to shoulder in our common struggle and commit ourselves to work together to organize and mobilize all community, workers, students, women, religious, sporting, and other organizations, under the banner of the United Democratic Front.

Bless our nation of Africa

To consult our people regularly and honestly and bravely, and strive to represent their views and aspirations.

Let it be so,

To educate all about the coming dangers and the need for unity. To build and strengthen all organizations of the people.

Forever and ever.

To unite in action against these bills and other day-to-day problems affecting our people.[34]

IN PROTEST

MORENA BOLOKA SECHABA SA HESO
O FEDISE DINTWA LE MATSOENYEHO
MORENA BOLOKA SECHABA SA HESO
O FEDISE DINTWA LE MATSOENYEHO
O SEBOLOKE—O SEBOLOKE
O SEBOLOKE—O SEBOLOKE
SECHABA SA HESO
SECHABA SA AFRIKA.

MAKUBE NJALO
KUZE KUBE NGUNA PHAKADE.

Amen.

EPILOGUE

When I was completing the manuscript of this book in October 1989, events in South Africa suggested a major detour in the country's lockstep march on the path of repressive minority rule. Newly elected President F. W. de Klerk legalized some anti-apartheid demonstrations, and unconditionally released Walter Sisulu and other old-guard anti-apartheid leaders after more than twenty years in prison. New allegations prompted public investigation of the state-sponsored hit squads that activists had long held responsible for the murders of Griffiths and Victoria Mxenge, David Webster, and others. For a while I held on to my manuscript, and added a footnote for each late-breaking event.

Now it's the beginning of March 1990. The ANC and other anti-apartheid organizations have been unbanned and un-restricted, and Nelson Mandela is a free man. Last year Mandela was an unquotable lifer; today he holds the top active post in the senior anti-apartheid organization in the country. Openly carrying banners that had been a criminal offense to display for the past thirty years, hundreds of thousands of South Africans now rally in streets and sports stadiums in the biggest demon-strations the country has ever seen. The ANC has announced plans to reestablish major offices inside South Africa and has agreed to meet with the Nationalist government to "talk about talks," with an ultimate goal of replacing apartheid with a nor-malized, democratic society. Last year all of this was unthink-able. And suddenly, today, I find myself with a three-day publishing deadline to write a last update and relate new political events to the singing that is, as it has always been, part of everything.

From inside South Africa, even people who were always more cautious than optimistic are calling events since February 2 the most significant steps in forty years. "The last three weeks have changed everything," a prominent civil rights attorney told me over the phone. "For years I've been telling you that revolution in South Africa is not around the corner. But today . . ." This person has always used words carefully.

But developments in South Africa are far from consistently positive, and outcomes are far from certain. I'm reminded that in Chinese, the character for "crisis" incorporates the one for "catastrophe" along with the one for "opportunity." South Africa is, indeed, in a crisis.

In one direction, the government has implicitly acknowledged the right of black people and their organizations to participate in the political process. Organizations have been legalized, names have been removed from the list of people who cannot be quoted, and activists have been freed from restrictions imposed after their release from detention. Detainees under the State of Emergency now have the right to legal and medical counsel. Prisoners who were convicted merely for belonging to banned organizations are promised release. The government has declared a moratorium on executions and lifted many media restrictions. A coup in the "independent" homeland of the Ciskei has just ousted the South African–supported president and replaced him with pro-ANC leaders who favor reincorporation into South Africa. Dissatisfaction is boiling over in other homelands as well, as national events give new courage to people who have felt powerless until now.

For the first time in anyone's memory, state-controlled South African television is broadcasting people discussing differing views on issues of serious national concern. Members of the ANC are being portrayed as human beings, rather than as incarnations of fire and brimstone. In a country where behavior and information are only just beginning to emerge from rigid government control, truth is no longer monolithic.

But there is another side. With the State of Emergency still in effect, police continue to fire lethal weapons on peaceful demonstrations, to interfere with emergency-room treatment of injured demonstrators, and to harass the families of high-profile activists—all with legal impunity and with visual media coverage prohibited. Detainees continue to die in prison; as many as 3,000 political prisoners remain in jail. A judicial inquiry into the death squads reveals one secret military unit with reported links to the Defense Minister. Army troops remain in black townships. As apartheid-induced frustration explodes in far-flung rural areas, the State continues to take whatever military action it deems necessary to contain violence and prop up the existing apartheid-based political structures.

Alongside the scrapping of some restrictive laws and the selective nonenforcement of others, several pillars of apartheid remain in place. The Population Registration Act still imposes an official racial classification on every man, woman, and child in the country. The Group Areas Act still regulates where people may live, on the basis of race. Education and health care are still separate—and grossly unequal—according to race. Black land ownership is still restricted to the 13 percent of overall territory that falls within homelands borders. Blacks still face chronic unemployment, malnutrition, and housing shortages, and they still have no official voice in the government that legislates their conditions. The Internal Security Act still gives the State sweeping, draconian powers against all opponents.

Conservative whites accuse President de Klerk of betraying his electoral mandate, and they demand his resignation. Right-wing militants talk of forming a white guerrilla movement. At mass demonstrations they wave Nazi flags, burn the Star of David, and call for Mandela and de Klerk to be hanged. Private citizens on the far right have filed treason charges against Mandela for the content of his first speech, on February 11, in Cape Town.

In everyday life, black friends tell me that optimism and hope have replaced some of the suspicion and fear that used to cloud every moment. But even hopeful blacks have not forgotten the Nationalist government's history of half truths and broken promises. South African blacks remain unequal in law, and in that position they know they can never be either safe or free.

When Mandela's release was announced on February 10, people sang in the streets in every township in the country. When rallies welcomed him in Cape Town and Soweto, tens of thousands of people sang for the whole world to hear. It is through their singing that black South Africans most publicly assert their cooperative identity. Through their singing they maintain the pride and resolute mass determination to win their long struggle for freedom. And we may be sure that when South Africa's people draft a constitution that allows them all to live together in true justice and equality, when they install their first truly democratically elected government, these political milestones will have the sound—quite literally—of more than 28 million voices singing.

March 8, 1990

APPENDIXES

NOTES

LET THEIR VOICES BE HEARD

RELATED RECORDINGS

BACKGROUND AND RELATED READINGS

NOTES

I. PEOPLE WHO SING

1. J. Blacking, "Trends in the Black Music of South Africa, 1959–1969," in *Musics of Many Cultures: An Introduction,* ed. E. May (Berkeley: University of California Press, 1980), 195–215.
2. G. Henry, from "Marching in Africa," © 1985. Used with kind permission. All rights reserved.

II. IN CHURCH

1. T. R. H. Davenport, *South Africa: A Modern History,* 2d ed. (Toronto: University of Toronto Press, 1978).
2. D. B. Coplan, *In Township Tonight! South Africa's Black City Music and Theatre* (London: Longman, 1980, 1985).
3. Ibid.
4. I played a tape of this hymn for exiled African National Congress song leader James Madhlope Phillips when we spent time together in 1985, two years before his death. At the time James was sixty-six; he had been in exile for thirty-two years. A trade unionist and prominent song leader in the 1940s and early 1950s, he was banned from all activity in 1953 and left his country a year later. James was a large man of extraordinary dignity. His voice, whether speaking or singing, was incomparably resonant. James listened to the Mothers sing of resurrection, and a tear rolled down his cheek. His face was excited, his voice choked as the words came out. "The Mandela song! So this is where it comes from! The most widely sung of freedom songs. The Mandela song. You can see how much it means to me. This song. I never knew where it came from!"
5. E. Roux, *Time Longer Than Rope: A History of the Black Man's Struggle for Freedom in South Africa* (Madison: University of Wisconsin Press, 1966).
6. B. G. M. Sundkler, *Bantu Prophets in South Africa,* 2d ed. (London: Oxford University Press for The International African Institute, 1961).
7. Roux, *Time Longer Than Rope.*
8. G. C. Oosthuizen, *Post-Christianity in Africa: A Theological and An-*

thropological Study (Grand Rapids, Mich.: William B. Eerdmans Publishing Company, 1968).

9. Sundkler, *Bantu Prophets in South Africa.*
10. Coplan, *In Township Tonight!*
11. Sundkler, *Bantu Prophets in South Africa.*
12. Oosthuizen, *Post-Christianity in Africa.*
13. Shembe hymn no. 216, in Sundkler, *Bantu Prophets in South Africa,* 288.
14. J. Blacking, "Political and Musical Freedom in the Music of Some Black South African Churches," in *The Structure of Folk Models,* eds. L. Holy and M. Stuchlik, ASA Monograph, no. 20 (London: Academic Press, 1980), 35–62.
15. Sundkler, *Bantu Prophets in South Africa.*
16. P. F. Larlham, *Black Theater, Dance, and Ritual in South Africa* (Ann Arbor, Mich.: UMI Research Press, 1982, 1985).
17. Shembe hymn no. 214, in Sundkler, 282.
18. Shembe hymn no. 112, in Sundkler, 197.
19. Larlham, *Black Theater, Dance, and Ritual in South Africa.*
20. C. Rickard, "The Strange Death of the Messiah's Kindly Grandson," *Weekly Mail* (5, no. 14) (April 14–20, 1989), 13. When Isaiah Shembe died in 1935, leadership of the church passed to his son Johannes Galilee. With Galilee's own death in 1976, a succession struggle ensued between his son Londa and his brother Amos. Church holy places were divided between the two men, and adherents expressed loyalty to one leader or the other. In the current climate of political violence in the Natal province, the two Shembe factions are cast—in somewhat oversimplified fashion—on opposite sides of the struggle. It is against this backdrop of religious division and political antagonism that Londa Shembe was murdered in April 1989. At the time of this writing the murder has not been solved, and the death is being used to deepen political and religious divisions in the province.
21. Shembe processional hymn, in Sundkler, 292.
22. Shembe hymn no. 112, in Sundkler, 197.
23. Shembe hymn no. 221, in Sundkler, 284.
24. Shembe hymn no. 112, in Sundkler, 197.
25. Shembe hymn no. 77, in Sundkler, 283.
26. Shembe hymn no. 197, in Sundkler, 283.
27. Shembe hymn no. 101, in Sundkler, 294.
28. Shembe hymn no. 134, in Sundkler, 282.
29. Shembe hymn no. 46, in Sundkler, 196.
30. Shembe hymn no. 112, in Sundkler, 197.

III. IN THE COUNTRY

1. R. Davies, D. O'Meara, and S. Dlamini, *The Struggle for South Africa: A Reference Guide to Movements, Organizations, and Institutions*, vols. 1 and 2 (London: Zed Books Ltd., 1984).

2. L. Platzky and C. Walker, for the Surplus People Project, *The Surplus People: Forced Removals in South Africa* (Johannesburg: Ravan Press, 1985), 112.

3. Ibid., 7–60.

4. Ibid., 17.

5. Ibid., 7–60.

6. A. Getz, "Police Again Clash with Demonstrators," *UPI Newswire*, September 8, 1989.

7. L. Platzky and C. Walker, *The Surplus People*, 113.

8. Study Commission on U.S. Policy Toward Southern Africa, *South Africa: Time Running Out* (Berkeley: University of California Press, 1981), 150.

9. Research Staff, South African Institute of Race Relations, *Race Relations Survey 1987/88* (Johannesburg: South African Institute of Race Relations, 1988), 865.

10. L. Platzky and C. Walker, *The Surplus People*.

11. R. Davies, D. O'Meara, and S. Dlamini, *The Struggle for South Africa*, vols. 1 and 2.

12. Research Staff, South African Institute of Race Relations, *Race Relations Survey 1983* (Johannesburg: South African Institute of Race Relations, 1984), 356.

13. Ibid. Dr. Boraine made these observations as a Member of Parliament from the liberal Progressive Federal Party. During 1989 the PFP was disbanded, and its liberal position taken over by the new, broader-based Democratic Party.

14. J. Blacking, "Music and the Historical Process in Vendaland," in *Essays on Music and History in Africa*, ed. K. P. Wachsmann (Evanston, Ill: Northwestern University Press, 1971), 185–212.

15. J. Blacking, *Venda Children's Songs: A Study in Ethnomusicological Analysis* (Johannesburg: Witwatersrand University Press, 1967).

16. Ibid.

17. J. Blacking, "Music and the Historical Process in Vendaland," 185–212.

18. J. Blacking, *How Musical Is Man?* (Seattle, Wash.: University of Washington Press, 1973).

19. J. Blacking, *Venda Children's Songs*, 18.

20. L. Platzky and C. Walker, *The Surplus People*, 126.

21. Ibid., 125–27.

22. Research Staff, South African Institute of Race Relations, *Race Re-*

NOTES

lations Survey 1985 (Johannesburg: South African Institute of Race Relations, 1986).

23. Ibid.
24. A. Isaacman and B. Isaacman, *Mozambique: From Colonialism to Revolution, 1900–1982* (Boulder, Colo.: Westview Press, 1983).
25. T. F. Johnston, "The Music of the Shangana-Tsonga" (Ph.D. diss., University of the Witwatersrand, 1972).

IV. MIGRANTS

1. J. Clegg, "Towards An Understanding of African Dance: The Zulu Isishameni Style," in *Papers Presented at the Second Symposium on Ethnomusicology*, ed. A. Tracey (Grahamstown: International Library of African Music, 1981), 8–14.
2. E. M. Sithole, *Zulu Music as a Reflection of Social Change* (Master's thesis, Wesleyan University, 1968).
3. V. Erlmann, *Mbube Roots: Zulu Choral Music from South Africa, 1930s–1960s*. Notes from record album. (Cambridge, Mass.: Rounder Records, 1987).
4. J. Clegg, "Towards an Understanding of African Dance," 8–14.
5. D. B. Coplan, *In Township Tonight! South Africa's Black City Music and Theatre* (London: Longman, 1980, 1985).
6. P. F. Larlham, *Black Theater, Dance, and Ritual in South Africa* (Ann Arbor, Mich: UMI Research Press, 1982, 1985).
7. Ibid.
8. J. Thomas, "Abafana Bomoya." Program notes for *Abafana Bomoya Live!* (Durban: Durban Arts Association; Department of Speech and Drama, University of Natal, 1984).
9. P. F. Larlham, *Black Theater, Dance, and Ritual in South Africa*.
10. All lyrics footnoted in this chapter are excerpted from English translations of songs written and recorded in Zulu by Joseph Shabalala. Used with Mr. Shabalala's kind permission. *Amabutho* © 1973; *Indlela Yase Zulwini* © 1978; *Umthombo Wamanzi* © 1982; Mavuthela Music Co., Johannesburg, Republic of South Africa. International copyright secured. All rights reserved.
11. From "Uligugu Lami," *Indlela Yase Zulwini*, 1978.
12. From "Isigcino," *Amabutho*, 1973.
13. From "Ungikhumbule," *Umthombo Wamanzi*, 1982.
14. From "Nqonqotha," *Amabutho*, 1973.
15. From "Isigcino," *Amabutho*, 1973.
16. S. R. Maile, Notes from record album *Ukukhanya Kwelanga* (Johannesburg: Mavuthela Music Co., 1975).
17. From "Nkosi Yamakhosi," *Amabutho*, 1973.
18. From "Sivuya Sonke," *Amabutho*, 1973.
19. From "Nomathemba," *Amabutho*, 1973.

20. From "Ungikhumbule," *Umthombo Wamanzi,* 1982.
21. All lyrics footnoted in this chapter are excerpted from English translations of songs written and recorded in Zulu by Joseph Shabalala. Used with Mr. Shabalala's kind permission. *Amabutho* © 1973, Mavuthela Music Co., Johannesburg, Republic of South Africa. International copyright secured. All rights reserved.
22. From "Ngelekelele," *Amabutho,* 1973.
23. From "Amabutho," *Amabutho,* 1973.
24. Ibid.
25. Ibid.
26. All lyrics footnoted in this chapter are excerpted from English translations of songs written and recorded in Zulu by Joseph Shabalala. Used with Mr. Shabalala's kind permission. *Amabutho* © 1973; *Umthombo Wamanzi* © 1982; Mavuthela Music Co., Johannesburg, Republic of South Africa. International copyright secured. All rights reserved.
27. From "Amabutho," *Amabutho,* 1973.
28. Ibid.
29. Ibid.
30. From "Yimani," *Umthombo Wamanzi,* 1982.
31–51. From "Uz'ube Nami Baba," *Umthombo Wamanzi,* 1982. Over the course of notes 31–51, a translation of nearly the entire song "Uz'ube Nami Baba" is presented.
52–55. From "Emafini," *Umthombo Wamanzi,* 1982.

V. IN THE CITY

1. J. Blacking, "Trends in the Black Music of South Africa, 1959–1969," in *Musics of Many Cultures: An Introduction,* ed. E. May (Berkeley: University of California Press, 1980), 195–215.
2. A. Tracey, "Some Key Words in African Music." Unpublished manuscript, International Library of African Music, Rhodes University, Grahamstown, 1982.
3. D. Rycroft, "Nguni Vocal Polyphony," *Journal of the International Folk Music Council* 19 (1967), 88–103.
4. D. B. Coplan, *In Township Tonight! South Africa's Black City Music and Theatre* (London: Longman, 1980, 1985).
5. Ibid.
6. In September and October 1989, the international media praised newly elected South African President F. W. de Klerk's legalization of many anti-apartheid demonstrations and his release of eight important, long-time political prisoners. Few sources mentioned that these months also saw a fresh wave of Emergency detentions of anti-apartheid activists, organizers, and leaders. On September 22, the Human Rights Commission (HRC) estimated the number of people

held under Emergency regulations to be at least 251, up roughly 500 percent from the previous month; the HRC estimated an additional 190 people being held without trial under other laws. G. Evans and V. Gunene, "Detentions Reach Record High," *Weekly Mail* 5, no. 37 (September 22–28, 1989), 4.

7. H. Joffe, "Nowhere to Stay. Nowhere to Go," *Weekly Mail* 4, no. 31 (1988), 14, 19.

8. A. Chaskalson and S. Duncan, "Influx Control: The Pass Laws." (Carnegie Conference Paper No. 81, delivered at the Second Carnegie Inquiry into Poverty and Development in Southern Africa, April 13–19, 1984).

9. H. Joffe, "Nowhere to Stay. Nowhere to Go," 14, 19.

10. Research Staff, South African Institute of Race Relations, *Race Relations Survey 1986, Part 1* (Johannesburg: South African Institute of Race Relations, 1987), 339–45.

11. Research Staff, South African Institute of Race Relations, *Race Relations Survey 1987/88* (Johannesburg: South African Institute of Race Relations, 1988), 865.

12. H. Joffe, "Nowhere to Stay. Nowhere to Go," 14, 19.

13. D. B. Coplan, *In Township Tonight! South Africa's Black City Music and Theatre,* 165.

14. J. Collins, with S. Moore, *African Pop Roots: The Inside Rhythms of Africa* (London: W. Foulsham & Co., Ltd., 1985), 71.

15. From "Bring Him Back Home," by Michael Timothy, Tim Daly and Hugh Masekela, © 1985 Warner Bros. Music Ltd/Anxious Music Ltd. Used with Mr. Masekela's kind permission. All rights reserved.

16. P. R. Kirby, *The Musical Instruments of the Native Races of South Africa* (Johannesburg: Witwatersrand University Press, 1968).

17. E. M. Sithole, *Zulu Music as a Reflection of Social Change* (Master's thesis, Wesleyan University, 1968).

18. P. F. Larlham, *Black Theater, Dance, and Ritual in South Africa* (Ann Arbor, Mich: UMI Research Press, 1982, 1985).

19. A. Brink, *Writing in a State of Siege: Essays on Politics and Literature* (New York: Summit Books, 1983).

VI. IN PROTEST

1. A. Tracey, "Some Key Words in African Music." Unpublished manuscript, International Library of African Music, Rhodes University, Grahamstown, 1982.

2. G. M. Gerhart, *Black Power in South Africa: The Evolution of An Ideology* (Berkeley: University of California Press, 1978), 94. Quoted from A. Luthuli, *Let My People Go: An Autobiography* (London: Collins, 1962), 82.

3. E. Roux, *Time Longer Than Rope: A History of the Black Man's Struggle*

for Freedom in South Africa (Madison: University of Wisconsin Press, 1966).

4. As I make final editorial changes on this manuscript, Walter Sisulu and five other members of the ANC high command are being released after over a quarter century behind bars. Lusaka-based ANC president Oliver Tambo suffered a stroke in August 1989, and he is recovering in Europe. (G. Myre, "South Africa—ANC," *AP Newswire,* October 16, 1989). Nelson Mandela was released from prison in February 1990.

5. Sixty-seven blacks were killed, including women and children; most were shot in the back. At least 186 others were wounded. The demonstration-turned-massacre took place on March 21, 1960. A State of Emergency was declared on March 30; the ANC was banned on April 8. Study Commission on U.S. Policy Toward Southern Africa, *South Africa: Time Running Out* (Berkeley: University of California Press, 1981).

6. V. Erlmann, "Black Political Song in South Africa—Some Research Perspectives." Unpublished paper, Durban, South Africa: University of Natal, 1984.

7. Ibid.

8. G. Evans, "Who Else Remains Inside? About 3500 Other Convicts," *Weekly Mail* 5, no. 14 (April 14–20, 1989), 4.

9. "Colored" Police Lieutenant Gregory Rockman publicly charged his colleagues with savagely beating schoolchildren and bystanders on September 5, 1989, in Mitchells Plain, as part of the anti-opposition violence that characterized the pre-election period. The regional magistrate found that although ". . . riot squad members did unlawfully assault members of the public," the order to use violence was authorized under the Emergency regulations. G. Davis, "Despicable! But Rockman Two Go Free," *Weekly Mail* 5, no. 14 (April 14–20, 1989), 1, 3.

10. Study Commission on U.S. Policy Toward Southern Africa, *South Africa: Time Running Out* (Berkeley: University of California Press, 1981).

11. Personal communication, 1984, Clive Thompson, Center for Applied Legal Studies, University of the Witwatersrand, Johannesburg.

12. D. B. Coplan, *In Township Tonight! South Africa's Black City Music and Theatre* (London: Longman, 1985).

13. Editorial Staff, "COSATU—A Recent Addition to the South African Political Arena," *Sash* 28, no. 4 (1986), 28–29.

14. K. Jacobs, "Tutu, Others Arrested in Protest March," *UPI Newswire,* February 29, 1988.

15. E. Koch, "COSATU Plans to Hit Back in Court," *Weekly Mail* 4, no. 7 (1988), 3.

16. B. Boyle, "South Africa: A Flicker of Hope After a Dark Year," *UPI Newswire,* December 18, 1987.

17. K. Jacobs, "Anti-apartheid Groups Fear Crackdown," *UPI Newswire,* May 8, 1987.

18. Staff, "Organizations restricted by Pretoria Edict," *UPI Newswire,* February 24, 1988.

19. Despite restrictions and harassment, COSATU membership eighteen months later was estimated to have increased to nearly one million. R. Minogue, "Unions Urge Boycott of Autumn Elections," *UPI Newswire,* July 16, 1989.

20. K. Jacobs, "Three Suspected Insurgents Killed in South Africa," *UPI Newswire,* September 23, 1988.

21. Government prohibitions notwithstanding, COSATU called for a boycott of parliamentary elections scheduled for the fall of 1989, and continues to call for international sanctions until the government meets its conditions for beginning acceptable negotiations for the transfer of power. R. Minogue, "Unions Urge Boycott of Autumn Elections," *UPI Newswire,* July 16, 1989.

22. Professor C. Thompson, Center for Applied Legal Studies, University of the Witwatersrand, Johannesburg, read from an interdict brought by the Goldfields Mining Group against the National Union of Mineworkers, February–March 1984, p. 37. The informer is describing an NUM meeting held on Monday, February 15, 1984, at the No. 2 compound.

23. Staff, "Protest Spreads, Postal Strikers Clash, Demonstrators Hurt," *UPI Newswire,* September 1, 1987.

24. B. Breytenbach, *The True Confessions of An Albino Terrorist* (Emmarentia, South Africa: Taurus, 1984).

25. Ibid.

26. In mid-September 1989, President de Klerk agreed to permit activists to hold some nonviolent anti-apartheid demonstrations without police intervention, provided they secured appropriate permission beforehand. For the first time in decades, tens of thousands of people marched in cities around the country. The international news media made much of South Africa's new freedom, and they all but ignored the lethal police violence that had crushed demonstrations just a few weeks before, and that continued to snuff out particular demonstrations even after de Klerk's liberalization.

Some analysts praised de Klerk's actions as an expansion of basic human rights. Others cited pre-election violence and subsequent strategic detentions as evidence that demonstrations were being permitted as an end in themselves, not as a real step toward societal change. These latter analysts predicted that new government crackdowns would follow signs that opposition groups were translating peaceful demonstration into meaningful organization. Ongoing detentions and severe restrictions against newly released detainees certainly suggest that silencing effective opposition leaders and crippling effective opposition remain very much part of Pretoria's agenda.

27. J. Iams, "Southern Africa," *UPI Newswire*, February 24, 1988.

28. University of the Witwatersrand anthropologist and human rights activist David Webster was shot dead outside his Johannesburg home on May 1, 1989. The last article he wrote discussed the government's use of assassination as a means of silencing its opposition when such lower-key methods as detention and explicit individual intimidation have failed. Before reports of the police investigation into the murder faded from the news, a police spokesman had categorically refuted the eyewitness account given by Webster's partner, Maggie Friedman, who was with him when he was shot. G. Evans "Police 'Must Scour Their Ranks' for the Webster Killers," *Weekly Mail* 5, no. 17 (1989), 1, 3, 5.

29. André Brink's 1979 novel *A Dry White Season* illustrates the patient, personal, and absolutely lethal way the authorities use informers against anyone perceived as dangerous to apartheid's status quo. (Great Britain: W. H. Allen & Co. Ltd., 1979).

30. Beginning in early August 1989, a loose coalition of anti-apartheid organizations calling itself the Mass Democratic Movement—including many UDF affiliates and called by some a regrouping of the UDF and COSATU—staged a nationwide defiance campaign opposing segregated hospitals, schools, buses, beaches, and other facilities. The Movement demanded sweeping societal change in the form of dismantling the whole apartheid structure. Their campaign elicited considerable police violence and gained international media attention during South Africa's presidential and parliamentary election campaigns.

31. Figures compiled by the Human Rights Commission indicate that since 1978, 61 anti-apartheid activists have been assassinated inside South Africa; in 60 of these cases no one has been arrested or charged. A 1988 Commission report lists 113 arson and other forms of attack on anti-apartheid organizations and individuals within the preceding four years; no arrests have been made in connection with these incidents. Staff "Apartheid Barometer," *Weekly Mail* 5, no. 17 (1989), 10.

In late October 1989, convicted murderer Butana Nofemela received a stay of execution (for the nonpolitical murder of a white farmer) after saying, in an affidavit, that he was one of four security police who killed attorney Griffiths Mxenge in 1981 under orders from senior officers. Nofemela also claimed partial responsibility for the murders of eight other political activists, all under orders from his superiors. The Pretoria-based organization Lawyers for Human Rights found Nofemela's affidavit to be credible, containing accurate details about Mxenge's murder. D. Crary, "SAfrica-Hangings," *AP Newswire*, October 20, 1989.

32. J. Blacking, "The Power of Ideas in Social Change: The Growth of the Africanist Idea in South Africa," *The Conceptualization and Explanation of Processes of Social Change*, vol. 3, ed. D. Riches. Queen's University Papers in Social Anthropology. (Belfast: Department of Social Anthropology, Queen's University of Belfast, 1979), 107–40.

33. A. Boesak. Speech delivered August 20, 1983. Transcribed from audiotape and used with Dr. Boesak's kind permission. All rights reserved.

34. Ibid.

LET THEIR VOICES BE HEARD

What I have tried to say in this book is fundamentally inseparable from the music that was my starting point. Indeed, the book began as an expansion of the written notes accompanying the two record albums of field recordings that I produced with Gary Gardner soon after our return from South Africa:

Let Their Voices Be Heard: Traditional Singing in South Africa. Rounder Records 5024.

Mbube! Zulu Men's Singing Competition. Rounder Records 5023. Grammy Nomination for Best Traditional Folk Recording, 1987.

In South Africa we recorded people singing as part of everyday experiences in church, in the country, in migrant hostels, at home, in city townships, and in protest against apartheid. With two exceptions, the artists we recorded are neither professional nor semiprofessional musicians. They are simply people who sing. *Let Their Voices Be Heard,* more than any other album, illustrates this book's underlying theme. In black South Africa songs and high-quality musicianship are not the property of professional performers; they are part and parcel of being alive.

Let Their Voices Be Heard was originally produced as a self-contained, aesthetic whole with album notes that completely annotate every cut. I will not repeat those notes here. However, so that the album can best function as a companion to this book, I have keyed each cut to the relevant book section(s), below. I have also provided summary translations.

SIDE A
1. Congregation, St. Paul's Church, Soweto (Zulu/Xhosa; Sotho)
   "NKOSI SIKELEL'I AFRIKA" (God bless Africa)
   (Public domain)
   In Church: "God bless Africa. Let the voice of the people be heard. Rise up, Spirit of the people. End the war and misery. God bless our people, our nation of Africa, forever."
2. Mothers' Union Celebration, St. Bede's Parish, Soshanguve (Sotho)
   "LERATO LA JESU" (Jesus' love)
   (Traditional)
   In Church: "Jesus' love is surprising. Go with it; stay with it."

3. Congregation, St. Barnabas Church, Soshanguve (English)
   "My, My, My"
   (Traditional)
   > **In Church:** "My, my my. Jesus is my Savior day by day."
4. Congregation, St. John's Apostolic Church, Echivini, KwaMashu
   (English) "Praise the Lord"
   (Traditional)
   > **In Church:** "Praise the Lord; Hallelujah amen!"
5. Mothers' Union Celebration, St. Bede's Parish, Soshanguve (Sotho)
   "TABA BUA" (Tell the news)
   (Traditional)
   > **In Church:** "Tell the news of Jesus. Tell the news, my mother's child."
6. Women, Village of Chief Makuleke, Gazankulu (Shangaan)
   "ME NA MA XANGU" (Hard times lie ahead)
   (Written by Amelia Makuleke; © Happy Valley Music)
   > **In the Country:** This song concerns marriage, which takes on special significance when a bride leaves her village to join her husband's family, knowing that for eleven months of every year he'll be working in the city and she won't even see him.
7. Nurses Phillipine Marumo, Cecilia Mdenge; Alexandra Health
   Centre, Alexandra (Shangaan)
   "NYIKA NYIKA" (Give, give)
   (Written by P. Marumo, C. Mdenge; © Happy Valley Music)
   > **In the Country; In the City:** "Add finely ground nuts and beans to make your child's porridge more nutritious."
8. Nurses Phillipine Marumo, Cecilia Mdenge; Alexandra Health
   Centre, Alexandra (Shangaan)
   "NCHULUKO WA VANA" (Diarrhea of children)
   (Written by P. Marumo, C. Mdenge; © Happy Valley Music)
   > **In the Country; In the City:** "Diarrhea is a serious enemy of children. Pour sugar and salt into a cup of water, and give it to your child to drink."
9. Vho Tshavhungwe Makhado, Vho Elisa Doyoyo, Vho Nyamutshagole
   Nemuramba; Venda (Venda)
   "A VHA VHULAHI" (They don't kill)
   (Written by Vho Nyamutshagole Nemuramba; © Happy Valley Music)
   > **In the Country:** The song concerns a woman who leaves her husband's family and village on very bad terms, to return to her own home.

10. Choir, Esikhawini College of Education, KwaZulu (Zulu)
    "ZIPHI NAZIYA" (Where are they?)
    (Traditional; *makwaya* arrangement with pronounced rural sound)
    In the City; In the Country: A traditional Zulu war song.
    "Where is our enemy? The gun has sounded!"
11. Petros Mabilu, Luvhengo Badaga; Venda (Venda)
    "DABADABA LIA VHANGA MUOFHE" (Venda nonsense
    song)
    (Written by Petros Mabilu; © Happy Valley Music)
    In the Country: This is either a nonsense song or is, among our
    consultants, simply untranslatable.
12. Choir, Esikhawini College of Education, KwaZulu (Zulu)
    "UTHI NGIMALE MALE" (You say I should reject him)
    (Traditional; *makwaya* arrangement)
    In the City: Traditional song about courtship. "You say I should
    reject him, but then whom should I love? A girl should follow her
    own heart!" "Hai, you skinny little girl! Where do you get the nerve
    to reject a fine man like me?"

SIDE B
1. Abafana Bomoya, Durban (Zulu)
    "SESIYADLALA" (We are singing and dancing)
    (Written by George Bhengu, Jeff Thomas; © Happy Valley Music)
    Migrants; In the Country; In the City: In their signature song,
    this ensemble participates in the Zulu tradition of self-praising. "Here
    are the boys of music! . . . We are singing and playing. We are really
    hot tonight!"
2. Utrecht, Zulu Men's Singing Competition, Dalton Road Hostel, Dur-
    ban; Onstage Performance and Exit (Zulu)
    "PHESHEYA MAMA" (Mama, they are overseas)
    (© Happy Valley Music)
    Migrants: This *isicathamiya* choir bemoans the political power-
    lessness of black South Africans in their own country. "We are being
    killed off because we have been compliant." They look to America
    for help, and they rely on internal leaders to speak for them to the
    world outside.
3. Wilba Choir, Soweto (Zulu)
    "IPH'INDLELA" (Where is the way?)
    (Traditional; *makwaya* arrangement)
    In the City: "Where is the way? My love, the way is wherever
    we make it."

4. Living Room Luncheon, Soweto (Sotho)
   "HE MOTSOALA" (Oh my cousin!)
   (Traditional; *makwaya* arrangement)

   In the City: This widely sung, traditional song concerns riding to Pretoria on a bicycle, to complete the paperwork necessary for legalizing a marriage.

5. Students, University of Zululand, KwaZulu (Zulu)
   "SHOSHOLOZA" (The train song)
   (Traditional; *makwaya* arrangement)

   In the City; Migrants: This traditional song concerns the train that carries migrants between Zimbabwe (or the rural homelands) and their work in South Africa's mines, in the shadow of mountainous mine dumps.

6. Mothers' Union Celebration, St. Bede's Parish, Soshanguve (Sotho)
   "BONANG HO HLAHILE MARU" (See those clouds!)
   (Traditional)

   In Church; In Protest: This resurrection hymn provides the melody for one of the country's most widely sung freedom songs, "Show us the way to freedom!" "Those clouds are the souls of the dead, returning from Heaven to bring all people together. The dead awake and rise from their graves, summoned by the Source of All Life. Hallelujah to all."

7. Dr. Alan Boesak, Launch of the United Democratic Front, Capetown (English; Zulu/Xhosa; Sotho)
   "As We Struggle On" (Written by A. Boesak; © Happy Valley Music)
   "NKOSI SIKELEL'I AFRIKA" (God bless Africa)
   (Public domain)

   In Protest: "God bless Africa. Let the voice of the people be heard. Rise up, Spirit of the people. End the war and misery. God bless our people, our nation of Africa, forever."

   Play this cut as a soundtrack for the last few pages of the book.

RELATED RECORDINGS

Music is central to the message of this book—not just verbal descriptions of music or translations of lyrics, but the actual sound of songs. The following discography can direct readers to record albums that exemplify the music discussed in each section of the book.

I. PEOPLE WHO SING

Let Their Voices Be Heard: Traditional Singing in South Africa. Various artists. Rounder Records 5024. Annotated 1984 field recordings of South Africans singing as part of everyday life. (See preceding appendix, "Let Their Voices Be Heard.")

Rhythm of Resistance: Music of Black South Africa. Various artists. Shanachie 43018. Collection of rural, migrant, and urban music illustrating the informal spirit of protest that pervades all facets of black life. Performances by several of South Africa's preeminent recording artists. Vocal and instrumental.

Shadow Man. Johnny Clegg and Savuka. EMI Capitol C1-90411. Every cut on this album is itself a mix of the musical styles of black South Africa. With his first interracial group Juluka, Johnny Clegg performed traditional Zulu music and dance, overlaid with elements of township jive. With this new group, Clegg creates music that mixes Zulu tradition, *mbaqanga,* and international pop in a rare glimpse of the multifaceted vitality that could infuse a nonracial South Africa. Vocal and instrumental. (Also *Third World Child,* Capitol CLT-46778.)

II. IN CHURCH

Bishop Desmond Tutu: Give Praise Where Praise is Deserved. Various artists. Shanachie 43057/8. Two-album set. On the first album, contemporary vocal and instrumental artists perform compositions expressing Archishop Tutu's central message of faith, strength, and resistance in the face of ungodly oppression at the hand of man. Musical styles include traditional African percussion, contemporary *mbaqanga,* Western gospel, and international pop-rock. On the second album, Archbishop Tutu delivers three speeches.

Let Their Voices Be Heard: Traditional Singing in South Africa. Various

RELATED RECORDINGS

artists. Rounder Records 5024. (See preceding appendix, "Let Their Voices Be Heard.")

Music from the Roadside No. 1, Music of Africa Series No. 18. Various artists. Gallo GALP 1110. Annotated collection of rural field recordings made in the 1950s and 1960s by Hugh Tracey, the founder of the International Library of African Music. The first cut on the album is a choral performance of the landmark *makwaya* religious composition "Ntsikana's Bell."

III. IN THE COUNTRY

Amampondo Live: Uyandibiza. Amampondo. Kijima Records BIG 004. This eight-person ensemble performs rural-based music using voices, dancing, and traditional percussion instruments (xylophones, marimbas, mbira, drums, bells, rattles) from the whole of black Africa.

Dinare. Mochini Oa Dikoro. Igagasi IAL 3003. Traditional Sotho women's singing, unaccompanied except for traditional drum.

Fashion Maswedi. Mzikayifani Buthelezi. Rounder Records 5032. Traditional Zulu music with some overlay of township jive; vocal and instrumental.

How Long. Philemon Zulu. Shanachie 43048. Traditional Zulu music with some overlay of urban instruments. Uses characteristic Zulu guitar style that involves intricate picking on specially strung instruments. Vocal and instrumental.

Let Their Voices Be Heard: Traditional Singing in South Africa. Various artists. Rounder Records 5024. (See preceding appendix, "Let Their Voices Be Heard.")

Mafube. Basotho Dihoba. Motella BL 196. Traditional Sotho men's singing. Vocals, accompanied by traditional drums and bows. (Also *Sekalakati,* Teal Records; Igagasi, IAL 4108.)

Music from the Roadside No. 1, Music of Africa Series No. 18. Various artists. Gallo GALP 1110. (See entry in section II, **In Church.**) Throughout roughly the middle third of this century, Hugh Tracey made an extensive collection of field recordings of traditional music in central, eastern, and southern Africa. The collection has been issued as two separate series of albums. The first is a commercial series, *Music of Africa,* issued on the Gallo label; this record comes from that series. The second is a 210-album scholarly series, available through the International Library of African Music, Andrew Tracey, Director, Rhodes University, Grahamstown, South Africa.

The Naked Prey. Various Artists. Folkways Records FS 3854. Traditional singing recorded in Venda, Xhosa, Shangaan, and Zulu villages for the sound track of the Paramount movie *The Naked Prey.* Vocal, with some accompaniment on traditional instruments.

Sangoma. Miriam Makeba. Warner Bros. Records 9 25673–1. Stunning arrangements of unaccompanied traditional women's singing. In this recent commercial recording, Ms. Makeba takes the talent and skill of a long, illustrious career, and returns to her musical roots. (Earlier albums are more popular-sounding, often carrying the lively sound of *mbaqanga* discussed in section V, **In the City**. Also, *Miriam Makeba in Concert*, Peters International PLD 2082.)

Scatterlings. Juluka. Warner Bros. Records 9 23898–1. Traditional Zulu music with an overlay of township jive, performed by the ground-breaking interracial group founded by Johnny Clegg and Sipho Mchunu. The group has now disbanded. Vocal and instrumental. (Other albums include: *Musa Ukungilandela*, Celluloid CEL 6783; *African Litany*, Minc MINC(L) 1020; *Universal Men*, CBS, DNW 2429; *Work For All*, Minc MINC(L) 1070; *Ubuhle Bemvelo*, Minc MINC(E) 1030; *The International Tracks*, Minc MINC(O) 1098; *The Good Hope Concerts*, EMI MINC(EV) 4051414.)

Sonqoba. Various artists. Kaya Records KHYL 3001. Traditional Zulu praise poetry and praise singing. Album recorded in praise of Prince Mangosuthu Gatsha Buthelezi, controversial Chief Minister of the KwaZulu homeland. Vocals, spoken and sung, occasionally acompanied by traditional instruments.

Sounds of the Transkei. Madlamini and her Witchdoctors. Gallo-Teal MFL BL 249. Traditional, rural Xhosa singing; female lead singer.

Zulu Songs from South Africa. Various artists. Lyrichord LLST 7401. Field recordings made in 1982 of rural Zulu singers accompanying themselves on traditional bows. Recordings and musicological annotations by ethnomusicologists Veit Erlmann and Bongani Mtetwa. Vocal with traditional instruments.

The Zulu Songs of Princess Constance Magogo, Music of Africa Series No. 37. Gallo SGALP 1678. Traditional Zulu songs performed by Princess Constance Magogo, accompanying herself on the Zulu *ugubu* bow. The late Princess Magogo was a senior member of the Zulu royal house and the mother of Prince Mangosuthu Gatsha Buthelezi, controversial Chief Minister of the KwaZulu homeland. (See *Music from the Roadside No. 1*, this section.)

IV. MIGRANTS

Bo-Tata. Venanda Lovely Boys. Rounder Records 5033. Durban-based *isicathamiya* group. Unaccompanied vocal.

Cothoza Mfana. Various artists. Motella DLPL 291/2. Two-record set featuring performances by a variety of Natal-based *isicathamiya* groups. Unaccompanied vocal.

Emakhabeleni. Abafana Bomoya. Ezomdabu BL469; distributed by Gallo. Instrumental and vocal music characteristic of migrants living in the city. Retains pronounced features of traditional, rural Zulu music.

Note the intricate guitar picking on specially strung guitars, characteristic of Zulu migrants. This multiracial group performs both music and dance. Quite different from the more familiar migrant idiom *mbube*.

Iscathamiya: Zulu Worker Choirs. Various artists. Heritage HT 313. *Isicathamiya* choirs recorded in the late 1970s and early 1980s in the Durban area. Comprehensive annotations. Unaccompanied vocal.

Let Their Voices Be Heard: Traditional Singing in South Africa. Various artists. Rounder Records 5024. (See preceding appendix, "Let Their Voices Be Heard.")

Mbube! Zulu Men's Singing Competition. Various artists. Rounder Records 5023. Annotated 1984 field recording of a complete men's singing competition at the Dalton Road Hostel in Durban. Unaccompanied vocal. Grammy Nomination, 1987.

Mbube Roots—Zulu Choral Music from South Africa, 1930s–1960s. Various artists. Rounder Records 5025. Compilation of *mbube* performances by groups whose careers have spanned nearly half a century. This is an archival album, making use of earlier-recorded material dating roughly from 1930 to 1970. Comprehensive annotations. Predominantly vocal. Grammy Nomination, 1987.

Scatterlings. Juluka. Warner Bros. Records 9 23898–1. Traditional Zulu music with an overlay of township jive. Much of Juluka's music reflects music and dance idioms developed in the migrant hostels. (See entry in section III, **In the Country**, for more information.)

Shaka Zulu. Ladysmith Black Mambazo. Warner Bros. Records 9 25582–1. The first American-recorded album by the group that made *mbube* or *isicathamiya* singing an international music sensation. This is the world's premier performing group and most prolific recording group in this genre. Unaccompanied vocal. Grammy Award, 1987. (Also *Journey of Dreams*, Warner Bros. Records 9 25753–1, Grammy Nomination, 1988; *Induku Zethu*, Shanachie 43021; *Ulwandle Oluncgwele*, Shanachie 43030; *Inala*, Shanachie 43040; *Umthombo Wamanzi*, Shanachie 43055; *Amabutho*, Motella BL 14; *Imbongi*, Motella BL 18; *Umama Lo!*, Mavuthela BL 23; *Isitimela*, Motella BL 27; *Ukukhanya Kwelanga*, Motella BL 35; *Amaqhawe*, Motella BL 81; *Shintsha Sithothobala*, Motella BL 91; *Phezulu Emafini*, Motella BL 92; *Ushaka*, Motella BL 129; *Indlela Yase Zulwini*, Ezomdabu BL 153; *Intokozo*, Ezomdabu BL 205; *Nqonqotha Mfana*, Ezomdabu BL 253; *Phansi Emgodini*, Ezomdabu BL 321; *Inkazimulo*, Ezomdabu BL 504.)

Sheshwe: The Sounds of the Mines. Four Sotho bands. Rounder Records 5031. Instrumental and vocal music played by Sotho migrant workers on the South African mines. The music retains pronounced features of traditional, rural Sotho music.

RELATED RECORDINGS

V. IN THE CITY

Bantu Choral Folk Songs. Various Artists. Folkways FW-6912. A group of young Americans sing *makwaya* arrangements of traditional South African songs as transcribed by staff and students at the Lovedale Missionary Institute, in the Eastern Cape, and delivered to Pete Seeger.

Back in Town. The Boyoyo Boys. Rounder Records 5026. Contemporary *mbaqanga* group whose sound kindled Paul Simon's interest in doing the project that eventually became *Graceland*. Primarily instrumental. (Also *TJ Today*, Rounder Records 5036.)

The Baragwanath Hospital Choir. Baragwanath Hospital Choir. Adcock-Ingram Group of Companies. *Makwaya* singing of South African compositions and folk songs in various South African languages, by one of South Africa's most renowned choirs. Choir members serve on the staff of Baragwanath Hospital, the largest hospital in the Southern Hemisphere and the primary medical facility for Soweto's estimated three million black residents. Vocal.

Fashion Maswedi. Mzikayifani Buthelezi. Rounder Records 5032. Traditional Zulu music that acquires overlays of township jive as rural musicians move to the cities. Vocal and instrumental.

Ford Choirs in Contest 1979. Various choirs. Kaya Records, Braamfontein, South Africa, KHYL 3002. *Makwaya* singing of South African compositions. Vocal.

Homeland—A Collection of South African Music. Various recording artists. Rounder Records 5009. Contemporary *mbaqanga* groups. Vocal and instrumental. Grammy Nomination, 1988.

Indestructible Beat of Soweto. Various recording artists. Shanachie Records 43033. Whole spectrum of urban styles, ranging from music that retains a predominantly traditional sound to contemporary *mbaqanga* with pronounced international pop influence. Includes two cuts by the upbeat, contemporary-sounding *mbaqanga* group Amaswazi Emvelo. Vocal and instrumental. (Also *Heartbeat of Soweto*, Shanachie 43041.)

Isina Muva Liyabukwa. Abafana Base Qhudeni. Gumba Gumba BL 207. Urban vocal and instrumental group incorporating elements of *mbaqanga*, *mbube*, and Western soul and gospel. This well-known male group formed in 1975 and often performs with the Mahotella Queens (see below). (Also *From Africa—The Cockerel Boys: From Soweto—Mbube, Jive, & Soul*, L&R Records LR 44.009; *Inkunzi Yimi*, Igagasi IAL 3001; *Bakhuphuka Izwe Lonke*, Gumba Gumba BL 146.)

Izagila Zesi Shingishane. Abafana Beshishingishane. WEA-Rainbow Records CHN 1015. Contemporary-sounding *mbaqanga* group. Vocal and instrumental.

Izibani Zomgqashiyo. Mahotella Queens. Shanachie Records 43036. One of South Africa's best known all-women *mbaqanga* groups. These five women have been singing together since 1964; they perform with various male musicians as backups. Vocal and instrumental. (Also *Khwatha O Mone,* Teal IAL 4005.)

Lazarus Kgagudi. Lazarus Kgagudi. Tusk Music 8003. *Mbaqanga* leaning toward rock. Vocal and instrumental.

Let Their Voices Be Heard: Traditional Singing in South Africa. Various Artists. Rounder Records 5024. (See preceding appendix, "Let Their Voices Be Heard.")

My Wife Bought a Taxi. Obed Ngobeni and the Kurhula Sisters. Shanachie Records 64003. Contemporary *mbaqanga* performed by male lead and female backup singers. Several cuts retain pronounced features of traditional Shangaan music. (Also *Gazankulu,* Heads Trutone LPEAD 1017.)

Poppie Nongena. Various artists, featuring Sophie Mgcina. Hannibal Records HNBL 6301. Original cast album of the Obie Award–winning South African musical *Poppie Nongena,* based on the novel by Elsa Joubert. Unaccompanied *makwaya* singing of traditional songs, arranged by Sophie Mgcina.

Rhythm of Resistance: Music of Black South Africa. Various artists. Shanachie 43018. (See entry in section I, **People Who Sing.**)

Sarafina! Various artists. Shanachie Records 43052. Original South African cast recording of the music from Mbongeni Ngema and Hugh Masekela's *mbaqanga* Broadway hit musical *Sarafina!.* Vocal and instrumental.

Siyahlabelela Kwazulu: Songs of Zululand. Student choir from the Madadeni Training College. Gallo-SABC Records BL 165. *Makwaya* performance of traditional Zulu songs. Unaccompanied vocal.

Sounds of Soweto. Various recording artists. Tusk Music 8001. *Mbaqanga* music with pronounced open, traditional sound. Vocal and instrumental.

Qeu Qeu Majoana. Soweto Teachers Choir. Mavutela CHL 2016. *Makwaya* singing of folk songs in most major South African languages, by one of the country's most renowned choirs. Choir members are teachers or administrators in the schools of Soweto. Vocal.

Tomorrow. Hugh Masekela and various artists. Warner Bros. Records 9 25566–1. Tracks draw on *mbaqanga,* popular music styles from throughout Africa, and classical jazz. Vocal and instrumental.

Ubuhle Bami. Tu Nokwe and various artists. RPM Records, South Africa, 7101. Artistically diverse, Zulu-based urban musical styles performed behind powerful female lead singer. Album produced and arranged by Mbongeni Ngema, most recently known for the *mbaqanga* musical *Sarafina!.* Vocal and instrumental.

Usobhuza Walitsatsa Ngenhlonipho. Kakai. Gallo-Mavuthela, BL 359. *Mbaqanga* with heavy Swazi influence. Vocal and instrumental.

Zulu Jive: Urban and Rural Zulu Beats from South Africa. Various artists. Earthworks ELP 2002. Contemporary *mbaqanga* performers. Album features the *kwela* pennywhistle. Vocal and instrumental.

Zulu Songs from South Africa. Various artists. Lyrichord LLST 7401. Field recording made in 1982 of rural Zulu singers accompanying themselves on traditional bows. (See entry in section III, **In the Country**.) These performances are characteristic of the bow music of Mrs. Ngwenyana, discussed in this section, in the chapter "Images of Home."

VI. IN PROTEST

Amandla. African National Congress Cultural Group; Musical Director, Jonas Gwangwa. C60–18207–08. Political music in idioms ranging from traditional African to modern rock and jazz, performed by ANC cultural workers. Artists are exiled from South Africa. Vocal and instrumental.

Change Is Pain. Mzwakhe Mbuli. Rounder Records 4024. Live recording of South African protest-poet-and-performance-artist, reading his stirring poems to music at a trade union rally. This recording was banned in South Africa soon after its release. Spoken word.

Fosatu Worker Choirs. Various artists. Shifty 6. Protest singing by union choirs in the Federation of South African Trade Unions. Vocal.

Freedom Is Coming. Various artists. Fjedur. Walton Music Corp. WB 528B. South African freedom songs. Vocal.

Let Their Voices Be Heard: Traditional Singing in South Africa. Various artists. Rounder Records 5024. (See preceding appendix, "Let Their Voices Be Heard.")

Malibongwe. James Madhlope Phillips and the Bremer Choir. Released by the ANC in Germany, LC 0972 (70111). The late James M. Phillips, exiled ANC songleader, leads a German choir in traditional South African freedom songs. (Also *"Inkululeko!."* Pläne 88244.)

Radio Freedom—Voice of the African National Congress and the People's Army Umkhonto We Sizwe. Various artists. Rounder Records 4019. Songs, chants, and commentary broadcast over the underground ANC radio station Radio Freedom.

South African Trade Union Worker Choirs. Various artists. Rounder Records 5020. Protest songs by choirs comprising members of black South African trade unions. Vocal.

This Land Is Mine: South African Freedom Songs. Various artists. Folkways FH 5588. Freedom songs sung by young South African exiles, recorded shortly after they crossed over the border into the country that was then called Tanganyika. Vocal.

Tomorrow. Hugh Masekela and various artists. Warner Bros. Records 9 25566–1. (See entry in section V, **In the City**.) Lyrics express uncompromising demand for freedom. Vocal and instrumental.

RELATED RECORDINGS

The following mail-order suppliers carry large selections of South African music in their catalogs:

Down Home Music, 10341 San Pablo Ave., El Cerrito, CA 94530.

Elderly Instruments, 1100 North Washington, P.O. Box 14210, Lansing, MI 48901.

Roundup Records, P.O. Box 154, North Cambridge, MA 02140.

BACKGROUND AND RELATED READINGS

In addition to the books and articles cited in Notes, the following readings—fiction and nonfiction; trade and academic—will enrich readers' understanding of the issues discussed in each section of the book. Most readings are relevant to more than one section; each reading is listed only once.

I. PEOPLE WHO SING

Andersson, M. *Music in the Mix: The Story of South African Popular Music.* Johannesburg: Ravan Press, 1981. Andersson discusses the ways political and economic forces in South Africa have influenced the development of the country's popular music and musicians.

Campschreur, W., and J. Divendal, eds. *Culture in Another South Africa.* New York: Olive Branch Press, 1989. A collection of papers and statements from a 1987 conference in Amsterdam where eight hundred South African artists, both exiles and "insiders," came together to discuss the cultural infrastructure of a nonracial and democratic South Africa.

Makeba, M. *Makeba: My Story.* New York: New American Library, 1987. Autobiography of long-exiled, anti-apartheid South African singer Miriam Makeba. Her life is a story of song and struggle.

II. IN CHURCH

Boesak, A. *Black and Reformed: Apartheid, Liberation and the Calvinist Tradition.* Maryknoll, N.Y.: Orbis Books, 1984. Collection of addresses and letters by the president of the International Reformed Church, discussing the struggle for black liberation as part of the Reformed Christian tradition.

Bundy, C. *The Rise and Fall of the South African Peasantry.* Berkeley: University of California Press, 1979. Bundy discusses the early role of missionization in the destruction of black South African agriculturalism at the hands of mining, industrialization, and apartheid legislation.

Randall, P., ed. *Not Without Honour: Tribute to Beyers Naudé.* Johannesburg: Ravan Press, 1982. Four essays in tribute to Beyers Naudé, the eminent dominee in the Dutch Reformed Church who decided that apartheid was inconsistent with the teachings of God. In acting on that decision Naudé was cast as a dangerous enemy by the ruling Afrikaners—

his own people who had, in his youth, identified him as the brightest and best of his generation.

Tutu, D. M. *Hope and Suffering: Sermons and Speeches*. Johannesburg: Skotaville Publishers, 1983. Addresses expressing Anglican Archbishop Desmond Tutu's message to oppressed blacks that the Christian God abhors evil and injustice, that freedom is inevitable, and that the new moral order must rest on a foundation of justice.

III. IN THE COUNTRY

Berliner, P. F. *The Soul of Mbira*. Berkeley: University of California Press, 1978, 1981. This ethnomusicological study of the music and traditions of the Shona people of Zimbabwe contains much that is relevant to understanding the music and traditions of the Shona's neighbors to the south, in South Africa.

Brink, A., and J. M. Coetzee, eds. *A Land Apart: A Contemporary South African Reader*. New York: Penguin Books, 1986. An anthology of South African writing (mostly short stories and poems) written from the early 1970s through 1985. Several of the pieces illustrate contemporary life in South Africa's rural areas.

Butler, J., R. I. Rotberg, and J. Adams. *The Black Homelands of South Africa: The Political and Economic Development of Bophuthatswana and KwaZulu*. Berkeley: University of California Press, 1977, 1978. Three scholars discuss the historical and political/legislative context of the overall homeland policy. They also provide a detailed description of politics and development in two of the three largest homelands.

Jabavu, N. *The Ochre People*. Johannesburg: Ravan Press, 1963, 1982. Born in 1920, raised Xhosa in the rural Eastern Cape, and educated in England from the age of thirteen, the sophisticated, well-educated Noni Jabavu writes of the life and traditions into which she was born, as she remembers them and experiences them on occasional visits home.

Research Staff, South African Institute of Race Relations. *Race Relations Survey 19—*. Johannesburg: South African Institute of Race Relations. The Institute has published an annual *Survey* every year since 1936. These surveys are comprehensive compilations of annual events and statistics concerning the ten homelands, South African national politics and legislation, development, administration, demographics, economics, and much more.

IV. MIGRANTS

Erlmann, V. *Iscathamiya: Zulu Worker Choirs*. Notes from record album *Iscathamiya: Zulu worker choirs*. Crawley, West Sussex, England: Heritage Records, 1986.

Kivnick, H. Q. *Mbube! Zulu Men's Singing Competition*. Notes from record album *Mbube! Zulu Men's Singing Competition.* Cambridge, Mass.: Rounder Records, 1987.

Joubert, E. *Poppie Nongena.* New York: W. W. Norton, 1978, 1980. This tale of a woman married to a migrant worker covers a whole family's experience over forty years. Poppie's story illustrates the lives of those whom the migrants must leave behind.

Marre, J., and H. Charlton. "Rhythm of Resistance: The Black Music of South Africa." In *Beats of the Heart: Popular Music of the World,* edited by J. Marre and H. Charlton 34–50. London: Pluto Press Limited, 1985. This chapter describes many genres of black music in South Africa, including *mbube.*

Rycroft, D. "Zulu Male Traditional Singing." *African Music* 1, no. 4 (1957): 33–36. David Rycroft is an English ethnomusicologist renowned for his knowledge of South African singing. This article provides an authoritative, interestingly dated, account.

V. IN THE CITY

Abrahams, P. *Tell Freedom.* New York: Knopf, 1954. Autobiography of the early life of "Colored" South African writer Peter Abrahams. Abrahams was born in 1917 and spent much of the period described in the book in the black locations outside Johannesburg. (See also *Mine Boy.* New York: Knopf, 1955.)

Callinicos, L. *Working Life: Factories, Townships, and Popular Culture on the Rand 1886–1940.* Vol. 2. Johannesburg: Ravan Press, 1987. Account of the development of South Africa's urban working class in response to the growth of the manufacturing industry on the Rand. Richly illustrated with photographs, drawings, and posters.

Dikobe, M. *The Marabi Dance.* London: Heinemann Educational Books, Ltd., 1973. Novelistic illustration of the Johannesburg slumyards in the 1930s, where people were caught between an increasingly distant, irrelevant-seeming rural traditional world on the one hand, and the fast, chaotic city-life of *marabi* parties and gangs on the other.

Finnegan, W. *Crossing the Line: A Year in the Land of Apartheid.* New York: Harper & Row, 1986. Memoir of an American writer's year teaching in a "Colored" school outside the city of Capetown, in the early 1980s.

Fugard, A. *Tsotsi.* Harmondsworth, Middlesex, England: Penguin Books, 1979, 1983. Novelistic account of life in the black locations of the 1950s, by one of South Africa's best-known playwrights.

Hodge, N., ed. *To Kill a Man's Pride.* Johannesburg: Ravan Press, 1984. Seventeen short stories illustrate black life in South Africa's urban areas.

Huddleston, T. *Naught for Your Comfort.* Glasgow: William Collins & Sons, 1956. In reaction to apartheid legislation of the early 1950s, this beloved mission priest from Sophiatown describes the raw dignity of life in black urban locations, and the ways then-new legislation stifled that dignity and suffocated life itself.

Lelyveld, J. *Move Your Shadow: South Africa, Black and White.* New York: Times Books, 1985. Pulitzer Prize–winning account of South Africa in the early 1980s, focusing largely on the cities.

Mathabane, M. *Kaffir Boy.* New York: New American Library, 1986. This memoir tells the story of a black young man's coming of age in Johannesburg's Alexandra location, in the 1960s and 1970s.

Matshoba, M. *Call Me Not a Man.* London: Longman, 1979, 1981. Seven powerful short stories give outsiders a glimpse of the forces that shaped the Soweto generation.

Omond, R. *The Apartheid Handbook.* Harmondsworth, Middlesex, England: Penguin Books, 1985. A roadmap through South Africa's intricate system of apartheid.

VI. IN PROTEST

Benson, M. *Nelson Mandela.* London: Panaf Books, 1980. The story of Nelson Mandela and the liberation movement in South Africa from the founding of the ANC to the late 1970s.

Bernstein, H. *For Their Triumphs & for Their Tears: Women in Apartheid South Africa.* London: International Defence and Aid Fund for Southern Africa, 1975, 1985. Describes the way oppression and exploitation of black women is integral to the apartheid system and how, therefore, women's resistance has always been integral to the liberation struggle.

Biko, S. *I Write What I Like.* San Francisco: Harper & Row, 1978. Collected writings of Steve Biko, the founder of South Africa's Black Consciousness movement, who was murdered in detention in 1977.

Bunn, D., and J. Taylor, eds. *From South Africa: New Writing, Photographs & Art. TriQuarterly 69.* Evanston, Ill.: Northwestern University, 1987. Collection of new expressions of South Africa's cultural struggle for liberation, by activists living in South Africa and in exile.

Cowell, A. *Why Are They Weeping? South Africans under Apartheid.* Text by Alan Cowell; photographs by David C. Turnley. New York: Steward, Tabori & Chang, 1988. Cowell was the Johannesburg Bureau Chief of *The New York Times* from 1983 to early 1987. His text describes the State of Emergency imposed since 1985 and provides necessary background. David C. Turnley is a photojournalist who was stationed in South Africa from 1985 to late 1987. His photo-essay documents life under the State of Emergency.

Cronin, J. *Inside.* Johannesburg: Ravan Press, 1983. Stunning collection of poems from the poet's seven years of political imprisonment.

Davis, S. M. *Apartheid's Rebels: Inside South Africa's Hidden War.* New Haven: Yale University Press, 1987. History and analysis of the African National Congress.

Dugard J. *Human Rights and the South African Legal Order.* Princeton, N.J.: Princeton University Press, 1978. Analysis of the South African legal system, placed in comparative, historical, and cultural contexts. Dugard is an Advocate of the Supreme Court of South Africa and a Professor of Law at the University of the Witwatersrand.

First, R. *117 Days.* Harmondsworth, Middlesex, England: Penguin Books, 1965, 1982. Memoir of 117 days in solitary confinement, in 1963, under South Africa's 90-day detention law. Written by activist journalist, ANC member Ruth First, assassinated by a South African letter bomb in 1982, in Maputo, Mozambique. First's period of activism inside South Africa is chronicled in the acclaimed film *A Land Apart,* written by her daughter, Shawn Slovo.

Frederikse, J. *South Africa: A Different Kind of War.* Boston: Beacon Press, 1986. South African resistance presented through a montage of interviews, press clippings, posters, poems, photographs, and author's narrative.

Friedman, S. *Building Tomorrow Today: African Workers in Trade Unions 1970–1984.* Johannesburg: Ravan Press, 1987. Traces the development of black trade unionism through the course of this century. Text is divided into a core, intended for lay readers, and a set of detailed notes for those with more specific interest.

Gordimer, N. *Burger's Daughter.* Harmondsworth, Middlesex, England: Penguin Books, 1979, 1980. The fictional story of a young white woman—the daughter of an activist attorney sentenced for life—struggling to find her personal, social, and political identity after her father's death in prison. (Also *A Sport of Nature; The Late Bourgeois World; A Guest of Honour; July's People; The Conservationist; Occasion for Loving; A World of Strangers.*)

Hanlon, J., and R. Omond. *The Sanctions Handbook: For or Against?* Harmondsworth, Middlesex, England: Penguin Books, 1987. Anti-apartheid movements inside South Africa continue to call for sanctions from outside. This book explores the arguments for and against sanctions, in the context of life under the apartheid regime.

Joseph, H. *Side by Side.* London: Zed Books Ltd., 1986. Autobiography of Helen Joseph, veteran white anti-apartheid activist and codefendant with Nelson Mandela in the 1958 Treason Trial.

Mandela, N. *No Easy Walk to Freedom.* London: Heinemann Educational Books Ltd., 1965, 1973. Collection of Nelson Mandela's leading speeches and articles.

Mandela, W. *Part of My Soul Went with Him.* Harmondsworth, Middlesex, England: Penguin Books, 1985. Autobiography of Winnie Mandela, wife of ANC leader Nelson Mandela. The book was assembled and edited outside South Africa to comply with government restrictions on Mrs. Mandela's activities inside the country.

Michelman, C. *The Black Sash of South Africa: A Case Study in Liberalism*. London: Institute of Race Relations, 1975. The Black Sash is a middle-class, white women's organization that has historically opposed apartheid through the use of moral influence rather than political power. In recent years the organization is perhaps best known for publishing and otherwise disseminating information the authorities would rather keep hidden, and for staffing advice offices throughout the country, to assist blacks in obtaining those rights the law guarantees them but that bureaucrats seek, nonetheless, to deny.

North, J. *Freedom Rising*. New York: Macmillan Publishing Company, 1985. A pseudonymous American journalist writes about South Africa based on four-and-one-half years in the country.

Rotberg, R. I. *Suffer the Future: Policy Choices in Southern Africa*. Cambridge, Mass.: Harvard University Press, 1980. Noted Africanist considers 1980 politics and future policy for South Africa, Namibia, and Zimbabwe in a regional and historical context. Discusses South African protest as an ongoing series of responses and counter-responses to political and legislative developments.

INDEX